T0159252

TOMATOES

TOMATOES

IN THE KITCHEN

The indispensable cook's guide to tomatoes, featuring a
list of varieties and over 180 delicious recipes

CHRISTINE FRANCE

LORENZ BOOKS

This edition is published by Lorenz Books,
an imprint of Anness Publishing Ltd,
Blaby Road, Wigston, Leicestershire LE18 4SE; info@anness.com

www.lorenzbooks.com; www.annesspublishing.com

If you like the images in this book and would like to investigate using them for publishing,
promotions or advertising, please visit our website www.practicalpictures.com for more information.

Publisher: Joanna Lorenz
Editorial Director: Helen Sudell
Project Editor: Emma Gray
Designer: Juliet Brown, Axis Design
Jacket Design: Adelle Morris
Additional text: Jenni Fleetwood, Richard Bird
Recipes: Catherine Atkinson, Alex Barker, Michelle Berriedale-Johnson, Angela Boggiano, Janet Brinkworth, Kathy Brown,
Carole Clements, Trish Davies, Patrizia Diemling, Tessa Evelegh, Silvano Franco, Shirley Gill, Brian Glover, Nicola Graimes,
Rosamund Grant, Carole Handslip, Shehzad Husain, Christine Ingram, Manisha Kanani, Soheila Kimberley, Lucy Knox,
Lesley Mackley, Sally Mansfield, Elizabeth Martin, Norma Miller, Jane Milton, Sallie Morris, Elisabeth Lambert Ortiz,
Maggie Pannell, Anne Sheasby, Liz Trigg, Elizabeth Wolf-Cohen, Jeni Wright
Variety Photography: Janine Hosegood

Recipe Photography: Karl Adamson, Edward Allwright, David Armstrong, Steve Baxter, James Duncan, Ian Garlick,
Michelle Garrett, Amanda Heywood, Janine Hosegood, David Jordan, Dave King, Don Last, William Lingwood, Patrick McLeavey,
Steve Moss, Thomas Odulate, Craig Robertson, Simon Smith, Sam Stowell

© Anness Publishing Ltd 2012

A CIP catalogue record for this book is available from the British Library.

NOTES
Bracketed terms are intended for American readers.
For all recipes, quantities are given in both metric and imperial measures and, where appropriate, in
standard cups and spoons. Follow one set of measures, but not a mixture, because they are not
interchangeable.Standard spoon and cup measures are level.
1 tsp = 5ml, 1 tbsp = 15ml, 1 cup = 250ml/8fl oz.
Australian standard tablespoons are 20ml. Australian readers should use 3 tsp in place of 1 tbsp for
measuring small quantities.American pints are 16fl oz/2 cups. American readers should use
20fl oz/2.5 cups in place of 1 pint when measuring liquids.
Electric oven temperatures in this book are for conventional ovens. When using a fan oven, the
temperature will probably need to be reduced by about 10–20°C/20–40°F. Since ovens vary, you
should check with your manufacturer's instruction book for guidance.
The nutritional analysis given for each recipe is calculated per portion (i.e. serving or item), unless
otherwise stated. If the recipe gives a range, such as Serves 4–6, then the nutritional analysis will be
for the smaller portion size, i.e. 6 servings. The analysis does not include optional ingredients, such
as salt added to taste. Medium (US large) eggs are used unless otherwise stated.

PUBLISHER'S NOTE

CONTENTS

THE TALE OF THE TOMATO

The early history of the tomato is not clear, but it is thought that the first known tomatoes grew wild in South America, to the west of the Andes in what is now Peru, Bolivia, Northern Chile and Ecuador. The ancestors of the Incas and Aztecs were the first to cultivate the tiny, cherry-sized fruits around 700AD.

Both the Aztecs and the Mayas farmed the little fruits for food, and their cultivation began to spread. By the time the Spaniards conquered Mexico in the early 16th century, tomatoes were widely domesticated there and throughout South America.

There is little doubt that we have the Spanish to thank for introducing tomatoes to Europe. Tradition has it that a Spanish priest returning from Peru brought the first seeds back to Seville, but in reality it seems more likely to have been an early Spanish explorer: perhaps Christopher Columbus or Hernando Cortés. Most people acknowledge Cortés as the person who brought the tomato to Europe. Plants would have arrived in Spain by boat, either from the expedition to the New World by Columbus in the 1490s, or brought back by Cortés after the Conquest of Mexico in 1519.

NAMING THE TOMATO

These early tomatoes introduced to Europe would have been small and yellow in colour, not bright red as is common today, and were named "Peruvian apples", or often "golden apples" – "pomo d'oro" in Italian, "pommes d'or" in French, and "goldapfel" in German.

Either through their supposed aphrodisiac qualities, or because folk medicine linked the appearance of plants to their therapeutic use (tomatoes look very like hearts), they also earned the name of "love apples" or "pomme d'amour" which may also be a simple corruption of "pomo d'oro". Many people believe that it was the

Above: Hernando Cortés, 1485–1547, one of the great Spanish explorers, is reputed to have introduced the tomato to Spain after the Conquest of Mexico in the early 16th century.

tomato, rather than the apple, that was the fruit that Eve used to tempt Adam in the Garden of Eden, and which led to the fall of mankind from grace.

The English word for tomato derives from the original Aztec word "tomatl", but the Latin name "lycopersicon esculentum" translates as "edible wolf's peach" – perhaps reflecting suspicions of its poisonous nature. Indeed, the tomato plant is a member of the deadly nightshade family and the tomato was at first believed to be highly poisonous. In fact, the fruits are not at all toxic, but the foliage is poisonous, and the leaves can cause bad stomach upsets if eaten.

Left: Christopher Columbus, the earliest explorer thought to have brought tomatoes to Europe.

Right: Though glasshouses were few and far between in the early 19th century, they were essential for the success of many tomato varieties which could not withstand the cool northern European climates, even in summer. This glasshouse was designed by George Tod in 1812, for Lady Jennings, who lived just outside London.

EARLY CULTIVATION

The tomato was first cultivated in England by John Gerard, who was the superintendent of the College of Physicians' gardens in London. In his book "Gerard's Herball", published in 1597, Gerard described the plant as "of ranke and stinking savour". This unfavourable view of the tomato dominated until the early 19th century in Britain and Northern Europe, and the plants were grown largely as an ornamental curiosity, for their climbing habit, decorative foliage and fruit, or for medicinal use. A poultice of tomato was thought to cure skin disorders, rheumy eyes and the "vapours in women".

Meanwhile, tomatoes flourished in the warm climates of Spain and Italy, and these were the first European nations to realize the potential of tomatoes in cooking, featuring them in recipes from the late 17th century. The early development of new and hardy strains was centred largely around the Mediterranean, and by the mid-18th century there were more than 1,000 tomato varieties, cultivated throughout Spain, Portugal, Italy and the South of France. Eventually the rest of Europe followed suit, helped greatly by the discovery that tomatoes would flourish in glasshouses, extending their season over months instead of weeks. The first glasshouses in England were built in Kent and Essex in the mid-19th century, when sheet glass production was quite a recent innovation.

The North American colonies were also surprisingly cautious about this native fruit, and treated tomatoes with great suspicion when they were reintroduced in the early 1800s.

Some tomato types in cultivation in the 19th century
Though there were many varieties of tomato available, few were cultivated in Europe until the 19th century. Below is a small selection of fruit grown in glasshouses and painted with meticulous accuracy in watercolour paints. They were all included in a cookery ingredients book published in 1879.

Right: cherry-formed red

Right: pear-shaped

Right: cherry-formed yellow

Right: large red

Right: Japanese striped

Above: currant-fruited red

Above: large yellow

Above: rose-fruited red

It's not certain who was responsible for reintroducing the tomato to North America, but from the mid-18th century, tomatoes were cultivated in Carolina, and by the late 1700s, the migration of farmers across North America took tomato cultivation north and west and to the central coast of Florida. By the early 19th century, tomatoes were widely used in cooking, and recipes reflected the influences of Spanish, Italian, Caribbean or French and other settlers.

THE PRESENT-DAY TOMATO

Once cultivation began on a commercial scale, there was no stopping the tomato, and there are now well over 7,000 varieties. New hybrids are constantly being introduced.

Tomatoes are grown all over the world, from Iceland to New Zealand. They are one of the main horticultural crops of Britain, about 80 per cent being grown in heated glasshouses, with the rest of the crop being grown almost entirely in unheated greenhouses.

Glasshouses allow the growers to maintain a constant environment for the tomato plants, and provide shelter from inclement weather, as well as consistent humidity, air, water, nutrients and light. This extends the length of the growing season and helps to increase the yield

Above: This tomato canning factory still uses hand sorting to choose the best tomatoes. Canned tomatoes have often been ripened on the vine and may have superior flavour to those picked green and artificially ripened for year-round supply to supermarkets.

Above: Markets are one of the best places to buy tomatoes. They are often fresher than those on many supermarket shelves, though the choice may be more seasonal.

Above: Tomato plants being grown on a small commercial scale.

of the plants. Even when tomatoes are grown on a large scale, bumble-bees are used to pollinate the flowers naturally, and natural predators are used whenever possible in preference to chemicals to control insect damage.

From the day the flowers appear on the tomato plants, it takes between 40 and 60 days for the fruits to reach their peak of ripeness, depending on the tomato variety. If they are grown in coldhouses, the weather will also be a factor. For the finest flavour, tomatoes need to be ripened in the sun and on the vine, and from the first sign of ripening it takes four to six days for a tomato to reach full ripeness.

Commercially, the fruit is picked when it is half-ripened, to allow it to reach the customer when it is at peak ripeness and to extend its shelf-life. Many tomatoes are now sold "on the vine" for aesthetic reasons which allows them to be picked a little later and keep a little bit longer.

Above: Basil is a suitable companion plant for tomatoes.

Below: Even when picked, tomatoes will ripen if left on the vine.

NUTRITION

The nutritional content of tomatoes is important because of the large quantities consumed. Each fruit is between 93 and 95 per cent water, they are a good source of vitamins A and C, and if eaten raw, contain significant amounts of vitamin E. This varies with the variety. Some cherry tomatoes, for instance, contain five times as much vitamin C as other types. Tomatoes also contain a natural bioflavonoid, lycopene. This is a powerful antioxidant that may help to lower the risk of cancer, particularly prostate and colon cancer, and heart disease. Lycopene is a fat-soluble nutrient and is most readily absorbed into the bloodstream when the tomatoes are cooked with a little oil.

Tomatoes also contain potassium, calcium and other mineral salts, and the fibre content is typically around 1.5 per cent. They contain only a trace of fat and just 14 calories/58 kilojoules per 100g/3½oz serving.

CULTIVATING TOMATOES

Tomatoes are probably the most widely grown of all vegetables. Even people without a garden often manage to grow a plant or two on a balcony or patio, or in a window box. One reason for this is that tomatoes are relatively easy to grow, but another must surely be that supermarket-bought tomatoes sometimes bear little resemblance to what a gardener knows as a tomato. Tomatoes grown at home can be so sweet that they really do live up to their official classification as a fruit, although most people would still consider them a vegetable. Another reason may well be the sheer range of tomatoes that can now be grown at home. They come in all shapes, sizes and colours. Flavours vary, too, and some of the old-fashioned varieties that taste superb are becoming more readily available. The largest, such as the beefsteak tomato, can weigh up to 1.3kg/3lb each, while the smallest are not much bigger than a grape.

Tomatoes can either be grown on cordons (upright plants) or as bushes. It is well worth not only growing your own particular favourite varieties each year, but also experimenting with at least one new one. This may well result in a glut of tomatoes, but they are wonderful

Above: A bed of tomato plants with good exposure to the sun for ripening.

things to give away or they can be made into sauces and frozen for later use. They make very decorative plants, with their red, yellow, green, orange or even purple fruits, and they are a valuable addition to ornamental gardens.

Tomatoes are used widely in raw and cooked dishes. They can even be used in their unripened state, so that any that have not ripened by the time the frosts arrive can still be used.

Tomatoes are half-hardy and can be grown under glass or outside. Growing under glass extends the growing season and results in heavier crops, but outside crops often taste better, particularly if the summer has been hot and the fruit has ripened well.

CULTIVATION IN A GREENHOUSE

If you are growing under glass, sow the seed in mid-spring in a very gentle heat or an unheated greenhouse. An earlier start can be made in a heated greenhouse to obtain earlier crops. When the seedlings are big enough to handle, prick them out into single pots. When the plants are large enough, transfer them to grow bags or a greenhouse border. Arrange some support, such as strings or stakes, for the tomatoes to be tied to as they grow. Remove any side shoots as they appear. Keep well watered and feed every ten days with a high-potash liquid fertilizer once the fruits begin to swell. Pinch out the top of the plant when it reaches the glass.

Above: A satisfying crop.

Above: A greenhouse is ideal for growing old favourites and new varieties.

CULTIVATION OUTDOORS

For cordons grown outside, follow the same procedure as in the greenhouse, but let the plants harden off. This simply means that the plants should be put outside in mild weather during the day for a week or so, before planting out. They should be planted in fertile soil in an open, sunny position. Bush forms are treated in the same way, except that the side shoots do not need to be removed and straw should be placed around the base of the plant to keep the fruit away from the ground.

Cultivation – the facts

Indoors
Sowing time early to mid-spring
Planting time mid- to late spring
Planting/sowing distance 45cm/18in
Harvesting summer onwards

Outdoors
Sowing time (inside) mid-spring
Planting-out time early summer
Planting distance (cordon) 45cm/18in
Planting distance (bush) 60cm/24in
Distance between sown rows
   75cm/30in
Harvesting late summer onwards

PESTS AND DISEASES

Tomato plants suffer from a number of pests and diseases. Fortunately, these are generally not troublesome enough to deter those who grow them. Pests include aphids, potato cyst eelworm, whitefly and red spider mite. Diseases include tomato blight, grey mould, potato mosaic virus, greenback, tomato leaf mould and scald. Many problems can be avoided by good ventilation, but you will need to consult a specialist if you have persistent problems. Cracked or split fruit are often the result of uneven watering, the last excessive watering being the final culprit. Watering regularly should avoid this.

GROWING TOMATOES

Using grow bags

Tomatoes can be grown in bags of compost (soil mix). Simply remove the marked sections and plant directly into the bag. The plastic bag helps to reduce water loss in hot weather.

Pinching out the side shoots

The side shoots on cordon varieties should be pinched or cut out when they appear. This helps to direct the plant's energy into its fruit rather than its leaf.

Harvesting the fruit

The colour of the tomato when ripe will depend on the variety. However, if the fruit comes away from the stem easily it is ready to be eaten.

Ripening green tomatoes

If the weather has been poor, and many tomatoes have failed to ripen on the plant, dig up any remaining plants and hang them upside down under protection. This may be in the kitchen or in a greenhouse or garage. They will ripen slowly and will often keep until mid-winter if treated in this way.

Hanging basket tomatoes

It is easy to grow small tomato varieties in hanging baskets. Simply ensure that the soil is fed with a potash or hanging basket fertilizer.

GUIDE TO BUYING TOMATOES

Nowadays, there is a wider choice of tomatoes available than ever before, and they vary in colour, shape and size as well as flavour.

In the past, the range of tomatoes sold in supermarkets was fairly limited, and if you wanted to try different varieties the only option was to grow your own. The market has now changed, and supermarkets recognize the consumers' distaste for tomatoes that have been picked too young, ripened artificially and as a consequence are bland and watery.

As a result, many more varieties of tomato are now on sale, and supermarkets commission growers to breed tomatoes that fit their requirements exactly: from sweetness and colour to skin thickness and shape. All these factors can be varied by careful cross-pollination and generations of selective breeding.

This has led to a situation unusual in the vegetable and fruit world, namely that the tomato is one of a few vegetables that have been branded. When a supermarket chain commissions a grower to breed a tomato exclusively for sale in their stores, a new "own-brand" name is chosen, which does not reveal the tomato's origins, even though it might be a hybrid of a familiar variety.

Fortunately, when shopping for tomatoes, we tend to be concerned with flavour, texture or shape and are not too worried about the name. Apart from these basic characteristics, ripeness and freshness most affect the quality. The best tomatoes are usually found at a local market, particularly those run by farmers themselves. The tomatoes will have been allowed to ripen longer than most and picked just before they are transported to the market.

When purchasing tomatoes, also look for those that have been organically grown. These tomatoes will have been cultivated using sustainable farming practices and without the use of pesticides and synthetic fertilizers. They have a naturally lower water content and so usually have a better flavour and texture than most. Whichever variety you choose, be adventurous and try something new.

Beefsteak tomatoes

These are pumpkin-shaped, large and sometimes ridged. They are usually deep red or orange in colour. They have a good firm texture, plenty of flesh, and a sweet, mellow flavour due to their low acidity and often high water content. They are best eaten raw in salads and sandwiches or stuffed and baked whole.

Round or salad tomatoes

The round or salad tomato is the most common type available, they vary in size according to the exact variety and the time of year. Their flavour varies considerably depending on whether they are grown and picked during their natural season. They are generally quite acidic with a full flavour, so are excellent for cooking or eating raw. For cooking, look for fruit that is soft and very red. Add a pinch of sugar to bring out the sweetness and season well with salt and pepper to bring out the flavour.

Cherry tomatoes

These small, dainty cherry-size tomatoes are mouthwateringly sweet. High in sugar and low in acid, they are good in salads or for cooking whole. The skin can be very delicate in summer months, but tends to toughen towards the end of the season. They are perfect as part of a cocktail snack as they are just the right size for one mouthful. Combine them with cheese on sticks, or if you have time, make them into a brightly coloured hors d'oeuvres by stuffing them with soft cheese mixed with red or green pesto. They were once prized treasures exclusive to gardeners but are now widely available in supermarkets. Although they are more expensive than the usual round or salad tomatoes, it's worth paying a little extra for the delicious flavour which, remarkably, improves even further with keeping. Red, yellow and orange varieties of cherry tomato are available.

Plum tomatoes

These tomatoes are elongated and are usually shaped like an egg, but are occasionally very long and almost hollow inside. They have a meaty flesh, a thick core, strong skin, which can be easily peeled, and are richly flavoured, with fewer seeds than round tomatoes. They are considered to be the best cooking tomatoes due to their concentrated flavour and high acidity. They are best used when they are fully ripe. Plum tomatoes are grown widely in Italy, and are available in various sizes and colours, but red plum tomatoes are best for cooking. They are the most popular variety for canning.

Yellow tomatoes

These have a sweet, slightly lemony, mild flavour and a lower acidity than red tomatoes. Yellow tomatoes come in different shapes and sizes, from pear, to plum and round. Yellow tomatoes should ideally be used in salads and also for garnishes for their decorative quality, but are quite suitable for cooking and are especially good in pickles and chutneys. The Yellow Pear variety, so called because of the shape, is particularly popular.

Orange tomatoes

Mild tomatoes, these have a sweet, delicate flavour and low acidity. Like red, round salad tomatoes, they have quite a high seed to flesh ratio. The seeds, however, are often smaller than in the red tomato. Orange tomatoes add a splash of colour to salads, create wonderful garnishes and are also good in soups. They make stunning sauces. Orange Bourgoin and Mini Orange are particularly pretty varieties.

Green tomatoes

The term "green tomato" was used for the tangy, unripened tomatoes traditionally used for relishes and chutneys. Ripe green tomatoes are also available now – such as the green cherry tomato "Green Grape", and the cordons "Evergreen" and stripy "Green Zebra". They have a bright green skin and flesh, and are tasty and very decorative used in salads and garnishes.

Vine tomatoes

These tomatoes were recently introduced in supermarkets, and were greeted with great enthusiasm. The tomatoes are just the same as other tomatoes, but are still attached to their stalk or vine and have the aromatic quality usually only present in home-grown tomatoes. This is mostly due to the chemicals coming from the green stalk and leaf of the plant, rather than the fruit itself. However, if you do not have home-grown tomatoes, choose rich red vine tomatoes over round, salad tomatoes.

Pear tomatoes

This small category includes some of the tastiest tomatoes of all. The name refers to the shape, not the flavour, and the tomatoes are generally quite small. Perhaps the best known is the Yellow Pear, a vigorous grower that produces masses of tiny yellow fruits. They look pretty on the plate, and have a mild, citrus flavour. Red Pear tomatoes have a richer flavour and are equally popular. In tomato tastings, these score very highly for flavour.

SELECTING TOMATOES

Tomatoes are at their best when they have ripened naturally in the sun – they should ideally be allowed to ripen slowly on the plant so that their flavour can fully develop. Therefore, home-grown tomatoes are best for flavour, followed by those grown and sold locally. Try to buy tomatoes loose so that you can smell them before you buy – they should have a wonderful aroma, not only from the green stalks, but also from the tomato itself. When buying tomatoes from a supermarket or greengrocer, look at the leafy green tops: the fresher they look the better. If you are buying red tomatoes, try to buy deep-red fruit. If buying yellow or orange, look for depth of colour. The fruit should have flesh that is firm, but gives slightly when pressed gently. Choose tomatoes according to how you wish to prepare them – buy locally grown beefsteak or cherry tomatoes for salads, and plum tomatoes for sauces.

STORING TOMATOES

If you are not using the tomatoes the same day, they will benefit from being removed from the packaging. To improve the flavour of a slightly hard tomato, leave it to ripen at room temperature and preferably in direct sunlight. Paler tomatoes or those tinged with green will redden if kept in a brown paper bag or fruit bowl with a ripe tomato or banana; the gases given off will ripen the tomatoes, though they cannot improve the basic flavour. Overripe tomatoes, where the skin has split and they seem to be bursting with juice, are excellent in soups and sauces. However, check for any sign of mould or decay, as this would spoil the flavour of the finished product. Tomatoes should not be stored in the refrigerator – chilling adversely affects the taste and the texture, so aim to make small, frequent purchases to enjoy them at their best.

USEFUL EQUIPMENT

The right tool for the job always makes life easier, and you may find that there are now pieces of equipment available that you haven't come across before. Although it is perfectly possible to use only basic kitchen tools for tomatoes, this list will help you to make the most of what is available.

FOOD PROCESSOR OR BLENDER

An invaluable asset when preparing tomatoes is a food processor. Use the main chopping blade to finely chop peeled or unpeeled tomatoes for recipes where the texture of the tomato or finished product is important. A food processor is perfect for dishes such as soups, stews and chunky salsas.

Below: A blender is perfect for quickly making a smooth tomato sauce.

MOULI GRATER

Use a mouli grater to produce a smooth tomato purée (paste) – the consistency will depend upon the ripeness of the tomatoes. Very ripe tomatoes will give a more liquid result, while firmer tomatoes will produce a thicker purée. Tomatoes can be cooked with other vegetables such as (bell) peppers or courgettes (zucchini) and then processed in the mouli to make tasty purées for babies.

KNIVES AND KNIFE SHARPENERS

You will need several types of knives to prepare tomatoes, and it is important that the appropriate knife should be used for each job – for efficiency and safety reasons. To slice tomatoes, the best knife is a small serrated one, which is easy to control and can be used to produce thick or thin slices according to preference. For smaller, awkward jobs, such as peeling or seeding tomatoes, a paring knife is ideal. Choose a knife with a short enough blade to allow you to use your thumb as well, but not too

Below: A mouli grater is handy for puréeing small quantities of food.

short or the balance will be less than ideal. For jobs other than slicing, the knife blade should be curved with a sharp point. Don't be tempted by those with removable peeler blades, as these are easily lost and remove too much skin. One of the handiest knives has a wide, serrated blade that ends in a round, flat surface for lifting the slice on to a sandwich or salad. It is now usually made of stainless steel with a wooden handle. This was designed in 1920, has recently been brought back into production by various companies and is available for purchase again. However, if you are lucky enough, you may find an original 1920s version.

Below: The knife on the left is a special tomato knife, the others are paring knives.

Knives must always be sharp and clean – a blunt knife is more likely to cause injury because excessive pressure has to be used. If you can't cut the skin of a tomato with a knife, the blade needs sharpening. There are several types of knife sharpener available, ranging from a traditional steel or carborundum, which gives the best results but can be quite tricky to use, to manual or electrical sharpeners, which will give a good edge. Whichever type of sharpener you use, make sure you sharpen your knives regularly and evenly – uneven sharpening can be dangerous. Knives will stay sharper if they are used on a cutting board.

Above: Sieves are handy for making smooth soups and sauces.

SIEVE

A sturdy sieve can be used to produce smooth purées (pastes), sauces and soups. A metal sieve is preferable to a plastic one because it can withstand higher temperatures and enables you to sieve hot and cold mixtures; it is also easier to keep clean. Conical sieves have the advantage of forcing the tomato sauce, soup or purée mixture out through a smaller surface area so there is less risk of splashing and the sieved food can be passed into a smaller container. To sieve tomato mixtures, the best method is to push down firmly using the back of a metal or wooden spoon – this ensures minimum wastage and maximum yield. It is best if the tomatoes have been skinned if this method is used.

HULLING TOOL

This is a handy little implement used to remove the stalk and green part from the top of individual tomatoes while leaving the fruit intact. It is especially useful and can save time, if you are preparing a large glut of home-grown tomatoes to make into sauces and soups for the freezer.

JUICER

There are principally two types of juicer on the market: mechanical and electrical. The electrical ones suit tomatoes best as they will separate out the skin and fibre, leaving a thick and delicious drink in moments. When buying a juicer, the best type for tomatoes is a centrifugal juicer – the tomatoes simply need to be cut into pieces (there is no need to peel or seed) and then put into the feeder. If you wish to experiment and make fruit and vegetable cocktails, you may need to check whether the juicer will process harder ingredients, such as carrots and celery, too.

Right: Peelers are useful when making garnishes.

SWIVEL-BLADE VEGETABLE PEELER

With their horizontal-angled blades, these easy-to-use peelers are ideal for peeling fine swirls of tomato skin to make garnishes such as tomato roses.

TOMATO PRESS

A tomato press is a useful piece of equipment for dealing with a glut of tomatoes. It looks rather like a modern version of an old-fashioned mincer or grinder, and clips to the work surface. Put the tomatoes in the bowl at the top, turn a handle, and smooth tomato pulp comes out of one side, while seeds and skin emerge from the other.

CRINKLE CUTTER

This is a specially designed knife, which has a crinkle-edged blade to give a decorative wavy edge to fruits and vegetables. It can be used to cut tomatoes in halves, quarters or slices for attractive garnishes.

Above: A juicer is great for making fresh, healthy tomato drinks.

PREPARING TOMATOES

For perfect results, use the following techniques to prepare tomatoes and make attractive garnishes.

PEELING

Add a professional finish to sauces and soups that are not being sieved by peeling and seeding the tomatoes.

1 Use a small, sharp knife to cut out the green stalk end, then make a cross in the skin on the base of each tomato.

2 Place the tomatoes in a bowl and add boiling water to cover. Leave for 30 seconds, then drain. Cool slightly.

3 Gently pull away the loosened skin from the tomato.

FLAME-SKINNING

If you have a gas cooker, this is the simplest and quickest method for skinning a small number of tomatoes. If you have many more than five or six tomatoes, then the first method is quicker.

1 Skewer one tomato at a time on a metal fork or skewer and hold in a gas flame for 1–2 minutes, turning the tomato until the skin splits and wrinkles.

2 Use a cloth to protect your hands and remove the tomato from the fork or skewer. Leave the tomatoes on a chopping board until cool enough to handle. Using your fingers or a knife, slip off and discard the skins.

PLAIN CUTTING

Tomato slices have a different appearance, depending on which way you cut them. Slice them across rather than downwards for salads and pizzas – the slices have a more attractive finish this way, and hold the seeds in the flesh better. For wedges, cut the tomato downwards, then quarter. If smaller pieces are needed, cut the quarters into two or three pieces, depending on the size of the tomato.

SEEDING

Using just the flesh of the tomato gives a meatier texture to a dish. Here are two methods that can be used.

Halve the tomatoes. Squeeze out the seeds or scoop them out with a teaspoon.

Cut the tomatoes into quarters. Slide a knife along the inner flesh, scooping out all the seeds.

CONCASSING

After peeling and seeding tomatoes, to add the final touch to the perfect sauce or soup ingredient, concass the flesh.

Using a sharp knife, cut the flesh into neat 5mm/¼in squares.

TOMATO ROSES

Use these classic tomato roses to decorate quiches or tarts or to garnish platters of cold meats.

1 Use a swivel-blade peeler to peel one long continuous strip from a whole tomato. Start at the base and work slowly to avoid breaking the strip.

2 With the skin side out, and starting at the stem end, coil the peel loosely to within 2cm/¾in of the end. Set the coil upright so that it resembles a rosebud and tuck the end loosely underneath.

3 Place a lettuce leaf underneath the rose to give a contrast and to add the finishing touch.

TOMATO SUNS

These pretty cherry tomato garnishes can be arranged on individual plates for a professional looking garnish.

1 Hull a cherry tomato, then place it stem-side down. Cut lightly into the skin across the top, edging the knife towards the base. Turn the tomato through 45° and repeat, until the skin has been cut into eight segments, joined at the base.

2 Slide the knife under the point of each segment and ease the skin away, stopping just short of the base.

3 With your fingers or the knife, gently fold the "petals" on each tomato back to mimic the sun's rays.

TOMATO FANS

This simply prepared garnish can transform a plain pâté or dip. It looks good next to a sandwich, too.

1 Quarter and seed a tomato. Make four cuts down most of the length of each piece. Fan out the "fingers".

2 Top each tomato fan with a sprig of parsley, to finish.

TOMATO LILIES

Using a small sharp knife, make identical zig-zag cuts around the central circumference.cut right into the centre of the tomato. Gently pull the tomato apart and garnish with cucumber.

PRESERVING TOMATOES

If you've got a glut of tomatoes or simply can't resist the bargain-priced tomatoes at the market, there are plenty of ways to keep your supply going right through the winter.

BOTTLED CHERRY TOMATOES

Cherry tomatoes bottled in their own juices with garlic and basil are sweetly delicious and a perfect accompaniment to thick slices of country ham.

MAKES 1KG/2¼LB

INGREDIENTS
   1kg/2¼lb cherry tomatoes
   5ml/1 tsp salt per 1 litre/1¾ pint/
   4 cup jar
   5ml/1 tsp granulated sugar per
   1 litre/1¾ pint/4 cup jar
   fresh basil leaves
   5 garlic cloves per jar

1 Preheat the oven to 120°C/250°F/ Gas ½. Prick each tomato with a fork. Pack them into clean, dry jars, adding the salt and sugar as you go.

2 Fill the jars to within 2cm/¾in of the top. Tuck the basil and garlic among the tomatoes. Rest the lids on the jars, but do not seal. Stand the jars on a baking sheet lined with a layer of newspaper and place in the oven. After about 45 minutes, when the juice is simmering, remove the jars from the oven and seal. Store in a cool place and use within 6 months.

DRYING AND PRESERVING IN OIL

Dried tomatoes have always been popular with the Italians – it's a wonderful way to enjoy the taste of summer in the winter months. To make your own dried tomatoes by "oven drying" them,

wash and seed the tomatoes and dry with kitchen paper. Place them, cut-sides down, on wire racks on a baking sheet and dry in the oven for 6–8 hours at 120°C/250°F/Gas ½.

   Home-dried tomatoes can be preserved in olive oil for up to 6 months. Simply place them in clean jars and top up with olive oil. The tomatoes will taste truly delicious and the oil will take on a wonderful tomato flavour which is delicious used in salad dressings.

FREEZING

Whole, fresh tomatoes do not freeze well, as they tend to go mushy once thawed. However, if you have a glut of tomatoes, they freeze very well once they have been puréed: skin and core the tomatoes, boil with minimal water for 5 minutes, then purée in a food processor. Allow to cool and then freeze. The purée (paste) can be added to stews, soups and casseroles.

TOMATO KETCHUP

The real tomato flavour of this home-made ketchup is delicious with burgers.

MAKES 2.75KG/6LB

INGREDIENTS
   2.25kg/5lb very ripe tomatoes
   1 celery heart, chopped
   30ml/2 tbsp soft light brown sugar
   65ml/4½ tbsp raspberry vinegar
   3 garlic cloves
   15ml/1 tbsp salt
   1 onion
   6 cloves
   4 allspice berries
   6 black peppercorns
   1 rosemary sprig
   25g/1oz fresh root ginger, sliced

1 Peel, seed and cut the tomatoes into small pieces, then place them in a large pan with the celery, sugar, vinegar, garlic and salt. Tie the onion, rosemary and spices in a double layer of muslin (cheesecloth) and add to the pan.

2 Bring the mixture to the boil, then simmer for 2 hours, stirring regularly to ensure the mixture does not stick to the base of the pan. Cook until the mixture is reduced by half. Remove the cloth bag containing the onion, rosemary and spices.

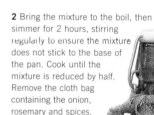

3 Purée the mixture in a blender or sieve, then return to the pan and simmer for 15 minutes. Bottle in clean, sterilized glass jars with a good seal. Store in the refrigerator and use within 2 weeks.

Left and above: Bottled tomatoes and ketchup are delicious and easy to make.

TOMATOES IN THE PANTRY

When fresh tomatoes are out of season or unavailable, or because it is more convenient, you'll be able to get a distinctive tomato flavour in seconds, simply by opening a jar, can or bottle. The following guide will help you to choose the most appropriate product for your recipe.

CANNED TOMATOES

Tomatoes are one of the few fruits that can be canned really successfully and they are the most popular tomato pantry product available. They are excellent in tomato sauces for pastas and pizzas, having an intense and distinct flavour, and can be puréed when passata is called for. Plum tomatoes are normally selected for canning and can be whole or chopped. Flavoured canned tomatoes are also available. These have added herbs or garlic, but it is preferable to avoid these as the flavours can be overwhelming. It is better to add your own flavourings.

PASSATA

Raw, ripe tomatoes that have been puréed and sieved to remove the skin and seeds are known and packaged as passata. Depending on the degree of sieving, it can be perfectly smooth or slightly chunky. The chunky variety is sold in tall jars, while the smoothest type is available in jars or cartons. It may separate, if it has been standing for some time, but will mix together again if it is shaken a few times. It is a useful pantry ingredient and is invaluable in recipes such as soups where you want a smooth finished result in minutes. With the addition of just a little salt and a few herbs, it makes an almost instant sauce for pasta dishes.

SUGOCASA

This is a combination of coarsely chopped plum tomatoes and tomato purée (paste). It has a rich, full flavour and is more concentrated than passata. Sold in jars, sugocasa is ideal for pizzas, pasta sauces and stews.

RED PESTO

Pesto, a traditional Italian ingredient, is usually made with basil, pine nuts, Parmesan or Pecorino cheese and olive oil. A red version of pesto is available that has either sun-dried tomatoes or red (bell) peppers added. The overwhelming flavour is of basil, with the tomato or pepper being added for colour and just a hint of flavour.

CREAMED TOMATOES

These are usually sold in cardboard and plastic cartons of varying sizes. They have a very smooth and thick consistency and often contain many preservatives. However, they are very convenient as you can buy a carton smaller than a can, which is the perfect quantity for a soup or sauce if you are cooking for just one or two people.

SUN-DRIED TOMATOES

These wonderfully rich tomatoes, which are actually more often air-dried by machine rather than by the sun, have an intense, sweet flavour. They are available either dried and sold in packets or preserved in olive oil in jars. The packet variety can be either eaten on their own as a snack or rehydrated in hot water until soft for cooking (use the tomato-flavoured water for soups or sauces). Sun-dried tomatoes preserved in oil can simply be drained and chopped and added straight to a dish or eaten as they are. The oil in which they are preserved takes on a wonderful tomato flavour and can be used for cooking or to make a fabulous salad dressing. Use these tasty preserved tomatoes in soups, pasta sauces or as an Italian-style appetizer, served with mozzarella, fresh tomatoes and basil.

TOMATO PURÉE

Available in cans or in tubes, tomato purée (paste) adds a strong flavour and a very bright colour to sauces and soups. It should be used very sparingly because the flavour is quite intense and could overpower the flavour of other ingredients. Sun-dried tomato paste is also available and has the rich taste of the dried tomatoes. It is even more concentrated than regular purée, because the tomatoes have been dried and preserved in oil. You may wish to reduce the amount of oil in a recipe if you are going to use this type of purée. Tomato purée should be stored in the refrigerator once opened – tubes will keep for up to 6 months and cans of purée can be kept for up to 1 week.

THE TASTIER TOMATO

A well-flavoured tomato needs little enhancement, but there are a number of herbs and spices that complement and enliven the flavour of tomato dishes particularly well.

GARLIC
Allium sativum

Intensely fragrant and pungent, garlic has an affinity with tomatoes in numerous dishes, both hot and cold. Like onions, garlic is much milder in flavour when cooked, and can be crushed, sliced or chopped. Cloves are delicous roasted whole with tomatoes and extra virgin olive oil.

CHIVES
Allium schoenoprasum

These familiar long, thin, tubular green leaves have a mild, onion-like flavour. Chinese, Welsh or garlic chives are also mild, but have a hint of garlic in their flavour. Snip into small pieces with scissors and add to tomato salads, dressings, dips, omelettes and soups, and use as a garnish. Chives look pretty when braided, tied in a bow, or simply placed on the side of a dish.

PAPRIKA
Capsicum annuum

This rich, bright red powder is derived from a pepper that looks very like the sweet red (bell) pepper. It is widely grown in Europe, especially Hungary, and the USA. It works well with tomatoes and is the principal flavouring in goulash. Look out for pimentón dulce, which is a delicious smoked paprika from Spain.

CHILLIES
Capsicum annuum

These are actually from the same family as the tomato, so they have a natural affinity. You'll find the hot spice of chilli and sweetness of tomatoes combined in many traditional Mexican and South American dishes. The heat varies, depending on variety, but generally the smaller the chilli, the hotter it is. For a milder flavour, discard the seeds.

CINNAMON
Cinnamomum zeylanicum

The fragrant bark of a tree that is native to Sri Lanka, cinnamon is used in both sweet and savoury dishes. Its warm flavour goes well with tomatoes and chillies, a combination that often appears in Moroccan and Greek cooking. Use sticks whole, or grind fresh for the finest flavour.

CORIANDER (CILANTRO)
Coriandrum sativum

Delicate green leaves with a strong, warm, earthy flavour. Use generously in raw tomato dishes, or add towards the end of cooking to retain the flavour. Good with chilli spiced dishes.

BAY
Laurus nobilis

The slightly sweet, astringent, spicy flavour of bay is ideal for infusing into long-cooked tomato dishes such as sauces or stews, as the flavour increases with cooking. Tie the leaves into bunches and remove them before serving. Dried bay leaves are less bitter in flavour than fresh.

MINT
Mentha spicata

Fresh green leaves with a clean, refreshing flavour, favoured by the ancient Romans. Spearmint or garden mint is the main variety, though there are many other types, such as applemint and peppermint. Use it to enliven tomato soups, relishes, dips or salads. For a delicious but unusual sandwich filling, try combining sweet red tomatoes and home-produced mint jelly.

NUTMEG AND MACE
Myristica fragrans

Both have a sweet, warm, rich flavour that adds a subtle depth to tomato sauces, soups and pasta dishes. It is used for this reason in Greek moussaka. Use nutmeg freshly grated for the best, most fragrant flavour.

BASIL
Ocimum basilicum

Tomatoes and basil are classic partners, particularly in Italian dishes. Basil has a strong, aromatic and peppery flavour. Tear the fresh leaves over a tomato salad, or use basil oil for a dressing. To keep the aromatic quality, it is best added to hot dishes at the very end of cooking.

MARJORAM
Origanum marjorana

A delicate, soft-leaved herb with a sweet, spicy, fragrant flavour. It is very good in egg-based tomato dishes, or when added to the filling for stuffed tomatoes and mild-flavoured vegetarian dishes.

OREGANO
Origanum vulgare

This is a form of wild marjoram, with a strong fragrant flavour similar to cultivated marjoram. It is widely used in Greek and Italian dishes, and is particularly good with tomatoes in fish dishes, in tomato sauces and on pizzas and sprinkled on to salads.

PARSLEY
Petroselinum crispum

Both flat leaved and curly varieties are used in cooking, but the flat leaved variety is superior in flavour and is more tender to eat. It is often used with tomatoes in classic dishes such as Middle-eastern Tabbouleh and along with coriander (cilantro), it often appears in Mexican salsa recipes.

PEPPERCORNS
Piper nigrum

Dried berries from a vine that originated in the East Indies, peppercorns are commonplace today, but were once treated like treasure. Used whole or ground, they add a warm spiciness to ketchup and other tomato sauces.

ROSEMARY
Rosmarinus officinalis

These aromatic, pungent, resinous leaves go well with tomatoes in cooked meat dishes or in marinades, or can be used as a garnish. They can be used finely chopped or in sprigs to remove after cooking.

SAGE
Salvia officinalis

Silver green sage and tomatoes are old friends. An early English cookbook recommended strewing sage over tomatoes before baking, and young leaves also taste good in a tomato salad, or snipped into the filling for a stuffed tomato.

WINTER SAVORY
Saturea montana

Both winter and summer savory (*saturea hortensis*) have a pungent, slightly peppery flavour that adds interest to tomato sauces, soups and drinks based upon tomato juice. It is a little-used herb, but really does taste wonderfully savoury with tomatoes. Use fresh or dried.

THYME
Thymus vulgaris

The scent of thyme is so sweet that it is sometimes planted on paths, so that when the leaves are crushed they will perfume the air. There are several types, the most common being a shrubby plant with a very pungent flavour. It is most often cultivated, but can occasionally be found wild. It goes well with tomatoes, aubergines (eggplant), courgettes (zucchini) and onions, so is often added to ratatouille.

Above: Tomatoes and fresh herbs are a match made in heaven.

GUIDE TO TOMATO VARIETIES

There are more than 7,000 varieties of tomato, with new hybrids coming on line all the time. In choosing which types to feature in this round-up, flavour was the first priority, but second was to give some idea of how varied this versatile ingredient can be. Tomatoes come in a range of sizes, from dwarf varieties, scarcely bigger than a grape, to heavies that weigh in at more than 1.3kg/3lb. They can be round, plum, or pear shaped; squat, smooth or ribbed, and their looks can even mimic (bell) peppers. Colours range from palest cream to dark purple, and there are striped varieties that particularly appeal to children. Some are perfect for snacks and salads, others are best cooked, but all are well worth getting to know. For the finest, freshest flavour, grow them yourself, or buy them from someone who shares your enthusiasm and grows several different varieties. Farmer's markets and organic growers are good sources. The tomatoes you see in the supermarket are often specific to that chain of stores, which is why the names may not be as familiar as those you grow at home.

AILSA CRAIG

This tomato was bred by a Scottish grower in Ayrshire, and takes its name from a rocky island in the Firth of Clyde. It is grown both outdoors and under glass. The mid-red fruits are medium-size, about 5cm/2in in diameter, with smooth, thick skin. Ailsa Craig has good sweet flavour. It is the source of several successful hybrids.

Below: Alicante

ALICANTE

An early maturing English cordon-type tomato, Alicante is regarded as a good choice for novice gardeners, as it is not difficult to grow, and crops very well. The medium-size fruits are uniform, smooth and red, with a very good flavour. Alicante tomatoes remain firm when grilled (broiled), roasted or baked, and are ideal for mixed vegetable kebabs.

Below: Ararat Flamed

ARARAT FLAMED

Bred from a Hungarian variety, Debrecen, this good-looking tomato is clearly flamed, with dark green stripes on the skin, which fade as the fruit ripens. It is a cordon type, with a big yield and good flavour.

Hybrid tomatoes

These are scientifically bred from at least two parent tomatoes, which possess desirable characteristics such as disease resistance or colour, with the aim of producing a tomato that combines both features.

BRANDYWINE

The original Brandywine was developed in America by Amish farmers in the latter half of the 19th century. The plants yield well and are disease-resistant, making them a popular choice with gardeners and growers alike. The vines grow quite tall, and have leaves that resemble those of potatoes. The reddish-pink fruits – up to 900g/2lb in weight – are noted for their succulent, rich flavour. The good balance of sweetness and acidity makes this tomato a top choice for salads.

Below: Brandywine

BRITAIN'S BREAKFAST

Thick-skinned, with a superb flavour, this tomato is shaped like a lemon and is about the size of a small hen's egg. It has a striking growth pattern, with very large spreading trusses, each capable of producing more than 60 fruits. Britain's Breakfast has a sweet taste and is good raw or cooked.

Above: Britain's Breakfast

Right: Ailsa Craig

CHADWICK

This bright red cherry tomato is named in honour of Alan Chadwick, who developed the biointensive method of gardening. The vigorous, disease-resistant plants bear extremely well. Chadwick tomatoes measure about 2.5cm/1in across, and grow in clusters of five or six. They have a tangy flavour and taste good raw in salads or cooked in soups or sauces.

Above: Chadwick

DAFFODEL

These canary yellow tomatoes were bred in Britain, and are based on Gardener's Delight, a popular cordon type. Tasty and sweet, they are perfect for lunch boxes, or can be incorporated in salads. Stuffed with cream cheese, they make unusual and tasty canapés.

Below: Dark Purple Beefsteak

DARK PURPLE BEEFSTEAK

There are a number of varieties of beefsteak tomato, all big on flavour as well as size. Some specimens are so large that a single slice can be sufficient to fill a roll or sandwich. These tomatoes are also good for stuffing. The solid, meaty flesh is full of old-fashioned tomato flavour. The classic beefsteak (or beef) tomato is red, but specialities such as this dark purple variety (more often deep pink) and the pale rose Florida Pink are becoming increasingly popular. Most weigh between 350g/12oz and 450g/1lb, but there are also giant varieties including the aptly named Goliath, which can top 1.3kg/3lb. For flavour, Aunt Ginny's Purple and Big Beef are consistent favourites.

FLAMME

This French cordon-type tomato is an excellent cropper. The spherical fruits, about the size of golf balls, are a beautiful apricot-orange colour and look extremely pretty when cut. The flesh is juicy, with an intense fruity flavour, making this tomato an excellent choice for salads and salsas. Flamme also makes a good pasta sauce, and can be dried successfully.

Right: Flamme

GARDENER'S DELIGHT

One of the older varieties of British tomato, this is perennially popular. It is easy to grow, both outdoors and in the greenhouse, and yields a heavy crop. Long trusses bear clusters of dark red fruits, about 4cm/1½in in diameter. This variety has a slight tendency to split, but the flesh is meaty, with a sweet yet tangy flavour that connoisseurs claim is what tomatoes used to taste like in the days before they were bred to meet commercial rather than culinary criteria.

Above: Daffodel

Left: Gardener's Delight

*Left:
Golden
Sunrise*

GOLDEN SUNRISE

This cordon type is a heavy, reliable cropper, producing masses of medium-size round fruit. As the name suggests, these are sunshine yellow in colour. The flavour is sweet and fruity, with a slight suggestion of citrus. Slices look pretty in a two-tomato salad, and these tomatoes make an excellent garnish. Try them diced, with a light vinaigrette and a dusting of chopped mint.

*Left: Green
Zebra*

GREEN ZEBRA

As you would expect from the name, this one has stripes (dark green on a yellowish-green background, which strengthen with ripening) and looks very attractive. The tomatoes are about 7.5cm/3in across and weigh around 75g/3oz apiece. Cut them to reveal emerald green flesh with an exquisitely sweet/spicy flavour and a subtle tang. Children love them, so put them into lunch boxes or serve in salads.

HARBINGER

This English cordon-type tomato was first bred around the beginning of the 20th century. It can be grown outdoors and under glass. It is indeed a harbinger of summer, and fruits early, producing medium-size tomatoes with thin, smooth skins. Harbingers have a balanced, old-fashioned tomato flavour. The fruits ripen rapidly, both on the plant and after picking. They are good tomatoes for salads and garnishes.

Above: Harbinger

JUBILEE

An American variety of tomato that requires staking, this yields medium to large globe-shaped fruits that are a rich golden yellow or orange colour. The flavour is mild and low in acidity. Alternate slices of Jubilee and Alicante look pretty on a tomato Tart Tatin, or make the most of their colour by combining them with shellfish and pasta in a creamy saffron sauce.

Below: Jubilee

*Below: Koenig
Humbert*

KOENIG HUMBERT

Named in honour of Italy's King Umberto, this is a very old medium-early variety. It was popular in North America in the early part of the 20th century. After 1920 it became somewhat less fashionable, but as an heirloom or heritage variety it is now making a comeback. The bright scarlet 50g/2oz fruits can be prune- or pear-shaped, and are very juicy and sweet.

*Below: Lycopersicon
Ribesforme*

LYCOPERSICON RIBESFORME

Despite the gravitas of its botanical name, this is a small fruit. It is a short-lived perennial that was bred from the wild cherry tomato, and has a semi-erect, scrambling habit. As with many of the smaller tomatoes, the ratio of skin to flesh is high, so these are best grown under glass for a more tender skin. Otherwise, if the trusses are picked whole, they make a magnificent table decoration and are ideal for garnishing.

MARMANDE

One of the few types of tomato that most people know by name, Marmande originated in Provence. It does particularly well in Mediterranean regions, but will also grow in cooler climes. Aromatic and fruity, these ribbed tomatoes are good for cooking and are frequently stuffed. They are best grown outdoors, as they need bees for pollination.

Right: Mirabelle

Above: Marmande

MINI ORANGE

Quite popular a few years ago, but now less frequently grown, this is a bush variety that produces masses of small (2.5–4cm/1–1½in) round fruits. It is particularly notable for its brilliant orange colour. This is a rewarding variety to grow.

Above: Mini Orange

MIRABELLE

Similar to Gardener's Delight in all but size and colour, this has small yellow fruits with a sweet flavour. Plants of medium height produce long, heavily laden trusses. Mirabelle tomatoes make a pretty garnish and are good in salsas and salads. If you are fortunate enough to have a heavy crop, they make a delicous chutney.

Below: Moon Beam

MOON BEAM

This early-ripening tomato is a beefsteak type. Unlike many beefsteaks, which tend to be squat, the glossy orange fruits are almost spherical. Slices taste good in sandwiches and hamburgers, and the tomatoes can also be used to make a very tasty tomato jam.

ORANGE BOURGOIN

About the same size as apricots, and almost the same colour, these juicy tomatoes have a superb flavour. Fruity, mild and sweet, they are perfect for nibbling, and taste delicious in a salad with sweet orange (bell) peppers and brightly orange segments on rocket (arugula) leaves.

Above: Orange Bourgoin

PENDULINA

This is a prolific, tumbling variety of cherry tomato, often grown in hanging baskets or tubs. The fruits are bite size, and have a distinctive pointed tip. They may be yellow, orange or red, and have sweet, juicy flesh.

Right: Pendulina Yellow

Try something new

It is tempting to grow the same tomatoes every year, especially when you are on to a winner such as Gardener's Delight, but do try some of the new varieties (or newly available heirlooms) as well.

Right:
Peruvian
Horn

PERUVIAN HORN

Also known as Andine Cornue, this variety was recently introduced by a collector who brought it back from the Andes. The fruits are very large and look rather like poblano chillies or sweet (bell) peppers with pointed ends. They are particularly good for cooking, and make fine soups and sauces.

Below: Phydra

PHYDRA

Perfect for growing in hanging baskets or tubs, this 30cm/12in-high plant produces cascades of very small fruits in various colours. Children love them for their appearance and sweet flavour, and they also look very good as a garnish, especially when left on the vine.

PINK PING PONG

A robust variety, this ripens early and produces masses of unusual pinkish-red fruits the size of ping pong balls. The fruits are juicy, with a very good, sweet flavour, perfect for eating in the hand, or adding to salads.

Above: Pink Ping Pong

PRINCIPE BORGHESE

Although largely identified as a paste tomato, this aromatic Italian bush variety tastes good raw, and can also be dried very successfully. The ovoid, medium-size fruits (about 50g/2oz) are carried on large trusses and are very sugary. When grown in cooler climes, the flavour is refreshing, slightly more acidic and not too sweet.

Below: Principe Borghese

PRUDEN'S PURPLE

Large and meaty, with few seeds, this recently rediscovered heirloom tomato resembles Brandywine, but ripens earlier on in the season. The dark pink fruit are globular, with deep pleats and can weigh anything from 225g/8oz to 450g/1lb. They look and taste good. Try them sliced in sandwiches with basil, or in salads. Alternatively, stuff them with fish or shellfish for a special Mediterranean-style treat.

Below: Pruden's
Purple

Growth habits

Tomatoes grow in different ways. Bush types, which stop growing at a certain, predetermined height, do not need to be pruned or pinched out. This type of tomato is sometimes described as "determinate". Most of the fruit is produced over a four-week period. Determinate tomatoes benefit from some sort of support, to keep the fruit off the ground, but staking is not as vital as it is with the cordon or "indeterminate" tomatoes. If left to themselves, these tomatoes will go on growing and fruiting over a long period, although gardeners usually limit the growth to improve the size of the individual fruit, especially in colder climes. A third category, semi-bush tomatoes, are "determinate" but must be staked.

Below: Red Peach

ROMA

A popular Italian plum tomato, this is a medium to late producing bush variety with large leaves. The scarlet fruits weigh around 50g/2oz each. If allowed to ripen on the bush, these tomatoes have a very good flavour. They have firm, thick flesh and very few seeds, so are very good cookers and are also often used for bottling.

Below: Roma

RED PEACH

Like a peach, this early-ripening bush tomato has a fine fuzz or bloom on the skin. It is a deep orange/rose colour. The soft flesh has a mild, sweet flavour. There is also a yellow variety, which ripens to a pale, whitish/creamy colour, and whose flavour is even more intense.

Right: Red Pear

Left: Rosadel

Heirloom or heritage tomatoes

These are old-fashioned varieties, often forgotten in the rush to find new and more commercially viable tomatoes. Unlike hybrids, the seeds produced from these tomatoes will produce the same fruiting characteristics of the parent plant. Traditionally, good gardeners have always saved seed and shared it with others. Now seed merchants are doing the same, so that we can all rediscover the tempting taste of traditional tomatoes that breed true.

ROSADEL

This is one of a series (the Del series) of tomatoes bred by Lewis Darby, formerly in charge of tomato breeding at the Glasshouse Crops Research Institute in Britain. All are based on the popular Gardener's Delight, but are less prone to splitting. Rosadel is a dainty blush-pink cordon-type cherry tomato with a wonderful flavour. It fruits quite early on in the season.

RED PEAR

Full of flavour, whether freshly picked or lightly cooked, this variety is particularly popular in the USA. The small fruits, which weigh around 25g/1oz, look like party light bulbs, and grow on strong, tall vines. They are well named, being decidedly pear shaped. There is also a yellow variety, which is equally popular but does not have quite such a rich taste. When sliced in half lengthways, these look pretty on a platter, epecially when interleaved with basil and drizzled with dark green olive oil.

RUFFLED

The name refers to the appearance of these tomatoes, the skin of which looks as though it has been tweaked into accordion pleats. The hollow seed cavity makes them perfect for stuffing, and they also look very attractive when hollowed out and filled with a salad. There are several varieties of ruffled tomatoes, both red and yellow.

Below: Ruffled

SAN MARZANO

Similar to Roma, but larger and tastier, this is a good all-rounder, suitable for eating fresh in salads and sandwiches, but also ideal for sun-drying or bottling. Of Italian origin, it has been described as the original Italian tomato for sauces and pastes.

Above: San Marzano

Improving taste

The taste of a tomato depends on three main factors: the variety, the weather and the growing medium. Of all three, the natural quality and nutrient content of the soil makes a remarkable impact on flavour – after all, it is mostly from the roots that the tomatoes are fed. So enrich your soil and enjoy your harvest.

Above: Sun Belle

SUN BELLE

This small yellow tomato is shaped like a plum. It is noted for its exceptional flavour, and is high in both acid and sugar. A heavy cropper, it can be grown in cold or heated greenhouses. Enjoy it fresh in salads or salsas.

TIGERELLA

The name gives it away. This is another striped tomato (also known as Mr Stripey), and typically has greenish-yellow or orange broken stripes on a dark red background, which is largely lost on ripening. The small, round fruits are 4–5cm/1½–2in in diameter. A very early cordon-type, Tigerella can be grown outdoors or under glass. It has a tangy, almost tart flavour, and makes a good addition to salads.

Above: Yellow Butterfly

YELLOW BUTTERFLY

As pretty as its name suggests, this is a cordon-type tomato, producing 25g/1oz slightly pear-shaped cherry tomatoes, with a very sweet taste. It is an exceptionally heavy cropper, and grows best under glass. It makes an excellent cocktail snack if filled with soft cheese and chives, or, if you are feeling adventurous, it makes a surprising dessert if stewed with apples and sugar and made into a crumble (crisp).

Above: Supersweet 100

Above: Tigerella

Below: Tiny Tim

SUPERSWEET 100

A hybrid version of Gardener's Delight, this salad tomato is usually grown under glass. Each truss produces up to 100 bright red cherry tomatoes, each about 2cm/¾in in diameter. The flavour is sweet, rich and well balanced. It is claimed that the Supersweet 100 tomato is higher in Vitamin C than any other variety.

TINY TIM

Only about 2cm/¾in across, these tasty red dwarf tomatoes grow on decorative bush-type plants, which look good in tubs and hanging baskets. They are perfect for salads and as snacks. Tiny Tims also look attractive sliced on cocktail-size pizzas.

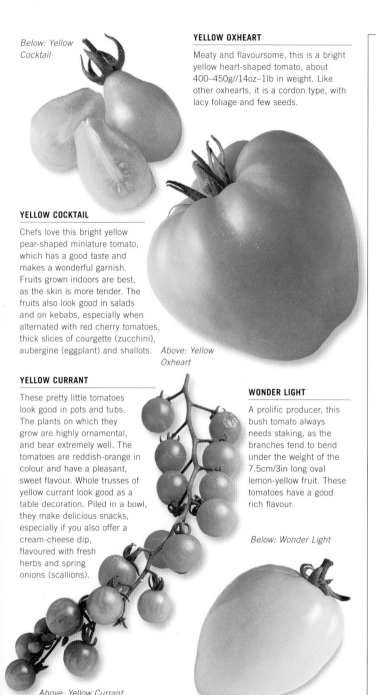

Below: Yellow Cocktail

YELLOW OXHEART

Meaty and flavoursome, this is a bright yellow heart-shaped tomato, about 400–450g//14oz–1lb in weight. Like other oxhearts, it is a cordon type, with lacy foliage and few seeds.

YELLOW COCKTAIL

Chefs love this bright yellow pear-shaped miniature tomato, which has a good taste and makes a wonderful garnish. Fruits grown indoors are best, as the skin is more tender. The fruits also look good in salads and on kebabs, especially when alternated with red cherry tomatoes, thick slices of courgette (zucchini), aubergine (eggplant) and shallots.

Above: Yellow Oxheart

YELLOW CURRANT

These pretty little tomatoes look good in pots and tubs. The plants on which they grow are highly ornamental, and bear extremely well. The tomatoes are reddish-orange in colour and have a pleasant, sweet flavour. Whole trusses of yellow currant look good as a table decoration. Piled in a bowl, they make delicious snacks, especially if you also offer a cream-cheese dip, flavoured with fresh herbs and spring onions (scallions).

Above: Yellow Currant

WONDER LIGHT

A prolific producer, this bush tomato always needs staking, as the branches tend to bend under the weight of the 7.5cm/3in long oval lemon-yellow fruit. These tomatoes have a good rich flavour.

Below: Wonder Light

OTHER POPULAR VARIETIES

Amish Paste

An American heirloom tomato from Wisconsin. The 225g/8oz fruits are a cordon type and are large and elongated, with a deep red colour. Firm and meaty, with few seeds and low acidity, Amish Paste tomatoes are used for canning and for sauces.

Black Krim

For a dramatic effect, there are few tomatoes to equal this one. The skin is of such a deep tone of red that it often appears to be black, with a hint of dark green on the heavy shoulders. It comes from the Black Sea port of Krymsk and is sometimes known as Black Russian. The very large, slightly irregular fruits can weigh up to 350g/12oz and have maroon flesh, noted for its delicate, melting tenderness and rich, complex flavour.

Costoluto Fiorentino

An Italian beefsteak-type tomato, grown outdoors. The fruits are large, up to 10cm/4in in diameter, with irregular ribbing. They have a fleshy texture and exceptionally good flavour, and are ideal for stuffing, slicing and serving raw in salads.

Costoluto Genovese

A prolific variety from the Italian Riviera, first recorded in 1805. This scarlet, ribbed tomato loves hot climates and is grown throughout the Mediterranean. The large, attractive fruits average about 200g/7oz. They have a meaty texture and are full-flavoured, with a hint of acidity. The ribbing ensures that they look good sliced in salads, but they also cook well and make fine pasta sauces. They look very similar to Pruden's Purple, but are more deeply lobed.

THE RECIPES

Although tomatoes taste wonderful when picked straight from the vine, they are equally at home in the kitchen, whether simply sandwiched between slices of fresh bread and drizzled with olive oil, topping a tart, or playing a supporting role in a salad or stew. Tomatoes are endlessly versatile, as is amply illustrated by the tempting recipes that follow. We enjoy tomatoes all day long, and they feature in starters, snacks, main courses, chutneys and drinks. We love tomatoes in all their guises, fresh, canned or dried; as juices, sauces or salsa; puréed or as paste. So, dedicating an entire volume to this indispensable ingredient wasn't difficult — just a tribute to good taste.

The best soups are packed with flavour, and there's nothing better than a few ripe tomatoes to add that extra richness that makes a chilled soup such as Iced Tomato and Vodka Soup so special, or a warming Onion and Tomato Soup so comforting. And what better way to start a meal than with the tangy flavour of juicy tomatoes? Try the delectable Tomato and Cheese Tarts or rustic Baked Polenta with Tomatoes; the possibilities are endless.

Soups and Appetizers

CHILLED TOMATO AND SWEET PEPPER SOUP

A RECIPE INSPIRED BY THE SPANISH GAZPACHO, WHERE RAW INGREDIENTS ARE COMBINED TO MAKE A CHILLED SOUP. IN THIS RECIPE THE INGREDIENTS ARE COOKED FIRST AND THEN CHILLED.

SERVES FOUR

INGREDIENTS
  2 red (bell) peppers, halved
  45ml/3 tbsp olive oil
  1 onion, finely chopped
  2 garlic cloves, crushed
  675g/1½lb ripe well-flavoured
    tomatoes
  150ml/¼ pint/⅔ cup red wine
  600ml/1 pint/2½ cups vegetable stock
  salt and ground black pepper
  chopped fresh chives, to garnish
For the croûtons
  2 slices day-old white bread,
    crusts removed
  60ml/4 tbsp olive oil

COOK'S TIP
Any juice that accumulates in the pan after grilling (broiling) the peppers, or in the bowl, should be stirred into the soup. It will add a delectable flavour.

1 Cut each pepper half into quarters and seed. Place skin-side up on a grill (broiling) rack and cook until the skins have charred. Transfer to a bowl and cover with a plate.

2 Heat the oil in a large pan. Add the onion and garlic, and cook until soft. Meanwhile, remove the skin from the peppers and roughly chop them. Cut the tomatoes into chunks.

3 Add the peppers and tomatoes to the pan, then cover and cook gently for 10 minutes. Add the wine and cook for a further 5 minutes, then add the stock and salt and pepper, and simmer for 20 minutes.

4 To make the croûtons, cut the bread into cubes. Heat the oil in a small frying pan, add the bread and fry until golden. Drain on paper towels, cool, then store in an airtight box.

5 Process the soup in a blender or food processor until smooth. Pour into a clean glass or ceramic bowl and leave to cool thoroughly before chilling for at least 3 hours. When the soup is cold, season to taste.

6 Serve the soup in bowls, topped with the croûtons and garnished with chopped chives.

CHILLED TOMATO AND BASIL-FLOWER SOUP

THIS IS A REALLY FRESH-TASTING SOUP, PACKED WITH THE COMPLEMENTARY FLAVOURS OF TOMATO AND BASIL, AND TOPPED WITH PRETTY PINK AND PURPLE SWEET BASIL FLOWERS.

SERVES FOUR

INGREDIENTS

15ml/1 tbsp olive oil
1 onion, finely chopped
1 garlic clove, crushed
600ml/1 pint/2½ cups vegetable
    stock
900g/2lb tomatoes, roughly chopped
20 fresh basil leaves
a few drops of balsamic vinegar
juice of ½ lemon
150ml/¼ pint/⅔ cup natural
    (plain) yogurt
granulated sugar and salt, to taste
For the garnish
30ml/2 tbsp natural (plain) yogurt
8 small basil leaves
10ml/2 tsp basil flowers, all green
    parts removed

COOK'S TIP
Basil flowers may be small but they certainly have a beautifully aromatic flavour and are surprisingly sweet. They can be used fresh in all sorts of ways by being added with basil leaves to tomato salads or pizza toppings, sprinkled on pastas, or used as flavourings in tomato juice. To remove the flowers from the stem, simply pull – they will come away easily. Purple-leaved basil has a pretty mauve flower, which is delicious too.

1 Heat the oil in a pan and add the finely chopped onion and garlic. Fry the onion and garlic in the oil for 2–3 minutes until soft and transparent, stirring occasionally.

2 Add 300ml/½ pint/1¼ cups of the vegetable stock and the chopped tomatoes to the pan. Bring to the boil, then lower the heat and simmer the mixture for 15 minutes. Stir it occasionally to prevent it from sticking to the base of the pan.

3 Allow the mixture to cool slightly, then transfer it to a food processor and process until smooth. Press through a sieve placed over a bowl to remove the tomato skins and seeds.

4 Return the mixture to the food processor and add the remainder of the stock, half the basil leaves, the vinegar, lemon juice and yogurt. Season with sugar and salt to taste. Process until smooth. Pour into a bowl and chill.

5 Just before serving, finely shred the remaining basil leaves and add them to the soup. Pour the chilled soup into individual bowls. Garnish with yogurt topped with a few small basil leaves and a sprinkling of basil flowers.

ICED TOMATO AND VODKA SOUP

THIS FRESH-FLAVOURED SOUP PACKS A PUNCH LIKE A FROZEN BLOODY MARY. IT IS DELICIOUS SERVED
AS AN IMPRESSIVE FIRST COURSE FOR A SUMMER'S DINNER PARTY WITH SUN-DRIED TOMATO BREAD.

SERVES FOUR

INGREDIENTS

    450g/1lb ripe, well-flavoured
      tomatoes, halved or
      roughly chopped
    600ml/1 pint/2½ cups jellied beef
      stock or consommé
    1 small red onion, halved
    2 celery sticks, cut into large pieces
    1 garlic clove, roughly chopped
    15ml/1 tbsp tomato purée (paste)
    10ml/2 tsp lemon juice
    10ml/2 tsp Worcestershire sauce
    a handful of small fresh basil leaves
    30ml/2 tbsp vodka
    salt and ground black pepper
    crushed ice, 4 small celery sticks and
      Sun-dried Tomato Bread, to serve

1 Put the halved or chopped tomatoes, jellied stock or consommé, onion and celery in a blender or food processor. Add the garlic, then spoon in the tomato purée. Pulse until all the vegetables are finely chopped, then process to a smooth paste.

2 Press the mixture through a sieve into a large bowl and stir in the lemon juice, Worcestershire sauce, basil leaves and vodka.

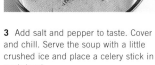

3 Add salt and pepper to taste. Cover and chill. Serve the soup with a little crushed ice and place a celery stick in each bowl.

COOK'S TIPS
• Canned beef consommé is ideal for this recipe, but vegetable stock, for vegetarians, will work well too.
• If you or your guests are fond of celery, you can stand more celery sticks in a jug (pitcher) of iced water on the table for people to help themselves. The celery sticks can be used as additional edible stirrers and taste delicious after being dipped into the soup.
• Making your own sun-dried tomato bread is easy and is bound to impress your guests. If you don't have time, however, look out for tomato-flavoured ciabatta or focaccia.

GAZPACHO WITH AVOCADO SALSA

TOMATOES, CUCUMBER AND PEPPERS FORM THE BASIS OF THIS CLASSIC, CHILLED SOUP. ADD A SPOONFUL OF CHUNKY, FRESH AVOCADO SALSA AND A SCATTERING OF CROÛTONS, AND SERVE FOR A LIGHT LUNCH OR SIMPLE SUPPER ON A WARM SUMMER DAY.

SERVES FOUR

INGREDIENTS

2 slices day-old white bread, cubed
600ml/1 pint/2½ cups chilled water
1kg/2¼lb tomatoes
1 cucumber
1 red (bell) pepper, halved, seeded
  and chopped
1 fresh green chilli, seeded
  and chopped
2 garlic cloves, chopped
30ml/2 tbsp extra virgin olive oil
juice of 1 lime and 1 lemon
a few drops of Tabasco sauce
salt and ground black pepper
8 ice cubes, to garnish
a handful of basil leaves, to garnish
For the croûtons
2 slices day-old bread,
  crusts removed
1 garlic clove, halved
15ml/1 tbsp olive oil
For the avocado salsa
1 ripe avocado
5ml/1 tsp lemon juice
2.5cm/1in piece cucumber, diced
½ red chilli, seeded and
  finely chopped

1 Place the bread in a large bowl and pour over 150ml/¼pint/ ⅔ cup of the water. Leave to soak for 5 minutes.

2 Meanwhile, place the tomatoes in a bowl and cover with boiling water. Leave for 30 seconds, then peel off the skin, remove the seeds and finely chop the flesh.

3 Thinly peel the cucumber, then cut it in half lengthways and scoop out the seeds with a teaspoon. Discard the inner part and chop the flesh.

4 Place the bread, tomatoes, cucumber, red pepper, chilli, garlic, olive oil, citrus juices and Tabasco in a food processor or blender with the remaining 450ml/ ¾ pint/scant 2 cups chilled water and blend until well combined but still chunky. Season to taste and chill for 2–3 hours.

5 To make the croûtons, rub the slices of bread with the garlic clove. Cut the bread into cubes and place in a plastic bag with the olive oil. Seal the bag and shake until the bread cubes are coated with the oil.

6 Heat a large non-stick frying pan and fry the croûtons over a medium heat until crisp and golden.

7 Just before serving, make the avocado salsa. Halve the avocado, remove the stone (pit), then peel and dice. Toss the avocado in the lemon juice to prevent it from browning, then place it in a serving bowl and add the cucumber and chilli. Mix well.

8 Ladle the soup into four chilled bowls and add a couple of ice cubes to each. Top each portion with a good spoonful of avocado salsa. Garnish with the basil and sprinkle the croûtons over the top of the salsa.

FRESH TOMATO SOUP

THE COMBINATION OF INTENSELY FLAVOURED SUN-RIPENED AND FRESH TOMATOES NEEDS LITTLE EMBELLISHMENT IN THIS TASTY ITALIAN SOUP. CHOOSE THE RIPEST-LOOKING TOMATOES AND ADD SUGAR AND BALSAMIC VINEGAR TO TASTE. THE QUANTITY WILL DEPEND ON THE NATURAL SWEETNESS OF THE FRESH TOMATOES. ON A HOT DAY, THIS SOUP IS ALSO DELICIOUS CHILLED.

SERVES SIX

INGREDIENTS
  1.3–1.6kg/3–3½lb ripe tomatoes
  400ml/14fl oz/1⅔ cups chicken or
    vegetable stock
  45ml/3 tbsp sun-dried tomato
    purée (paste)
  30–45ml/2–3 tbsp balsamic vinegar
  10–15ml/2–3 tsp sugar
  a small handful of fresh basil leaves,
    plus extra to garnish
  salt and ground black pepper
  toasted cheese croûtes and crème
    fraîche, to serve

COOK'S TIP
Use a sharp knife to cut a cross in the base of each tomato before plunging it into the boiling water. The skin will then peel back easily from the crosses.

1 Plunge the tomatoes into boiling water for 30 seconds, then refresh in cold water. Peel off the skins and quarter the tomatoes. Put them in a large pan and pour over the chicken or vegetable stock. Bring just to the boil, reduce the heat, cover and simmer gently for 10 minutes until the tomatoes are pulpy.

2 Stir in the tomato purée, vinegar, sugar and basil. Season with salt and pepper, then cook gently, stirring, for 2 minutes. Process the soup in a blender or food processor, then return to a clean pan and reheat gently. Serve in bowls, topped with one or two toasted cheese croûtes and a spoonful of crème fraîche, garnished with basil leaves.

FRAGRANT TOMATO SOUP

ALTHOUGH BASIL IS TRADITIONALLY USED TO PARTNER TOMATOES, FRESH CORIANDER ALSO COMPLEMENTS THEIR FLAVOUR. THIS WARMING SOUP IS EXCELLENT ON A COLD WINTER'S DAY.

3 Add the salt, garlic, peppercorns and fresh coriander to the tomato mixture. Add the water and bring to the boil, lower the heat and simmer for 15–20 minutes.

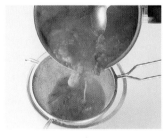

4 Dissolve the cornflour in a little cold water. Remove the soup from the heat and press it through a sieve.

SERVES FOUR

INGREDIENTS
  675g/1½lb tomatoes
  30ml/2 tbsp vegetable oil
  1 bay leaf
  4 spring onions (scallions), chopped
  5ml/1 tsp salt
  1 garlic clove, crushed
  5ml/1 tsp black peppercorns, crushed
  30ml/2 tbsp chopped fresh
    coriander (cilantro)
  750ml/1¼ pints/3 cups water
  15ml/1 tbsp cornflour (cornstarch)
  1 spring onion (scallion), chopped and
    30ml/2 tbsp single (light) cream,
    to garnish

COOK'S TIP
In winter when fresh tomatoes can be rather pale and under-ripe, add 15ml/ 1 tbsp tomato purée (paste).

1 Plunge the tomatoes into boiling water for 30 seconds, then refresh in cold water. Peel away the skins and chop the tomatoes.

2 In a medium pan, heat the oil and fry the chopped tomatoes, bay leaf and spring onions for a few minutes until the spring onions are soft and the tomatoes have cooked down a little.

5 Return the soup to a clean pan, add the cornflour paste and stir over a very gentle heat for about 3 minutes or so until thickened. Pour the soup into individual serving dishes and garnish with the chopped spring onion and cream. Serve.

TOMATO AND FRESH BASIL SOUP

A SOUP FOR LATE SUMMER WHEN FRESH TOMATOES ARE AT THEIR MOST FLAVOURSOME. SERVE WITH ONE OF THE MANY FLAVOURED BREADS YOU CAN BUY — A PESTO, OLIVE OR ROSEMARY LOAF WOULD GO PARTICULARLY WELL WITH THIS SOUP, OR SERVE WARM SODA BREAD.

SERVES FOUR TO SIX

INGREDIENTS

15ml/1 tbsp olive oil
25g/1oz/2 tbsp butter
1 medium onion, finely chopped
900g/2lb ripe plum tomatoes, chopped
1 garlic clove, chopped
750ml/1¼ pints/3 cups chicken stock
120ml/4fl oz/½ cup dry white wine
30ml/2 tbsp sun-dried tomato
   purée (paste)
30ml/2 tbsp shredded fresh basil
150ml/¼ pint/⅔ cup double
   (heavy) cream
salt and ground black pepper
fresh basil, to garnish

1 Heat the oil and butter in a large pan until foaming. Add the onion and cook gently for about 5 minutes, stirring frequently with a wooden spoon, until softened but not brown.

2 Stir in the chopped tomatoes and garlic, then add the stock, wine and sun-dried tomato purée, with salt and pepper to taste. Bring to the boil, then lower the heat, half cover the pan and simmer gently for 20 minutes, stirring occasionally to stop the tomatoes sticking to the base of the pan.

3 Process the soup with the shredded basil in a blender or food processor, then press through a sieve into a clean pan.

4 Add the double cream and heat through very gently, stirring. Do not allow the soup to overheat. Check the consistency and add a little more stock or water if necessary, then taste for seasoning. Pour into heated bowls and garnish with basil. Serve at once.

VARIATION
This soup can also be served chilled. Pour it into a container after sieving, allow to cool to room temperature and then chill in the refrigerator for at least 4 hours. Serve in chilled bowls.

ROASTED GARLIC AND BUTTERNUT SQUASH SOUP WITH TOMATO SALSA

THIS IS A WONDERFUL, RICHLY-FLAVOURED DISH. A SPOONFUL OF THE HOT AND SPICY TOMATO SALSA GIVES BITE TO THE SWEET-TASTING SQUASH AND GARLIC SOUP.

SERVES FOUR TO FIVE

INGREDIENTS

2 garlic bulbs, outer papery
 skin removed
a few fresh thyme sprigs
75ml/5 tbsp olive oil
1 large butternut squash, halved
 and seeded
2 onions, chopped
5ml/1 tsp ground coriander
1.2 litres/2 pints/5 cups vegetable or
 chicken stock
30–45ml/2–3 tbsp chopped fresh
 oregano or marjoram
salt and ground black pepper
For the salsa
4 large ripe tomatoes, halved
 and seeded
1 red (bell) pepper, seeded
1 large fresh red chilli, halved
 and seeded
30ml/2 tbsp extra virgin olive oil
15ml/1 tbsp balsamic vinegar
pinch of caster (superfine) sugar

1 Preheat the oven to 220°C/425°F/
Gas 7. Place the garlic bulbs on a piece
of foil, add the thyme and drizzle over
half the olive oil, then fold the foil
around the garlic bulbs to enclose them.

2 Transfer the foil parcel to a baking
sheet with the butternut squash and
brush the squash with 15ml/1 tbsp of
the remaining olive oil. Place the
tomatoes, red pepper and fresh chilli
for the salsa on the baking sheet.

3 Roast the vegetables for 25 minutes,
then remove the tomatoes, pepper and
chilli. Reduce the temperature to 190°C/
375°F/Gas 5 and cook the squash and
garlic for 20–25 minutes more, or until
the squash is tender.

4 Heat the remaining oil in a large,
heavy pan and cook the onions and
ground coriander gently for about
10 minutes, or until softened and just
beginning to brown.

5 Meanwhile, skin the pepper and
chilli, then process them in a food
processor or blender with the tomatoes
and the olive oil for the salsa. Stir in the
balsamic vinegar and seasoning to
taste, adding a pinch of caster sugar,
if necessary, to moderate the taste.

6 Squeeze the roasted garlic out of its
papery skin into the onions and scoop
the squash out of its skin, adding it
to the pan too. Add the stock, 5ml/1 tsp
salt and plenty of black pepper. Bring to
the boil, then simmer for 10 minutes.

7 Stir in half the fresh oregano or
marjoram and cool the soup slightly
before processing it in a blender or food
processor. Alternatively, use a wooden
spoon to press the soup through a fine
sieve placed over a bowl.

8 Reheat the soup without allowing it
to boil, then taste for seasoning before
ladling it into warmed bowls. Top each
with a spoonful of salsa and sprinkle with
the remaining chopped oregano or
marjoram. Serve immediately.

ONION <u>AND</u> TOMATO SOUP

THIS WARMING WINTER SOUP COMES FROM UMBRIA, IN ITALY, WHERE IT WAS TRADITIONALLY
THICKENED WITH BEATEN EGGS AND LOTS OF GRATED PARMESAN CHEESE. IT WAS THEN SERVED
ON TOP OF HOT TOASTED CROÛTES – RATHER LIKE SAVOURY SCRAMBLED EGGS.

SERVES FOUR

INGREDIENTS
115g/4oz pancetta, rind removed,
    roughly chopped
30ml/2 tbsp olive oil
15g/½oz/1 tbsp butter
675g/1½lb onions, thinly sliced
10ml/2 tsp granulated sugar
350g/12oz ripe plum tomatoes
about 1.2 litres/2 pints/5 cups
    chicken stock
a few fresh basil leaves, shredded
salt and ground black pepper
ciabatta and a chunk of Parmesan
    cheese, to serve

1 Put the chopped pancetta in a large
pan and heat gently, stirring constantly,
until the fat runs. Increase the heat to
medium, add the oil, butter, onions and
sugar, and stir well to mix.

2 Half cover the pan and cook the
onions gently for about 20 minutes until
golden. Lift the lid and stir frequently,
lowering the heat if necessary.

3 Plunge the tomatoes into boiling
water for 30 seconds, refresh in
cold water, drain and peel.

4 Chop the tomatoes and add to the
pan with the stock. Add salt and pepper
and bring to the boil, stirring. Lower the
heat, half cover the pan and simmer,
stirring occasionally, for about
30 minutes.

5 Check the consistency of the soup
and add a little more stock or water if it
is too thick.

6 Just before serving, stir in most of
the basil and taste for seasoning. Serve
hot, garnished with the remaining basil.
Serve with ciabatta and invite guests to
grate in their own Parmesan.

COOK'S TIPS
• Beefsteak tomatoes are good in this
soup as they are very fleshy with few
seeds. You could try adding a few whole
cherry tomatoes just before the end of
the cooking time, which will add an
interesting look to the dish.
• Look for Vidalia onions to make this
soup. They are often available at
large supermarkets, and have a very
sweet, mild flavour and attractive
yellowish flesh.

PISTOU

A DELICIOUS CHUNKY VEGETABLE SOUP FROM NICE IN THE SOUTH OF FRANCE, SERVED WITH A
TOMATO PESTO, AND FRESH PARMESAN CHEESE. SERVE IN SMALL PORTIONS AS AN APPETIZER, OR
IN LARGER BOWLS WITH CRUSTY BREAD AS A FILLING LUNCH.

SERVES FOUR TO SIX

INGREDIENTS

   1 courgette (zucchini), diced
   1 small potato, diced
   1 shallot, chopped
   1 carrot, diced
   400g/14oz can chopped tomatoes
   1.2 litres/2 pints/5 cups vegetable
    stock
   50g/2oz green beans, cut into
    1cm/½in lengths
   50g/2oz/½ cup frozen petits pois
    (baby peas)
   50g/2oz/½ cup small pasta shapes
   60–90ml/4–6 tbsp pesto
   15ml/1 tbsp tomato purée (paste)
   salt and ground black pepper
   freshly grated (shredded) Parmesan
    or Pecorino cheese, to serve

1 Place the courgette, potato, shallot, carrot and tomatoes, with the can juices, in a large pan. Add the vegetable stock and season with salt and plenty of ground black pepper. Bring to the boil over a medium to high heat, then lower the heat, cover the pan and simmer for 20 minutes.

2 Bring the soup back to the boil and add the green beans and petits pois to the pan. Cook the mixture briefly, for about a minute.

VARIATION
To strengthen the tomato flavour, try using tomato-flavoured spaghetti, broken into small lengths, instead of the small pasta shapes. Sun-dried tomato purée (paste) can be used instead of regular.

3 Add the pasta. Cook the mixture for a further 10 minutes, until the pasta is tender. Taste and adjust the seasoning.

4 Ladle the soup into bowls. Mix together the pesto and tomato purée, and stir a spoonful into each serving. Sprinkle with freshly grated cheese.

MOROCCAN HARIRA

THIS IS A HEARTY MAIN-COURSE MEAT AND VEGETABLE SOUP, EATEN DURING THE MONTH OF RAMADAN, WHEN THE MUSLIM POPULATION FASTS BETWEEN SUNRISE AND SUNSET.

SERVES FOUR

INGREDIENTS
  450g/1lb well-flavoured tomatoes
  225g/8oz lamb, cut into pieces
  2.5ml/½ tsp ground turmeric
  2.5ml/½ tsp ground cinnamon
  25g/1oz/2 tbsp butter
  60ml/4 tbsp chopped fresh coriander
    (cilantro)
  30ml/2 tbsp chopped fresh parsley
  1 onion, chopped
  50g/2oz/¼ cup split red lentils
  75g/3oz/½ cup dried chickpeas,
    soaked overnight in cold water
  600ml/1 pint/2½ cups water
  4 baby (pearl) onions or shallots
  25g/1oz/¼ cup fine noodles
  salt and ground black pepper
  fresh coriander (cilantro), lemon
    slices and ground cinnamon,
    to garnish

COOK'S TIPS
• Most of the vitamins in fruits and vegetables are just under the skin. So, if you wish to improve the nutritional content, or simply save some time, the skins of the tomatoes can be left on.
• For maximum cinnamon flavour, grind a broken cinnamon stick in a spice grinder or a coffee grinder kept especially for the purpose.

1 Plunge the tomatoes into boiling water for 30 seconds, then refresh in cold water. Peel off the skins. Cut into quarters and remove the seeds. Chop the flesh roughly.

2 Put the pieces of lamb, ground turmeric, cinnamon, butter, fresh coriander, parsley and onion into a large pan, and cook over a medium heat, stirring, for 5 minutes.

3 Add the chopped tomatoes and continue to cook for 10 minutes, stirring the mixture frequently.

4 Rinse the lentils under running water and drain them well. Stir them into the contents of the pan, with the drained chickpeas and the measured water. Season with salt and pepper. Bring to the boil, lower the heat, cover, and simmer gently for 1½ hours.

5 Add the onions or shallots. Cook for 25 minutes. Add the noodles and cook for 5 minutes more. Spoon into bowls and garnish with the coriander, lemon slices and cinnamon.

SUMMER VEGETABLE SOUP

THIS BRIGHTLY COLOURED, FRESH-TASTING TOMATO SOUP MAKES THE MOST OF SUMMER VEGETABLES IN SEASON. ADD LOTS OF RED AND YELLOW PEPPERS TO MAKE A SWEETER VERSION.

SERVES FOUR

INGREDIENTS
450g/1lb ripe plum tomatoes
225g/8oz ripe yellow tomatoes
45ml/3 tbsp olive oil
1 large onion, finely chopped
15ml/1 tbsp sun-dried tomato
  purée (paste)
225g/8oz green courgettes (summer
  squash), trimmed and roughly chopped
225g/8oz yellow courgettes, trimmed
  and roughly chopped
3 waxy new potatoes, diced
2 garlic cloves, crushed
about 1.2 litres/2 pints/5 cups
  chicken stock or water
60ml/4 tbsp shredded fresh basil
50g/2oz/⅔ cup freshly grated
  (shredded) Parmesan cheese
sea salt and freshly ground
  black pepper

1 Plunge all the tomatoes in boiling water for 30 seconds, refresh in cold water, then peel and chop finely. Heat the oil in a large pan, add the onion and cook gently for about 5 minutes, stirring constantly, until softened. Stir in the sun-dried tomato purée, chopped tomatoes, courgettes, diced potatoes and garlic. Mix well and cook gently for 10 minutes, shaking the pan often.

2 Pour in the stock or water. Bring to the boil, lower the heat, half cover the pan and simmer gently for 15 minutes or until the vegetables are just tender. Add more stock or water if necessary.

3 Remove the pan from the heat and stir in the basil and half the cheese. Taste for seasoning. Serve hot, sprinkled with the remaining cheese.

TORTILLA TOMATO SOUP

THERE ARE SEVERAL TORTILLA SOUPS. THIS ONE IS AN AGUADA — OR LIQUID — VERSION, AND IS INTENDED FOR SERVING AS AN APPETIZER OR LIGHT MEAL. IT IS VERY EASY AND QUICK TO PREPARE, OR MAKE IT IN ADVANCE AND FRY THE TORTILLA STRIPS AS IT REHEATS. THE CRISP TORTILLA PIECES ADD INTEREST AND GIVE THE SOUP AN UNUSUAL TEXTURE.

SERVES FOUR

INGREDIENTS
4 corn tortillas
15ml/1 tbsp vegetable oil, plus extra,
   for frying
1 small onion, chopped
2 garlic cloves, crushed
350g/12oz ripe plum tomatoes
400g/14oz can plum tomatoes, drained
1 litre/1¾ pints/4 cups chicken stock
small bunch of fresh coriander (cilantro)
50g/2oz/½ cup grated (shredded)
   mild Cheddar cheese
salt and ground black pepper

1 Using a sharp knife, cut each tortilla into four or five strips, each measuring about 2cm/¾in wide. Pour vegetable oil to a depth of 2cm/¾in into a frying pan. Heat until a small piece of tortilla, added to the oil, floats on the top and bubbles at the edges.

2 Add a few tortilla strips to the hot oil and fry until crisp and golden brown.

3 Remove the tortilla chips with a slotted spoon and drain on kitchen paper. Cook the remaining tortilla strips in the same way.

4 Heat the 15ml/1 tbsp vegetable oil in a large pan. Add the onion and garlic and cook over a medium heat for 2–3 minutes, until the onion is soft and translucent. Do not let the garlic turn brown or it will give the soup a bitter taste.

5 Skin the fresh tomatoes by plunging them into boiling water for 30 seconds, refreshing them in cold water, draining them and then peeling off the skins with a sharp knife.

6 Chop the fresh and canned tomatoes and add them to the onion mixture. Pour in the chicken stock. Bring to the boil, then lower the heat and simmer for 10 minutes, until the liquid has reduced slightly. Stir occasionally.

7 Roughly chop or tear the coriander into pieces. Add it to the soup and season with salt and ground black pepper to taste.

8 Place a few of the crisp tortilla pieces in each of four large heated soup bowls. Ladle the soup on top. Sprinkle each portion with some of the grated mild Cheddar cheese and serve immediately.

COOK'S TIP
An easy way to chop fresh herbs is to put them in a mug and snip with a pair of scissors. Hold the scissors vertically with one hand on each handle and work the blades back and forth until the herbs are finely and evenly chopped. If you are using woody herbs, such as rosemary or thyme, remember to strip the leaves from the stalks before putting them in the mug. They are then ready to be chopped.

RIBOLLITA

THIS SOUP IS RATHER LIKE AN ITALIAN MINESTRONE. IT IS BASED ON TOMATOES, BUT WITH BEANS INSTEAD OF PASTA. IN ITALY IT IS TRADITIONALLY LADLED OVER BREAD AND A GREEN VEGETABLE.

SERVES SIX TO EIGHT

INGREDIENTS
    350g/12oz well-flavoured tomatoes,
        preferably plum tomatoes
    45ml/3 tbsp extra virgin olive oil or
        sunflower oil
    2 onions, chopped
    2 carrots, sliced
    4 garlic cloves, crushed
    2 celery sticks, thinly sliced
    1 fennel bulb, trimmed and chopped
    2 large courgettes (zucchini),
        thinly sliced
    400g/14oz can chopped tomatoes
    30ml/2 tbsp pesto
    900ml/1½ pints/3¾ cups vegetable
        stock
    400g/14oz can haricot (navy) or
        borlotti beans, drained
    salt and ground black pepper
To finish
    15ml/1 tbsp extra virgin olive oil,
        plus extra for drizzling
    450g/1lb fresh young spinach
    6–8 slices white bread
    Parmesan or Pecorino
        cheese shavings

1 To skin the tomatoes, plunge them into boiling water for 30 seconds, refresh in cold water and then peel off the skins. Chop the tomato flesh and set it aside.

2 Heat the oil in a large pan. Add the onions, carrots, garlic, celery and fennel and fry gently for 10 minutes. Add the courgettes and fry for a further 2 minutes.

3 Stir in the chopped fresh and canned tomatoes, pesto, stock and beans, and bring to the boil. Lower the heat, cover the pan and simmer gently for 25–30 minutes, until the vegetables are completely tender and the stock is full of flavour. Season the soup with salt and pepper to taste.

4 To finish, heat the oil in a frying pan and fry the spinach for 2 minutes or until wilted. Place a slice of bread in each serving bowl, top with the spinach and then ladle the soup over the spinach. Serve with extra olive oil for drizzling on to the soup, and Parmesan cheese to sprinkle on top.

BORLOTTI BEAN AND PASTA SOUP

A COMPLETE MEAL IN A BOWL, THIS IS A VERSION OF A CLASSIC ITALIAN SOUP. TRADITIONALLY, THE PERSON WHO FINDS THE BAY LEAF IS HONOURED WITH A KISS FROM THE COOK.

SERVES FOUR

INGREDIENTS

    1 onion, chopped
    1 celery stick, chopped
    2 carrots, chopped
    75ml/5 tbsp olive oil
    1 bay leaf
    1 glass white wine (optional)
    1 litre/1¾ pints/4 cups vegetable
      stock
    400g/14oz can chopped tomatoes
    300ml/½ pint/1¼ cups passata
      (bottled strained tomatoes)
    175g/6oz/1½ cups dried pasta shapes,
      such as farfalle or conchiglie
    400g/14oz can borlotti
      beans, drained
    salt and ground black pepper
    250g/9oz spinach, washed
      and drained
    50g/2oz/⅔ cup freshly grated
      (shredded) Parmesan cheese, to serve

VARIATION
Other pulses, such as cannellini beans, haricot (navy) beans or chickpeas, are equally good in this soup.

1 Place the chopped onion, celery and carrots in a large pan with the olive oil. Cook over a medium heat for 5 minutes or until the vegetables soften, stirring occasionally.

2 Add the bay leaf, wine, vegetable stock, tomatoes and passata, and bring to the boil. Lower the heat and simmer for 10 minutes until the vegetables are just tender.

3 Add the pasta and beans, and bring the soup back to the boil, then simmer for 8 minutes until the pasta is *al dente*. Stir frequently to prevent the pasta from sticking.

4 Season to taste with salt and pepper. Remove any thick stalks from the spinach and add it to the mixture. Cook for a further 2 minutes. Serve in heated soup bowls sprinkled with the freshly grated Parmesan.

VARIATIONS
• This soup is also delicious with chunks of cooked spicy sausage or pieces of crispy cooked pancetta or bacon – simply add to the soup at the end of Step 3 and stir in, ensuring that the meat is piping hot before serving.
• For vegetarians, you could use fried chunks of smoked or marinated beancurd (tofu) as an alternative to meat.

PROVENÇAL FISH SOUP

*THE ADDITION OF RICE MAKES THIS A SUBSTANTIAL MAIN MEAL SOUP. BASMATI OR THAI RICE HAS
THE BEST FLAVOUR, BUT ANY LONG GRAIN RICE COULD BE USED. IF YOU PREFER A STRONGER TOMATO
FLAVOUR, REPLACE THE WHITE WINE WITH EXTRA PASSATA.*

SERVES FOUR TO SIX

INGREDIENTS

450g/1lb fresh mussels
about 250ml/8fl oz/1 cup white wine
675–900g/1½–2lb mixed white fish
  fillets such as monkfish, plaice,
  flounder, cod or haddock
6 large scallops
30ml/2 tbsp olive oil
3 leeks, chopped
1 garlic clove, crushed
1 red (bell) pepper, seeded and cut
  into 2.5cm/1in pieces
1 yellow (bell) pepper, seeded and
  cut into 2.5cm/1in pieces
175g/6oz fennel bulb, cut into
  4cm/1½in pieces
400g/14oz can chopped tomatoes
150ml/¼ pint/⅔ cup passata (bottled
  strained tomatoes)
about 1 litre/1¾ pints/4 cups well-
  flavoured fish stock
generous pinch of saffron threads,
  soaked in 15ml/1 tbsp hot water
175g/6oz/scant 1 cup basmati
  rice, soaked
8 large raw prawns (shrimp), peeled
  and deveined
salt and ground black pepper
30–45ml/2–3 tbsp fresh dill, to garnish

1 Clean the mussels, discarding any
that do not close when tapped with a
knife. Place them in a heavy pan. Add
90ml/6 tbsp of the wine, cover, bring to
the boil over a high heat and cook for
about 3 minutes or until all the mussels
have opened.

2 Strain, reserving the liquid. Discard
any mussels that have not opened. Set
aside half the mussels in their shells for
the garnish; shell the rest and put them
in a bowl.

3 Cut the fish into 2.5cm/1in cubes.
Detach the corals from the scallops and
slice the white flesh into three or four
pieces. Add the scallops to the fish and
the corals to the shelled mussels.

4 Heat the olive oil in a pan and fry the
leeks and garlic for 3–4 minutes, until
softened. Add the pepper chunks and
fennel, and fry for 2 minutes more until
just softened.

COOK'S TIP
To make your own fish stock, place about
450g/1lb white fish trimmings – bones,
heads, but not gills – in a large pan. Add
a chopped onion, carrot, bay leaf, parsley
sprig, 6 peppercorns and a piece of
pared lemon rind. Pour in 1.2 litres/
2 pints/5 cups water, bring to the boil,
then simmer gently for 25–30 minutes.
Strain through muslin (cheesecloth).

5 Add the tomatoes, passata, stock,
saffron water, mussel liquid and wine.
Season and cook for 5 minutes. Drain
the rice, stir it into the mixture, cover
and simmer for 10 minutes.

6 Carefully stir in the white fish and
cook over a low heat for 5 minutes. Add
the prawns, cook for 2 minutes, then
add the scallop corals and shelled
mussels and cook for 2–3 minutes
more, until all the fish is tender. Add a
little extra white wine or stock if needed.
Spoon into warmed soup dishes, top
with mussels in their shells and
sprinkle with the dill. Serve immediately.

MEDITERRANEAN LEEK AND FISH SOUP WITH TOMATOES

THIS CHUNKY SOUP, WHICH IS ALMOST A STEW, MAKES A ROBUST AND WONDERFULLY AROMATIC MEAL IN A BOWL. SERVE IT WITH CRISP-BAKED CROÛTES SPREAD WITH A TASTY, GARLIC MAYONNAISE.

SERVES FOUR

INGREDIENTS

2 large thick leeks
30ml/2 tbsp olive oil
5ml/1 tsp crushed coriander seeds
a good pinch of dried red chilli flakes
300g/11oz small salad potatoes,
  peeled and thickly sliced
400g/14oz can chopped tomatoes
600ml/1 pint/2½ cups fish stock
150ml/¼ pint/⅔ cup white wine
1 fresh bay leaf
1 star anise
strip of pared orange rind
good pinch of saffron threads
450g/1lb white fish fillets, such as
  monkfish, sea bass, cod or haddock
450g/1lb small squid, cleaned
250g/9oz raw peeled prawns (shrimp)
30–45ml/2–3 tbsp chopped flat
  leaf parsley
salt and ground black pepper
To serve
  1 short French loaf, sliced and toasted
  garlic mayonnaise

3 Add the potatoes and tomatoes, and pour in the stock and wine. Add the bay leaf, star anise, orange rind and saffron. Bring to the boil, lower the heat and partially cover the pan. Simmer for 20 minutes or until the potatoes are tender. Taste and adjust the seasoning.

4 Cut the white fish fillets into chunks. Cut the squid sacs into rectangles and score a criss-cross pattern into them without cutting right through.

5 Add the fish to the soup and cook gently for 4 minutes. Add the prawns and cook for 1 minute. Add the squid and the sliced white part of the leek and cook, stirring occasionally, for a further 2 minutes.

6 Finally, stir in the chopped parsley and serve immediately, ladling the soup into warmed bowls. Offer the toasted French bread and the garlic mayonnaise with the soup.

1 Slice the leeks, keeping the green tops separate from the white bottom pieces. Wash the leek slices thoroughly in a colander and drain them well. Set the white slices aside for later.

2 Heat the oil in a heavy pan over a low heat, then add the green leek slices, the crushed coriander seeds and the dried red chilli flakes. Cook, stirring occasionally, for 5 minutes.

Seafood Soup WITH Rouille

This is a really chunky, aromatic mixed fish and tomato soup from France, flavoured with plenty of saffron and herbs. Rouille, a fiery hot paste, is served separately for everyone to swirl into their soup to flavour.

SERVES FOUR

INGREDIENTS

  3 gurnard, red mullet or snapper,
    scaled and gutted
  12 large prawns (shrimp)
  675g/1½lb white fish, such as cod,
    haddock, halibut or monkfish
  225g/8oz live mussels
  1 onion, quartered
  ½ litre/1 pints/2½ cups vegetable
    stock
  5ml/1 tsp saffron threads
  75ml/5 tbsp olive oil
  1 fennel bulb, roughly chopped
  4 garlic cloves, crushed
  3 strips pared orange rind
  4 fresh thyme sprigs
  900g/2lb tomatoes
  30ml/2 tbsp sun-dried tomato
    purée (paste)
  3 bay leaves
For the rouille
  1 red (bell) pepper, seeded
  1 fresh red chilli, seeded and sliced
  2 garlic cloves, chopped
  75ml/5 tbsp olive oil
  15g/½oz/¼ cup fresh breadcrumbs

1 To make the rouille, process the pepper, chilli, garlic, oil and breadcrumbs in a blender or food processor until smooth. Transfer to a serving dish and chill.

2 Fillet the gurnard, mullet or snapper by cutting away the flesh from either side of the backbone, reserving the heads and bones for the stock.

3 Cut the fillets into small chunks. Shell half the prawns and reserve the trimmings to make the fish stock.

4 Skin the white fish, discarding any bones, and cut into large chunks. Scrub the mussels well, discarding any damaged ones and any open ones that do not close when sharply tapped.

5 To make the stock, put the fish and prawn trimmings in a pan with the onion and the water. Bring to the boil, then simmer gently for 30 minutes. Cool slightly and strain.

6 Soak the saffron in ½ litre/1 pint/ 2½ cups vegetable stock. Heat 30ml/ 2 tbsp of the oil in a large sauté pan. Add all the fish and fry over a high heat for 1 minute. Drain and set aside.

7 Heat the remaining oil and fry the fennel, garlic, orange rind and thyme until beginning to colour. Make up the strained stock to about 1.2 litres/2 pints/ 5 cups with the vegetable stock.

8 Skin the tomatoes by plunging them into boiling water for 30 seconds, then refreshing them in cold water. Peel and chop. Add the stock to the pan with the saffron, tomatoes, tomato purée and bay leaves. Season, bring almost to the boil, then simmer gently, covered, for 20 minutes.

9 Stir in the gurnard, mullet or snapper, white fish and prawns, and add the mussels. Cover the pan tightly and cook for 3–4 minutes. Remove from the heat and take off the lid. Discard any mussels that do not open. Serve the soup piping hot with the rouille served separately in a small dish.

COOK'S TIPS
• To save time, order the fish and ask the fishmonger to fillet the gurnard or mullet for you.
• To temper the flavour of the rouille, blend a chopped tomato with the other ingredients or leave out the fresh chilli.

ROASTED TOMATO AND MOZZARELLA WITH BASIL OIL AND MIXED LEAF SALAD

ROASTING THE TOMATOES IN OLIVE OIL ADDS A NEW DIMENSION TO THIS DELICIOUS DISH AND A SUPERB SWEETNESS TO THE TOMATOES. MAKE THE BASIL OIL JUST BEFORE SERVING TO RETAIN ITS FRESH FLAVOUR AND VIVID EMERALD-GREEN COLOUR.

SERVES FOUR

INGREDIENTS
    olive oil, for brushing
    6 large plum tomatoes
    350g/12oz fresh mozzarella cheese,
        cut into 8–12 slices
    fresh basil leaves, to garnish
For the basil oil
    25 fresh basil leaves
    60ml/4 tbsp extra virgin olive oil
    1 garlic clove, crushed
For the salad
    90g/3½oz/4 cups salad leaves
    50g/2oz/2 cups mixed salad herbs,
        such as coriander (cilantro), basil
        and rocket (arugula)
    25g/1oz/3 tbsp pumpkin seeds
    25g/1oz/3 tbsp sunflower seeds
For the salad dressing
    60ml/4tbsp extra virgin olive oil
    15ml/1 tbsp balsamic vinegar
    2.5 ml/½ tsp Dijon mustard

1 Preheat the oven to 200ºC/400ºF/ Gas 6 and oil a baking sheet. Cut the tomatoes in half lengthwise and remove the seeds. Place skin-side down on a baking sheet and roast for 20 minutes or until the tomatoes are tender.

2 Meanwhile, make the basil oil. Place the basil leaves, olive oil and garlic in a food processor and process until smooth. Transfer to a bowl and chill.

3 Start to prepare the salad. Put the salad leaves in a large bowl. Add the mixed salad herbs and toss lightly with your hands to mix.

4 Toast the pumpkin and sunflower seeds in a dry frying pan over a medium heat for 2 minutes until golden, tossing frequently. Let the seeds cool before sprinkling them over the salad.

5 To make the salad dressing, combine the ingredients in a screw-top jar or bowl. Shake or mix with a small whisk or fork until combined. Pour the dressing over the salad and toss with your hands until the leaves are well coated.

6 For each serving, place the tomato halves on top of 2 or 3 slices of mozzarella and drizzle over the basil oil. Season well. Garnish with basil leaves. Serve with the salad.

TOASTED CIABATTA WITH TOMATOES, CHEESE AND MARJORAM FLOWERS

HERE IS A VERY SIMPLE BUT TASTY METHOD OF USING MARJORAM FLOWERS. THE COMBINATION OF CHEESE, TOMATO AND MARJORAM IS POPULAR, BUT LOTS OF EXTRAS CAN BE ADDED, SUCH AS CAPERS, OLIVES, ANCHOVIES OR SLICES OF ROASTED PEPPERS.

SERVES TWO

INGREDIENTS
1 ciabatta loaf
4 tomatoes
115g/4oz mozzarella or
   Cheddar cheese
15ml/1 tbsp olive oil
15ml/1 tbsp marjoram flowers
salt and ground black pepper

COOK'S TIP
Add marjoram flowers to your favourite pizza topping. Sprinkle over 7.5–15ml/ ½–1 tbsp flowers or flowering tops and add a few of the leaves. The flavours are strong, so marjoram flowers should be used with care, especially if you haven't tried them before. The amount you use will depend on your own palate.

1 Preheat the grill (broiler) to high. Cut the loaf in half lengthwise and toast very lightly under the grill until it has turned a pale golden brown.

2 Meanwhile, skin the tomatoes by plunging them in boiling water for 30 seconds, then refreshing them in cold water. Peel and cut into thick slices.

3 Slice or grate the cheese. Lightly drizzle the olive oil over the bread and top with the tomato slices and sliced or grated cheese. Season with salt and pepper and scatter the marjoram flowers over the top. Drizzle with a little more olive oil. Return to the grill until the cheese bubbles and is just starting to brown.

GRIDDLED TOMATOES <u>ON</u> SODA BREAD

NOTHING COULD BE SIMPLER THAN THIS DISH, YET A DRIZZLE OF OLIVE OIL AND BALSAMIC VINEGAR
AND SHAVINGS OF PARMESAN CHEESE TRANSFORM TOMATOES ON TOAST INTO SOMETHING REALLY SPECIAL.

<u>SERVES FOUR</u>

INGREDIENTS
  olive oil, for brushing and drizzling
  6 tomatoes, thickly sliced
  4 thick slices soda bread
  balsamic vinegar, for drizzling
  salt and ground black pepper
  shavings of Parmesan cheese,
    to serve

VARIATIONS
• For a more substantial meal, place a couple of slices of prosciutto on the toast before adding the tomatoes.
• This recipe is also delicious with slices of mozzarella cheese instead of the shaved Parmesan.
• Anchovies go well with tomatoes. If you like them, try tearing a few anchovy fillets into strips and arranging them on top of the tomatoes. Omit the Parmesan.

1 Brush a griddle pan with a little olive oil and heat. Add the tomato slices and cook for about 4 minutes, turning once, until softened and slightly blackened. Alternatively, heat a grill (broiler) to high and line the rack with foil. Grill (broil) the tomato slices for 4–6 minutes, turning once, until softened.

2 Meanwhile, lightly toast the soda bread until pale golden.

3 Place the tomatoes on top of the toast and drizzle each portion with a little olive oil and balsamic vinegar. Season with salt and ground black pepper to taste and serve immediately with thin shavings of Parmesan.

COOK'S TIP
Using a griddle pan reduces the amount of oil required for cooking the tomatoes and gives them a barbecued flavour.

MOZZARELLA ᴬᴺᴰTOMATO SKEWERS

STACKS OF FLAVOUR — LAYERS OF OVEN-BAKED MOZZARELLA, TOMATOES, BASIL AND BREAD. THESE COLOURFUL KEBABS WILL BE POPULAR WITH ADULTS AND CHILDREN ALIKE.

SERVES FOUR

INGREDIENTS
12 slices white country bread, each about 1cm/½in thick
45ml/3 tbsp olive oil
225g/8oz mozzarella cheese, cut into 5mm/¼in slices
3 ripe plum tomatoes, cut into 5mm/¼in slices
15g/½oz/½ cup fresh basil leaves, plus extra to garnish
salt and ground black pepper
30ml/2 tbsp chopped fresh flat leaf parsley, to garnish

COOK'S TIPS
• If you use wooden skewers, soak them in water first, to prevent them from scorching during the cooking time.
• The bread for these skewers needs to be quite robust, so don't be tempted to use slices from a soft white sandwich loaf.

1 Preheat the oven to 220°C/425°F/ Gas 7. Trim the crusts from the bread and cut each slice into four equal squares. Arrange on a baking sheet and brush with half the olive oil. Bake for 3–5 minutes until the squares are a pale golden colour.

2 Remove the bread squares from the oven and place them on a chopping board with the other ingredients.

3 Make 16 stacks, each starting with a square of bread, then a slice of mozzarella topped with a slice of tomato and a basil leaf. Sprinkle with salt and pepper, then repeat, ending with a piece of bread. Push a skewer through each stack and place on the baking sheet. Drizzle with the remaining oil and bake for 10–15 minutes until the cheese begins to melt. Garnish with basil and flat leaf parsley.

CANNELLINI BEAN AND TOMATO BRUSCHETTA

THIS TRADITIONAL ITALIAN-STYLE DISH IS A SOPHISTICATED VERSION OF BEANS ON TOAST. THE BEANS ADD FLAVOUR WHILE MAKING THIS APPETIZER MORE SUBSTANTIAL.

SERVES FOUR

INGREDIENTS

150g/5oz/¾ cup dried
    cannellini beans
5 tomatoes
45ml/3 tbsp olive oil, plus extra
    for drizzling
2 sun-dried tomatoes in oil, drained
    and finely chopped
2 garlic cloves
30ml/2 tbsp chopped fresh rosemary
12 slices Italian-style bread, such
    as ciabatta
salt and ground black pepper
a handful of fresh basil leaves,
    to garnish

VARIATION
Bruschetta can be served with a variety
of toppings. Make the tomato base as
in steps 2 and 3 and mix with canned,
flaked tuna, olives or pieces of cooked
ham instead of the beans.

1 Soak the beans in water overnight.
Drain and rinse the beans, then place
in a pan and cover with fresh water.
Bring to the boil and boil rapidly for
10 minutes. Reduce the heat and
simmer for 50–60 minutes or until
tender. Drain and return to the clean pan.

2 Meanwhile, place the tomatoes in a
bowl, cover with boiling water, leave for
30 seconds, then refresh in cold water.
Peel, seed and chop the flesh.

3 Heat the oil in a pan and add the
fresh and sun-dried tomatoes. Crush
1 garlic clove and add it with the
rosemary. Cook for 2 minutes until the
tomatoes begin to break down.

4 Add the tomato mixture to the
cooked cannellini beans, season to taste
with salt and ground pepper, and mix
well. Heat through gently.

5 Cut the remaining garlic clove in half
and rub the cut sides of the bread
slices with it. Toast the bread lightly.
Spoon the cannellini bean mixture on
top of the toast. Sprinkle with basil
leaves and drizzle with a little extra olive
oil before serving.

COOK'S TIP
Canned beans can be used instead of
dried; use 275g/10oz/2 cups drained,
canned beans and add to the tomato
mixture in step 4. If the beans are
canned in brine, then rinse and drain
them well before use.

PIPÉRADE <u>WITH</u> CROSTINI

THIS MIXTURE OF RIPE PLUM TOMATOES, SWEET PEPPERS AND EGGS HAS ALL THE FLAVOURS OF THE
MEDITERRANEAN. IT IS PERFECT FOR A TASTY APPETIZER OR A LIGHT LUNCH-TIME SNACK.

SERVES SIX

INGREDIENTS
   60ml/4 tbsp bacon fat, duck fat or
      olive oil
   2 small onions, coarsely chopped
   4 red or yellow (bell) peppers, seeded
      and chopped
   2 large garlic cloves, finely chopped
   pinch of chilli powder
   675g/1½lb ripe plum tomatoes,
      peeled, seeded and chopped
   15ml/1 tbsp chopped fresh oregano
      or 5ml/1 tsp dried oregano
   1 long French stick
   60–90ml/4–6 tbsp olive oil
   25g/1oz/2 tbsp butter
   6 eggs, beaten
   salt and ground black pepper
   fresh basil leaves, to serve

VARIATION
To make a quick party version, cut the
bread into thick slices and mix about
200ml/7fl oz/scant 1 cup ready-made
sweet pepper and tomato pasta sauce
into the eggs in Step 4.

1 Heat the fat or oil in a large, heavy
frying pan. Add the onions and cook
over a gentle heat, stirring occasionally,
for about 5 minutes until softened but
not coloured.

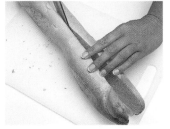

2 Add the peppers, garlic and chilli
powder. Cook for a further 5 minutes,
stirring, then add the plum tomatoes,
seasoning and oregano, and cook over
a medium heat for 15–20 minutes until
most of the liquid has evaporated.

3 Preheat the oven to 200°C/400°F/
Gas 6. Cut the bread in half lengthways,
trim off the ends, then cut into six equal
pieces and brush with olive oil. Place on
baking sheets; bake for 8–10 minutes
until crisp and just turning golden.

4 Heat the butter until it bubbles, add
the eggs and stir until soft scrambled.
Turn off the heat and stir in the tomato
mixture. Divide evenly among the pieces
of bread and sprinkle with the basil
leaves. Serve hot or warm.

HERBY POLENTA WITH TOMATOES

GOLDEN POLENTA FLAVOURED WITH A SELECTION OF FRESH SUMMER HERBS IS PAN-FRIED WITH
SEASONAL TOMATOES FOR A DELICIOUS TASTE OF NORTHERN ITALIAN CUISINE.

SERVES FOUR

INGREDIENTS
  750ml/1¼ pints/3 cups vegetable
    stock or water
  5ml/1 tsp salt
  175g/6oz/1 cup polenta
  25g/1oz/2 tbsp butter
  75ml/5 tbsp chopped mixed fresh
    parsley, thyme, chives and basil,
    plus extra, to garnish
  olive oil, for greasing and brushing
  6 large plum or beefsteak tomatoes
  salt and ground black pepper

COOK'S TIPS
• To get the criss-cross effect on the
polenta, turn each round through
90 degrees, halfway through cooking
each side on the griddle pan.
• Any mixture of fresh herbs can be
used, or try using just basil or chives
alone, for a really distinctive flavour.
Garlic chives taste very good.
• If you like garlic, simply add one
minced (ground) clove when adding the
rest of the herbs.

1 Prepare the polenta in advance:
place the stock or water in a heavy pan,
with the salt, and bring to the boil.
Lower the heat, slowly pour in the
polenta and stir with a wooden spoon.

2 Stir the mixture constantly, using a
figure-eight action, over a medium heat
for 5 minutes, until the polenta begins
to thicken and come away from the
sides of the pan.

3 Remove from the heat and continue
stirring for another minute or two. Stir
in the butter, freshly chopped parsley,
thyme, chives and basil, and season
with black pepper.

4 Tip the mixture into a wide, greased
tin (pan) or a glass or ceramic dish.
Using a flexible spatula, spread the
polenta mixture out evenly. Cover the
surface closely with greaseproof (waxed)
paper, then put it in a cool place until it
has set completely and is cold.

5 Turn out the polenta on to a board
and stamp out 8 rounds using a large
biscuit or cookie cutter. Alternatively,
you can cut the polenta into 8 squares
with a knife. Brush with oil.

6 Heat a griddle pan and lightly brush
it with oil. Cut the tomatoes in two, then
brush them with oil and sprinkle with
salt and pepper. Cook the tomato halves
and polenta patties on the pan for
5 minutes, turning them once. Serve
garnished with fresh herbs.

CROSTINI <u>WITH</u> TOMATO AND VEGETABLE TOPPING

THIS POPULAR ITALIAN HORS D'OEUVRE WAS ORIGINALLY A WAY OF USING UP LEFTOVERS AND THE OVERABUNDANCE OF TOMATOES FROM THE HARVEST. PLUM TOMATOES ARE TRADITIONALLY USED, BUT CHERRY TOMATOES ARE A DELICIOUS ALTERNATIVE.

MAKES SIXTEEN

INGREDIENTS
 1 ciabatta loaf
For the tomato, (bell) pepper and
anchovy topping
 400g/14oz can or bottle Italian
  roasted red (bell) peppers
  and tomatoes
 50g/2oz can anchovy fillets
 extra virgin olive oil, for drizzling
 15–30ml/1–2 tbsp balsamic vinegar
 1 garlic clove
 red pesto, for brushing
 30ml/2 tbsp chopped fresh chives,
  oregano or sage, to garnish
 15ml/1 tbsp capers, to garnish
For the mozzarella and tomato topping
 green pesto sauce, for brushing
 120ml/4fl oz/½ cup thick home-made
  or bottled tomato sauce or
  pizza topping
 115g/4oz good quality mozzarella
  cheese, cut into thin slices
 2–3 ripe plum tomatoes, seeded and
  cut into strips
 fresh basil leaves, to garnish

COOK'S TIP
For an extra healthy version, use
wholemeal or whole-wheat toast instead
of a ciabatta loaf.

1 Cut the ciabatta or French bread into
16 slices. Toast until crisp and golden
on both sides. Cool on a wire rack.

2 For the tomato, pepper and anchovy
topping, drain the tomatoes and
peppers and wipe dry with kitchen paper.
Cut into 1 cm/½in strips and place in a
shallow dish.

3 Rinse and dry the anchovy fillets and
add to the peppers and tomatoes.
Drizzle with olive oil and sprinkle with
the balsamic vinegar.

4 Using a sharp knife peel and halve
the garlic clove. Rub 8 toasts with the
cut edge of the clove and brush the
toast with a little red pesto. Arrange the
tomatoes, peppers and anchovies
decoratively on the toasts and sprinkle
with herbs and capers.

5 For the mozzarella and tomato
topping, brush the remaining toasts with
the green pesto and spoon on some
tomato sauce. Arrange a slice of
mozzarella on each and cover with the
tomato strips. Garnish with basil leaves.

TOMATO <u>AND</u> CHEESE TARTS

THESE CRISP LITTLE TARTLETS LOOK REALLY IMPRESSIVE BUT ARE ACTUALLY VERY EASY TO MAKE. THEY ARE BEST EATEN FRESH FROM THE OVEN AND MAKE IDEAL SNACKS WITH DRINKS.

SERVES FOUR

INGREDIENTS
  2 sheets filo pastry
  cornflour (cornstarch),
    for dusting
  1 egg white
  115g/4oz/½ cup cream cheese
  a handful of fresh basil leaves
  4 tomatoes, sliced
  salt and ground black pepper

VARIATIONS
• For a stronger cheese taste, sprinkle the tartlets with grated Cheddar or Parmesan cheese or top with a slice of mozzarella cheese before baking.

1 Preheat the oven to 200°C/400°F/ Gas 6. Lay out the filo pastry on a board dusted with cornflour (cornstarch). Brush the sheets of filo pastry lightly with egg white and cut into 16 10cm/4in squares.

2 Layer the squares in twos, in a tartlet tin (muffin pan). Divide the cheese among the pastry cases. Season with black pepper and top with a few basil leaves.

3 Arrange the tomato slices on the cheese, season well and bake the tarts for 10–12 minutes, until golden and crisp. Serve warm.

COOK'S TIPS
• When you are using filo pastry it is important to prevent it from drying out; cover any you are not using with a dishtowel or clear film (plastic wrap).
• Using egg white to brush the sheets of filo is quite unusual, but makes a change from the traditional – and much richer – melted butter. Of course, you can use butter if you prefer, but if you like the low-fat option, stick to the egg white and use a low-fat cream cheese.
• These tartlets are delicious served with chutney or salsa. Alternatively, serve with pesto mayonnaise – mix 90ml/6 tbsp mayonnaise into 15ml/1 tbsp pesto.

EGG-STUFFED TOMATOES

THIS SIMPLE DISH IS JUST THE KIND OF THING YOU MIGHT FIND IN A CHARCUTERIE IN FRANCE.
IT IS EASY TO MAKE AT HOME AND MAKES A DELICIOUS APPETIZER OR A LIGHT LUNCH.

SERVES FOUR

INGREDIENTS

175ml/6fl oz/¾ cup mayonnaise
30ml/2 tbsp chopped fresh chives
30ml/2 tbsp chopped fresh basil
30ml/2 tbsp chopped fresh parsley
4 hard-boiled (hard-cooked) eggs
4 ripe tomatoes
salt and ground black pepper
salad leaves, to serve

1 In a small bowl, mix together the mayonnaise and herbs. Set aside. Using an egg slicer or sharp knife, cut the eggs into thin slices, taking care to keep the slices intact.

2 Make deep cuts to within 1cm/½in of the base of each tomato. (There should be the same number of cuts in each tomato as there are slices of egg.)

3 Fan open the tomatoes and sprinkle with salt, then insert an egg slice into each slit. Place each stuffed tomato on a plate with a few salad leaves, season and serve with the herb mayonnaise.

SCRAMBLED EGGS

THIS DISH IS A SPECIALITY OF NORTHERN IRAN WHERE IT IS CALLED MIRZA GHASEMI. *SERVE IT WITH WARM PITTA BREAD FOR A COLOURFUL AND MOST UNUSUAL FIRST COURSE.*

SERVES FOUR TO SIX

INGREDIENTS
   4 aubergines (eggplant)
   115g/4oz/½ cup butter
   1 large onion, finely chopped
   2 garlic cloves, crushed
   4 large tomatoes, peeled, seeded
     and chopped
   4 eggs, beaten
   salt and ground black pepper
   warm pitta bread, to serve

COOK'S TIP
Small pitta breads can be used as scoops for the delicious aubergine and egg mixture; alternatively, open up the pockets in larger pitta breads and fill them with the mixture. For a more Mediterranean feel, use ciabatta, panini, rustic brown bread or sun-dried tomato and olive bread as a scoop.

1 Preheat the oven to 190°C/375°F/ Gas 5. Carefully score the skins of the aubergines with a sharp knife, place them on a baking sheet and bake in the oven for 30–40 minutes until the skins begin to split open.

2 Meanwhile, melt 50g/2oz/¼ cup of the butter in a large frying pan and fry the onion and garlic for 4–5 minutes until softened. Add the tomatoes and fry for a further 2–3 minutes.

3 Peel the aubergines, finely chop the flesh and stir it into the pan with the onion and tomatoes. Cook for about 4–5 minutes, stirring frequently.

4 Melt the remaining butter in a small frying pan, add the beaten eggs and cook over a low heat until the eggs are just beginning to set, stirring occasionally with a wooden spoon. Stir the eggs into the aubergine mixture, season and serve with pitta bread.

TOSTADAS <u>WITH</u> TOMATO SALSA

*A TOSTADA IS A CRISP, FRIED TORTILLA USED IN THIS RECIPE AS A BASE ON WHICH TO PILE THE
TOPPING OF YOUR CHOICE. THIS VARIATION ON A SANDWICH MAKES A VERY TASTY SNACK.*

<u>SERVES SIX</u>

INGREDIENTS
    30ml/2 tbsp oil, plus extra
      for frying
    1 onion, chopped
    2 garlic cloves, chopped
    2.5ml/½ tsp chilli powder
    400g/14oz can borlotti or pinto
      beans, drained
    150ml/¼ pint/⅔ cup chicken stock
    15ml/1 tbsp tomato purée (paste)
    30ml/2 tbsp chopped fresh
      coriander (cilantro)
    6 wheat or corn tortillas
    30ml/2 tbsp sour cream
    50g/2oz/½ cup grated (shredded)
      Cheddar cheese
    salt and ground black pepper
    6 sprigs of fresh coriander,
      to garnish
For the tomato salsa
    1 small onion, chopped
    1 garlic clove, crushed
    2 fresh green chillies, seeded and
      finely chopped
    450g/1lb tomatoes, chopped
    30ml/2 tbsp chopped fresh
      coriander (cilantro)

1 To make the salsa, put the onion and
garlic in a serving bowl and stir in the
chillies, tomatoes and fresh coriander.
Season generously and mix well.

2 Heat 30ml/2 tbsp oil in a heavy-
based frying pan and fry the chopped
onion for 3–5 minutes until softened.
Add the garlic and chilli powder, and
fry for 1 minute, stirring constantly.

3 Add the beans. Pour in the stock and
mix well. Mash the beans very roughly.
Add the tomato purée, chopped
coriander and seasoning to taste. Mix
thoroughly and cook for a few minutes.

4 Fry 2 tortillas in hot oil for 1 minute,
turning once, until crisp, then drain on
kitchen paper. Fry the remaining tortillas
in the same way.

5 Put a spoonful of the refried beans
on each tostada, spoon over some
tomato salsa, then some sour cream,
sprinkle with grated Cheddar cheese
and garnish with coriander.

COOK'S TIP
When you are in a hurry, use canned
refried beans. Thin them with a little
stock if necessary.

BAKED POLENTA ^WITH^ TOMATOES

THESE HERB-FLAVOURED POLENTA SQUARES INTERLEAVED WITH TOMATO AND TOPPED WITH CHEESE ARE AN EASY VERSION OF PIZZA! THE IMPORTANT THING TO REMEMBER IS TO ALLOW TIME FOR THE POLENTA TO COOL AND SET, BEFORE CUTTING AND TOPPING IT.

SERVES SIX

INGREDIENTS
  750ml/1¼ pints/3 cups chicken or
    vegetable stock
  175g/6oz/1 cup polenta
  60ml/4 tbsp finely chopped
    fresh sage
  15ml/1 tbsp extra virgin olive oil,
    for greasing
  3 beefsteak tomatoes,
    thinly sliced
  15ml/1 tbsp freshly grated
    (shredded) Parmesan cheese
  salt and ground black pepper

1 Bring the stock to the boil in a large pan, then gradually stir in the polenta, using a wooden spoon.

2 Continue stirring the polenta over a medium heat for about 5 minutes, until the mixture begins to come away from the sides of the pan.

3 Stir in the chopped sage and season well, then spoon into a lightly oiled, shallow 33 x 23cm/13 x 9in tray and spread evenly. Leave to cool.

4 Preheat the oven to 200°C/400°F/ Gas 6. Cut the cooled polenta into 24 squares, using a sharp knife.

5 Arrange the polenta squares in a lightly oiled, shallow ovenproof dish, slipping a slice of tomato between each square. Sprinkle with Parmesan and bake for 20 minutes or until golden brown. Serve hot.

COOK'S TIP
If you dip the knife in a jug of boiling water from time to time, the polenta will be easier to cut.

BAKED VEGETABLE SLICES <u>WITH</u> CHEESE

IN THE PAST, IT WAS NECESSARY TO SALT AUBERGINES TO DRAW OUT THEIR BITTERNESS, BUT THIS IS NO LONGER NECESSARY, THANKS TO THE DEVELOPMENT OF MILDER EXAMPLES THAT ARE SOLD WHEN THEY ARE YOUNG AND TENDER. TODAY, THEY CAN BE SLICED AND USED IMMEDIATELY, AS IN THIS TASTY DISH.

SERVES FOUR

INGREDIENTS

45–60ml/3–4 tbsp olive oil,
  for brushing
1 large aubergine (eggplant)
1 large or 2 medium tomatoes,
  thickly sliced
a few fresh basil leaves, shredded
115g/4oz mozzarella cheese, sliced
salt and ground black pepper
fresh basil, to garnish

COOK'S TIP
These aubergine slices are substantial
enough to be served as a light lunch, or
as part of a vegetarian meal.

1 Preheat the oven to 190°C/375°F/
Gas 5. Brush a baking sheet with a little
oil. Trim the aubergine and cut it
lengthways into four slices about 5mm/
¼in thick. Arrange the slices on the
greased baking sheet.

2 Brush the aubergine slices liberally
with oil and sprinkle with seasoning.

3 Arrange about three or four tomato
slices on top of each aubergine slice,
overlapping them slightly, if necessary.
Sprinkle over about half of the
shredded basil.

4 Top with the cheese or interleave it
with the tomato. Brush with more oil.
Bake for 15 minutes, or until the
aubergine is tender and the cheese is
bubbling. Garnish and serve.

Tomatoes are just as delicious raw or cooked, so it is hardly surprising that they are used all over the world to add a splash of colour as well as a delicious flavour to an astonishingly wide variety of dishes. Cherry tomatoes add a sweet tangy bite to Country Pasta Salad while beefsteak tomatoes give a meaty texture to refreshing Mango, Tomato and Red Onion Salad. And if there's a glut of tomatoes, what better way to use them than in cooked dishes such as Braised Fennel with Tomatoes or classic Ratatouille.

Salads and
Side Dishes

TURKISH TOMATO SALAD

THIS CLASSIC SALAD IS A WONDERFUL COMBINATION OF TEXTURES AND FLAVOURS. THE SALTINESS OF THE CHEESE IS PERFECTLY BALANCED BY THE REFRESHING SALAD VEGETABLES.

SERVES FOUR

INGREDIENTS
    1 cos (romaine) lettuce heart
    1 green (bell) pepper
    1 red (bell) pepper
    ½ cucumber
    4 tomatoes
    1 red onion
    225g/8oz feta cheese, crumbled
    black olives, to garnish
For the dressing
    45ml/3 tbsp extra virgin olive oil
    45ml/3 tbsp lemon juice
    1 garlic clove, crushed
    15ml/1 tbsp chopped fresh parsley
    15ml/1 tbsp chopped fresh mint
    salt and ground black pepper

1 Chop the lettuce into bitesize pieces. Seed the peppers, remove the cores and cut the flesh into thin strips. Chop the cucumber and slice or chop the tomatoes. Cut the onion in half, then slice finely.

2 Place the chopped lettuce, peppers, cucumber, tomatoes and onion in a large bowl. Sprinkle the feta over the top and toss together lightly.

3 To make the dressing: blend together the extra virgin olive oil, lemon juice and garlic in a small bowl or a screw-top jar. Stir in the freshly chopped parsley and mint, and season with salt and pepper to taste.

4 Pour the dressing over the salad, toss lightly with your hands until well coated, then garnish with a few black olives. Serve immediately.

PERSIAN SALAD WITH TOMATOES

THIS VERY SIMPLE SALAD IS ESPECIALLY GOOD SERVED WITH MEAT OR RICE DISHES – DON'T ADD THE DRESSING UNTIL JUST BEFORE YOU ARE READY TO SERVE.

SERVES FOUR

INGREDIENTS
    4 tomatoes
    ½ cucumber
    1 onion
    1 cos (romaine) lettuce heart
For the dressing
    30ml/2 tbsp olive oil
    juice of 1 lemon
    1 garlic clove, crushed
    salt and ground black pepper

VARIATION
Use lime juice for this dressing – it will add a deliciously aromatic flavour and be slightly sweeter too.

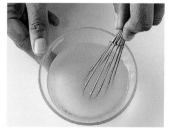

1 Peel and seed the tomatoes if you like, then cut them into small cubes. Cube the cucumber, leaving the skin on or removing it. Finely chop the onion and tear the lettuce into pieces.

2 Place the tomatoes, cucumber, onion and lettuce in a large salad bowl and mix lightly together.

3 To make the dressing, pour the olive oil into a small bowl. Add the lemon juice, garlic and seasoning, and whisk together well. Alternatively, combine the dressing ingredients in a screw-top jar, close tightly and shake vigorously. Pour the dressing over the salad and toss lightly to mix. Sprinkle with black pepper before serving.

CUCUMBER AND TOMATO SALAD

*THIS SALAD COMES FROM BULGARIA, WHERE IT WAS TRADITIONALLY MADE WITH THE LOCAL YOGURT.
IT IS CLAIMED THAT YOGURT WAS FIRST MADE IN BULGARIA.*

SERVES FOUR

INGREDIENTS
    450g/1lb firm ripe tomatoes
    ½ cucumber
    1 onion
    1 small fresh red or green chilli,
      seeded and chopped, or fresh
      chives, chopped into 2.5cm/1in
      lengths, to garnish
    crusty bread or pitta breads, to serve
For the dressing
    60ml/4 tbsp olive or vegetable oil
    90ml/6 tbsp thick Greek (US strained
      plain) yogurt
    30ml/2 tbsp chopped fresh parsley
      or chives
    2.5ml/½ tsp vinegar
    salt and ground black pepper

1 Skin the tomatoes by plunging them
in boiling water for 30 seconds, then
drain and plunge into cold water. Skin
the tomatoes and seed and chop into
even-size pieces.

2 Chop the cucumber and onion into
pieces of similar size to the tomatoes
and put them all in a bowl.

3 Mix all the dressing ingredients
together and season to taste. Pour the
dressing over the salad and toss all
the ingredients together.

4 Sprinkle over black pepper and
garnish with the chopped chilli or
chives. Serve with chunks of crusty
bread or pile into pitta pockets.

BLACK OLIVE, TOMATO AND SARDINE SALAD

*THE COMBINATION OF INGREDIENTS IN THIS SALAD — SARDINES, OLIVES, TOMATOES AND WINE
VINEGAR — BRING A REAL BURST OF FLAVOUR TO A DELIGHTFUL LIGHT SUMMER DISH.*

SERVES SIX

INGREDIENTS
    8 large firm ripe tomatoes
    1 large red onion
    60ml/4 tbsp white wine vinegar
    90ml/6 tbsp good olive oil
    18–24 small sardines, cooked
    75g/3oz/¾ cup pitted black olives,
      well drained
    salt and ground black pepper
    45ml/3 tbsp chopped fresh parsley,
      to garnish

1 Slice the tomatoes into 5mm/
¼in slices. Slice the onion thinly.

2 Arrange the tomatoes on individual
plates, overlapping the slices, then top
with the red onion.

4 Top each salad with 3–4 sardines
and a few black olives. Sprinkle the
chopped parsley over the top.

COOK'S TIPS
• Use extra virgin olive oil for the dressing.
• You may not need all the vinegar as the
juice from the tomatoes will contribute
some acidity.

3 Mix together the wine vinegar, olive
oil and seasoning, and spoon over each
plate of salad.

VARIATION
This recipe works equally well if the
sardines are replaced with 6 shelled and
halved hard-boiled (hard-cooked) eggs.

ASPARAGUS, TOMATO AND ORANGE SALAD

THIS SALAD COMES FROM SPAIN, WHERE COMPLICATED SALAD DRESSINGS ARE SELDOM USED. SPANISH COOKS SIMPLY RELY ON THE WONDERFUL TASTE OF A GOOD-QUALITY OLIVE OIL. USE EXTRA VIRGIN OIL FOR THE BEST FLAVOUR IN THIS RECIPE.

SERVES FOUR

INGREDIENTS

225g/8oz asparagus, trimmed and
  cut into 5cm/2in pieces
2 large oranges
2 well-flavoured tomatoes, cut
  into eighths
50g/2oz cos (romaine) lettuce
  leaves, shredded
30ml/2 tbsp extra virgin olive oil
2.5ml/½ tsp sherry vinegar
salt and ground black pepper

VARIATIONS
• Little Gem (Bibb) lettuce can be used
in place of cos lettuce.
• Grapefruit segments also work well in
this salad. Use 1 ruby grapefruit instead
of the oranges.

1 Cook the asparagus in a pan of
boiling, salted water for 3–4 minutes,
until just tender. Drain and refresh
under cold water.

2 Grate the rind from half an orange and
reserve. Peel both the oranges and cut
into segments. Squeeze out the juice from
the membrane and reserve it.

3 Put the asparagus, orange segments,
tomatoes and lettuce into a salad bowl.
Make the dressing by whisking together
the oil and vinegar and adding 15ml/
1 tbsp of the reserved orange juice and
5ml/1 tsp of the rind. Season with salt
and pepper. Just before serving, pour
the dressing over the salad and mix
gently to coat.

AVOCADO, TOMATO AND ORANGE SALAD

THIS SALAD HAS A FEEL OF THE MEDITERRANEAN – AVOCADOS ARE GROWN IN MANY PARTS OF THE REGION AND ADD A DELICIOUS FLAVOUR AND TEXTURE TO THIS DISH. TAKE CARE TO FIND AVOCADOS THAT ARE FULLY RIPE, BUT NOT OVER-RIPE.

SERVES FOUR

INGREDIENTS

2 oranges
4 well-flavoured tomatoes
2 small avocados
60ml/4 tbsp extra virgin olive oil
30ml/2 tbsp lemon juice
15ml/1 tbsp chopped fresh parsley
1 small onion, sliced into rings
salt and ground black pepper
25g/1oz/¼ cup flaked (sliced)
    almonds and olives, to garnish

COOK'S TIP

Use avocados that are just ripe for this salad. They should yield to gentle pressure. Avoid any avocados with bruised areas, or that feel very soft. Unripe avocados will ripen in 4–7 days if stored at room temperature; sooner if you have bananas in the same bowl.

1 Peel the oranges and slice into thick rounds. Plunge the tomatoes into boiling water for 30 seconds, then refresh in cold water. Peel off the skins, cut the tomatoes into quarters, remove the seeds and chop roughly.

2 Cut the avocados in half, remove the stones (pits) and carefully peel away the skin. Cut into chunks.

3 Whisk together the olive oil, lemon juice and parsley. Season with salt and pepper. Toss the avocados and tomatoes in half the dressing.

4 Arrange the sliced oranges on a plate and scatter over the onion rings. Drizzle with the rest of the dressing. Spoon the avocados, tomatoes, almonds and olives on top of the salad.

GREEK SALAD

ANYONE WHO HAS SPENT A HOLIDAY IN GREECE WILL HAVE EATEN A VERSION OF THIS SALAD — THE GREEKS' EQUIVALENT OF A MIXED SALAD. ITS SUCCESS RELIES ON USING ONLY THE FRESHEST INGREDIENTS, INCLUDING SUN-RIPENED TOMATOES, AND A GOOD OLIVE OIL.

SERVES SIX

INGREDIENTS
    450g/1lb well-flavoured plum
      tomatoes, skinned
    1 small cos (romaine) lettuce, sliced
    1 cucumber, seeded and chopped
    200g/7oz feta cheese, crumbled
    4 spring onions (scallions), sliced
    50g/2oz/½ cup pitted black
      olives, halved
For the dressing
    90ml/6 tbsp extra virgin olive oil
    25ml/1½ tbsp lemon juice
    salt and ground black pepper

1 Place the tomatoes on a chopping board. Using a sharp cook's knife or a serrated knife, cut into quarters and then into eighths. Put them in a bowl and add the lettuce, cucumber, feta, spring onions and olives.

2 Make the dressing. In a bowl, whisk together the olive oil and lemon juice, then season with salt and ground black pepper, and whisk again. Pour the dressing over the salad. Mix well and serve immediately.

SPICED TOMATO SALAD

SERVE THIS MIDDLE-EASTERN INFLUENCED SALAD WITH WARM PITTA BREAD AS AN APPETIZER OR TO ACCOMPANY A MAIN-COURSE RICE PILAFF. IT IS ALSO GREAT WITH FLAME-GRILLED MEATS.

SERVES FOUR

INGREDIENTS
    2 small aubergines (eggplant), sliced
    75ml/5 tbsp olive oil
    60ml/4 tbsp red wine vinegar
    2 garlic cloves, crushed
    15ml/1 tbsp lemon juice
    2.5ml/½ tsp ground cumin
    2.5ml/½ tsp ground coriander
    7 well-flavoured tomatoes
    ½ cucumber
    30ml/2 tbsp natural (plain) yogurt
    salt and ground black pepper
    chopped flat leaf parsley, to garnish

VARIATION
An equally delicious warm salad can be made by dicing the aubergines, then frying them in olive oil with 1 chopped onion and 2 crushed garlic cloves. Stir in 5–10ml/1–2 tsp mild curry powder and 3 chopped tomatoes. Cook until soft. Serve with natural yogurt.

1 Preheat the grill (broiler). Brush all the aubergine slices lightly with some of the oil and cook under a high heat, turning once, until golden and tender. Cut each slice into quarters.

2 In a bowl, mix together the remaining oil, vinegar, garlic, lemon juice, cumin and coriander. Season with salt and pepper, and mix thoroughly. Add the warm aubergines, stir well and chill for at least 2 hours.

3 Using a sharp knife, slice, or if you prefer, cut the tomatoes into quarters. Slice the cucumber finely, leaving the seeds intact. Add both cucumber and tomato to the aubergine mixture.

4 Transfer the salad vegetables to an attractive serving dish and arrange them decoratively. Spoon the natural yogurt over the aubergine mixture. Sprinkle with the freshly chopped flat leaf parsley and serve.

FATTOUSH

THIS IS A DELICIOUS LEBANESE DISH, FULL OF THE FLAVOUR OF FRESH HERBS AND LEMONS. IT MAKES A DELICIOUS SNACK OR AN EXCITING ADDITION TO A BUFFET TABLE.

SERVES FOUR

INGREDIENTS

1 yellow or red (bell) pepper
1 large cucumber
4–5 tomatoes
1 bunch spring onions (scallions)
30ml/2 tbsp finely chopped
  fresh parsley
30ml/2 tbsp finely chopped
  fresh mint
30ml/2 tbsp finely chopped fresh
  coriander (cilantro)
2 garlic cloves, crushed
75ml/5 tbsp olive oil
juice of 2 lemons
salt and freshly ground black pepper
4 pitta breads

1 Slice the pepper, discarding the seeds and core, then slice or chop the flesh. Leaving the skin on the cucumber, roughly chop it. Dice the tomatoes. Place them in a large salad bowl.

2 Slice the spring onions. Add to the cucumber, tomatoes and pepper with the parsley, mint and coriander.

3 To make the dressing, mix the garlic with the olive oil and lemon juice. Whisk well, then season to taste.

4 Pour the dressing over the salad and toss lightly to mix.

5 Toast the pitta breads in a toaster or under a hot grill (broiler) until crisp and serve them with the salad.

COOK'S TIP
Although the recipe calls for only 30ml/2 tbsp of each of the herbs, if you have plenty to hand, you can add as much as you like to this aromatic salad.

VARIATION
If you prefer, make this salad in the traditional way. After toasting the pitta breads until crisp, crush them in your hand and then sprinkle them all over the salad before serving.

MANGO, TOMATO AND RED ONION SALAD

THIS SALAD MAKES AN APPETIZING SIDE DISH. THE MANGO HAS A SUBTLE SWEETNESS AND ITS FLAVOUR BLENDS WELL WITH THE TOMATO, ONION AND CUCUMBER.

SERVES FOUR

INGREDIENTS

1 firm mango
2 large tomatoes or 1 beefsteak
   tomato, sliced
½ red onion, sliced into rings
½ cucumber, peeled and thinly sliced
30ml/2 tbsp sunflower oil
15ml/1 tbsp lemon juice
1 garlic clove, crushed
2.5ml/½ tsp hot pepper sauce
salt and ground black pepper
sugar, to taste
chopped chives, to garnish

COOK'S TIP
Choose a mango that is slightly under-ripe. The flesh should be fairly firm for this salad, but not hard.

1 Cut away two thick slices either side of the mango stone (pit) and cut into finer slices. Peel off the skin.

2 Arrange the mango, tomato, onion and cucumber slices in circles on a large serving plate.

3 Blend the oil, lemon juice, garlic, hot pepper sauce, salt and pepper in a blender or food processor, or place in a small jar and shake vigorously. Add a pinch of sugar to taste and mix again.

4 Using a teaspoon, drizzle the dressing over the salad, taking care not to disturb the slices of mango, tomato, onion and cucumber. Sprinkle with the chopped chives and serve.

CHAYOTE AND TOMATO SALAD

COOL AND REFRESHING, THIS TOMATO SALAD IS IDEAL ON ITS OWN OR WITH FISH OR CHICKEN DISHES. THE SOFT FLESH OF THE CHAYOTES ABSORBS THE FLAVOUR OF THE DRESSING BEAUTIFULLY.

SERVES FOUR

INGREDIENTS
2 chayotes
2 firm tomatoes
1 small onion, finely chopped
finely sliced strips of fresh red and
  green chilli, to garnish
For the dressing
2.5ml/½ tsp Dijon mustard
2.5ml/½ tsp ground anise
90ml/6 tbsp white wine vinegar
60ml/4 tbsp olive oil
salt and ground black pepper

1 Bring a pan of water to the boil. Peel the chayotes, cut them in half and remove the seeds. Add them to the boiling water. Lower the heat and simmer for 20 minutes or until the chayotes are tender. Drain and set them aside to cool.

2 Meanwhile, skin the tomatoes by cutting a cross in the blossom end of each of them and plunging them into boiling water for 30 seconds. Lift the tomatoes out using a slotted spoon and drop them into a bowl of cold water. Drain. The skins will have begun to peel back from the crosses. Remove the skins completely and cut the tomatoes into wedges.

3 Make the dressing by combining all the ingredients in a screw-top jar. Close the lid tightly and then shake the jar vigorously to mix.

4 Cut the chayotes into wedges and place them in a bowl with the tomato and onion. Pour over the dressing and serve garnished with the strips of fresh red and green chilli.

ROASTED PEPPER AND TOMATO SALAD

THIS IS ONE OF THOSE LOVELY RECIPES THAT BRINGS TOGETHER PERFECTLY THE COLOURS, FLAVOURS AND TEXTURES OF SOUTHERN ITALIAN FOOD. EAT THIS DISH AT ROOM TEMPERATURE.

SERVES FOUR

INGREDIENTS
    3 red (bell) peppers
    6 large plum tomatoes
    2.5ml/½ tsp dried red chilli flakes
    1 red onion, finely sliced
    3 garlic cloves, finely chopped
    grated (shredded) rind and juice
       of 1 lemon
    45ml/3 tbsp chopped fresh flat
       leaf parsley
    30ml/2 tbsp extra virgin olive oil
    salt
    black and green olives and extra
       chopped flat leaf parsley, to garnish

COOK'S TIP
These peppers will keep for several weeks if the peeled pepper pieces are placed in a jar of olive oil, with a tight-fitting lid. Store in the refrigerator.

1 Preheat the oven to 220°C/425°F/ Gas 7. Place the peppers on a baking sheet and roast for 10 minutes until the skins are slightly blackened. Add the tomatoes and bake for 5 minutes more.

2 Place the peppers in a plastic bag. Close the top loosely, trapping in the steam, and then set them aside, with the tomatoes, until they are cool.

3 Skin and seed the peppers. Chop the peppers and tomatoes roughly and place them both in a mixing bowl.

4 Add the chilli flakes, onion, garlic, lemon rind and juice. Sprinkle over the parsley. Mix well, then transfer to a serving dish. Season with salt, drizzle over the olive oil and sprinkle the olives and extra parsley over the top.

GRILLED LEEK AND FENNEL SALAD
WITH SPICY TOMATO DRESSING

*THIS IS AN EXCELLENT SALAD TO MAKE IN THE EARLY AUTUMN, WHEN YOUNG LEEKS ARE AT THEIR
BEST AND RIPE TOMATOES ARE FULL OF FLAVOUR. SERVE WITH GOOD BREAD AS AN APPETIZER OR
SERVE TO ACCOMPANY SIMPLY COOKED WHITE FISH FOR A MAIN COURSE.*

SERVES SIX

INGREDIENTS
675g/1½lb leeks
2 large fennel bulbs
120ml/4fl oz/½ cup extra virgin
  olive oil
2 shallots, chopped
150ml/¼ pint/⅔ cup dry white wine or
  white vermouth
5ml/1 tsp fennel seeds, crushed
6 fresh thyme sprigs
2–3 bay leaves
good pinch of dried red chilli flakes
350g/12oz tomatoes, peeled, seeded
  and diced
5ml/1 tsp sun-dried tomato
  paste (optional)
good pinch of sugar (optional)
75g/3oz/¾ cup small black olives
salt and ground black pepper

2 Trim the fennel bulbs, reserving any tops for the garnish, if you like, and cut the bulbs either into thin slices or into thicker wedges, according to taste.

3 Cook the fennel in the reserved cooking water for about 5 minutes, then drain thoroughly and toss with 30ml/ 2 tbsp of the olive oil. Season to taste with black pepper.

6 Add the diced tomatoes and cook briskly for 5–8 minutes, or until they have reduced and the consistency has thickened.

7 Add the tomato paste, if using, and adjust the seasoning, adding a good pinch of sugar if you think the dressing needs it.

1 Cook the leeks in boiling salted water for 4–5 minutes. Use a slotted spoon to remove the leeks and place them in a colander to drain thoroughly and cool. Reserve the cooking water in the pan. Squeeze out excess water and cut the leeks into 7.5cm/3in lengths.

COOK'S TIP
When buying fennel, look for rounded bulbs; they have a better shape for this dish. The flesh should be crisp and white, with no signs of bruising. Avoid specimens with broken leaves or with brown or dried-out patches.

4 Heat a ridged cast-iron griddle under the grill (broiler). Arrange the leeks and fennel on the griddle and cook until tinged deep brown. Remove the vegetables from the griddle, place in a large shallow dish and set aside.

5 Place the remaining olive oil, the shallots, white wine or vermouth, crushed fennel seeds, thyme, bay leaves and chilli flakes in a large pan and bring to the boil over a medium heat. Lower the heat and simmer for 10 minutes.

8 Pour the dressing over the leeks and fennel, toss to mix and leave to cool. The salad may be made several hours in advance and kept in the refrigerator, but bring it back to room temperature before serving.

9 When ready to serve, stir the salad then sprinkle the chopped fennel tops, if using, and black olives over the top of the dish.

PANZANELLA

IN THIS LIVELY ITALIAN SPECIALITY, A SWEET TANGY BLEND OF TOMATO JUICE, RICH OLIVE OIL AND RED WINE VINEGAR MAKES A MARVELLOUS DRESSING FOR A COLOURFUL SALAD.

SERVES FOUR TO SIX

INGREDIENTS
    225g/8oz ciabatta
    150ml/¼ pint/⅔ cup extra virgin
        olive oil
    3 red (bell) peppers
    3 yellow (bell) peppers
    50g/2oz can anchovy fillets
    675g/1½lb ripe plum tomatoes
    4 garlic cloves, crushed
    60ml/4 tbsp red wine vinegar
    50g/2oz/⅓ cup capers, drained
    115g/4oz/1 cup pitted black olives
    salt and ground black pepper
    fresh basil leaves, to garnish

1 Preheat the grill (broiler) and line the pan with foil. Also preheat the oven to 200°C/400°F/Gas 6. Cut the ciabatta into 2cm/ ¾in chunks and drizzle with 60ml/4 tbsp of the oil. Place on the lined grill pan and grill (broil) lightly until just golden. Set aside.

2 Put the peppers on a foil-lined baking sheet and bake for about 45 minutes, turning them occasionally, until the skins begin to char. Remove from the oven, cover with a dishtowel and leave to cool slightly.

3 Skin and quarter the peppers, remove the stalk and seeds. Drain and then roughly chop the anchovies. Set aside. Halve the tomatoes and scoop the seeds into a sieve set over a bowl.

4 Using the back of a spoon, press the tomato pulp in the sieve to extract as much juice as possible. Discard the pulp and add the remaining oil, the garlic and vinegar to the juices.

5 Layer the bread, peppers, tomatoes, anchovies; capers and olives in a salad bowl. Season the tomato dressing and pour it over the salad. Leave to stand for about 30 minutes. Serve garnished with plenty of basil leaves.

ROASTED PEPPERS WITH TOMATOES

IF YOU HAVE TIME, MAKE AND DRESS THIS SALAD AN HOUR OR TWO BEFORE SERVING, AS THIS WILL
ALLOW THE JUICES TO MINGLE AND CREATE THE BEST MOUTHWATERING Sicilian-STYLE SALAD.

SERVES FOUR

INGREDIENTS
 1 red (bell) pepper
 1 yellow (bell) pepper
 4 ripe plum tomatoes, sliced
 2 canned artichokes, drained
 and quartered
 4 sun-dried tomatoes in oil, drained
 and thinly sliced
 15ml/1 tbsp capers, drained
 1 garlic clove, sliced
For the dressing
 15ml/1 tbsp balsamic vinegar
 5ml/1 tsp lemon juice
 75ml/5 tbsp extra virgin olive oil
 chopped fresh mixed herbs
 salt and ground black pepper

VARIATION
The flavour of the salad can be varied
by using different herbs in the salad
dressing. For a nutty flavour add a
handful of pine nuts.

1 Cut the peppers in half, and remove
the seeds and stalks. Cut into quarters
and place on a grill (broiler) pan covered
with foil. Cook, skin-side up, under a
grill (broiler) set on high, until the skin
chars. Transfer to a bowl and cover with
a plate or tuck a dishtowel around the
peppers on the grill pan, to trap the
steam. Leave the peppers to cool.

2 Use your fingers to peel the skin off
the peppers and then cut into strips.

3 Arrange the peppers, fresh tomatoes
and artichokes on a serving dish.
Sprinkle over the sun-dried tomatoes,
capers and garlic.

4 To make the dressing, put the
balsamic vinegar and lemon juice in a
bowl and whisk in the olive oil, then the
chopped herbs. Season with salt and
pepper. Pour the dressing over the
salad an hour or two before the salad is
served, if possible.

BULGUR WHEAT AND CHERRY TOMATO SALAD

THIS APPETIZING SALAD IS IDEAL SERVED WITH FRESH CRUSTY BREAD AND HOME-MADE CHUTNEY OR PICKLE. IT ALSO MAKES A VERY GOOD ACCOMPANIMENT TO GRILLED MEAT OR FISH.

SERVES SIX

INGREDIENTS
    350g/12oz/2 cups bulgur wheat
    225g/8oz frozen broad (fava) beans
    115g/4oz/1 cup frozen petits pois
      (baby peas)
    225g/8oz cherry tomatoes, halved
    1 sweet onion, chopped
    1 red (bell) pepper, seeded and diced
    50g/2oz mangetouts (snow
      peas), chopped
    50g/2oz watercress or American cress
    45ml/3 tbsp chopped fresh herbs,
      such as parsley, basil and thyme
For the dressing
    75ml/5 tbsp olive oil
    15ml/1 tbsp white wine vinegar
    5ml/1 tsp mustard powder
    salt and ground black pepper

1 Put the bulgur wheat into a large bowl. Add enough cold water to come 2.5cm/1in above the level of the wheat. Leave to soak for approximately 30 minutes, then tip into a sieve lined with a clean dishtowel. Drain the wheat well and use the dishtowel to squeeze out any excess water.

2 Cook the broad beans and petits pois in a pan of boiling water for about 3 minutes, until tender. Drain thoroughly and mix with the prepared bulgur wheat in a bowl.

3 Add the cherry tomatoes, onion, pepper, mangetouts and watercress to the bulgur wheat mixture and mix. Combine all the ingredients for the dressing, season and stir well.

4 Add the herbs, seasoning and enough dressing to taste, tossing the ingredients together. Serve immediately or cover and chill in the refrigerator first.

TABBOULEH WITH TOMATOES AND APRICOTS

ALSO KNOWN AS BULGAR OR BURGHUL, BULGUR WHEAT HAS BEEN PARTIALLY COOKED, SO IT REQUIRES ONLY A SHORT SOAKING BEFORE BEING USED IN A SALAD.

SERVES FOUR

INGREDIENTS

250g/9oz/1½ cups bulgur wheat
4 tomatoes
4 baby courgettes (zucchini), thinly
sliced lengthways
4 spring onions (scallions), sliced
8 ready-to-eat dried
apricots, chopped
40g/1½oz/¼ cup raisins or sultanas
(golden raisins)
juice of 1 lemon
30ml/2 tbsp tomato juice
45ml/3 tbsp chopped fresh mint
1 garlic clove, crushed
salt and ground black pepper
sprig of fresh mint, to garnish

1 Put the bulgur wheat into a large bowl. Add enough cold water to come 2.5cm/1in above the level of the wheat. Leave to soak for 30 minutes, then tip into a sieve lined with a clean dishtowel. Drain well and squeeze out any excess water.

2 Meanwhile, plunge the tomatoes into boiling water for 30 seconds and then refresh in cold water. Peel off the skins. Halve the tomatoes, remove the seeds and cores, and chop roughly.

3 In a bowl, mix the tomatoes, courgettes, spring onions and dried fruit with the bulgur wheat.

4 Put the lemon and tomato juice, mint, garlic clove and seasoning into a small bowl and whisk with a fork. Pour over the salad and mix well. Chill for at least 1 hour. Serve garnished with a sprig of mint.

WARM CHICKEN ^{AND} TOMATO SALAD WITH HAZELNUT DRESSING

THIS SIMPLE, WARM SALAD COMBINES PAN-FRIED CHICKEN AND SPINACH WITH A LIGHT, NUTTY DRESSING. SERVE IT FOR LUNCH ON AN AUTUMN DAY.

SERVES FOUR

INGREDIENTS
    45ml/3 tbsp olive oil
    30ml/2 tbsp hazelnut oil
    15ml/1 tbsp white wine vinegar
    1 garlic clove, crushed
    15ml/1 tbsp chopped fresh mixed herbs
    225g/8oz baby spinach leaves
    250g/9oz cherry tomatoes, halved
    1 bunch spring onions
      (scallions), chopped
    2 skinless, boneless chicken breasts,
      cut into thin strips
    salt and ground black pepper

VARIATIONS
• Use other meat or fish, such as steak,
pork fillet or salmon fillet, in place of the
chicken breasts.
• Any salad leaves can be used instead
of the baby spinach.

1 First make the dressing: place 30ml/
2 tbsp of the olive oil, the hazelnut oil,
vinegar, garlic and chopped herbs in a
small bowl or jug and whisk together
until thoroughly mixed. Set aside.

2 Trim any long stalks from the spinach
leaves, then place in a large serving
bowl with the tomatoes and spring
onions, and toss together to mix.

3 Heat the remaining olive oil in a
frying pan, and stir-fry the chicken over
a high heat for 7–10 minutes until it is
cooked, tender and lightly browned.

4 Arrange the cooked chicken pieces
over the salad. Give the dressing a
quick whisk to blend, then drizzle it
over the salad. Add salt and pepper to
taste, toss lightly and serve immediately.

MOROCCAN TUNA AND TOMATO SALAD WITH BEANS AND EGGS

THIS SALAD IS SIMILAR TO THE CLASSIC SALAD NIÇOISE AND USES TUNA OR SWORDFISH STEAKS, WITH GREEN BEANS, CHERRY TOMATOES AND A HERB AND SPICE MARINADE.

SERVES SIX

INGREDIENTS

6 tuna or swordfish steaks, about
    900g/2lb total weight
For the marinade
    1 onion
    2 garlic cloves, halved
    ½ bunch fresh parsley
    ½ bunch fresh coriander (cilantro)
    10ml/2 tsp paprika
    45ml/3 tbsp olive oil
    30ml/2 tbsp white wine vinegar
    15ml/1 tbsp lime or lemon juice
For the salad
    450g/1lb green beans
    450g/1lb broad (fava) beans
    1 cos (romaine) lettuce
    450g/1lb cherry tomatoes, halved
    30ml/2 tbsp coarsely chopped fresh
      coriander (cilantro)
    3 hard-boiled (hard-cooked) eggs
    45ml/3 tbsp extra virgin olive oil
    10–15ml/2–3 tsp lime or lemon juice
    ½ garlic clove, crushed
    175–225g/6–8oz/1½–2 cups pitted
      black olives

1 First make the marinade. Skin and cut the onion into quarters or eighths. Place the onion, garlic, parsley, coriander, paprika, olive oil, wine vinegar and lime or lemon juice in a food processor, add 45ml/3 tbsp water and process for 30–40 seconds until all the ingredients are finely chopped.

2 Prick the tuna or swordfish steaks all over with a fork, place in a shallow dish that is large enough to hold them in a single layer and pour over the marinade, turning the fish so that each piece is coated. Cover and leave in a cool place for 2–4 hours.

3 To prepare the salad, cook the green beans and broad beans in boiling salted water for 5-10 minutes or until tender. Drain, refresh in cold running water and drain again.

4 Discard the outer shells from the broad beans and place them in a large serving bowl with the green beans. Remove the outer leaves from the lettuce and tear the inner leaves into pieces. Add to the bowl with the tomatoes and coriander.

5 Shell the eggs and cut into eighths with a sharp knife. To make the dressing, whisk the olive oil, citrus juice and garlic in a bowl.

6 Preheat the grill (broiler) and arrange the fish steaks on a grill pan. Brush with the marinade mixed with a little extra olive oil and grill for 5–6 minutes on each side, until the fish is tender. Brush with marinade and more olive oil when turning the fish over.

7 Allow the fish to cool a little and then break the steaks into large pieces. Toss into the salad with the olives and dressing. Add the eggs and serve.

SPICY TUNA, CHICKPEA AND CHERRY TOMATO SALAD

A QUICK AND EASY SALAD USING CANNED CHICKPEAS AND TUNA WITH A TASTY SPICY TOMATO DRESSING. IT WOULD BE PERFECT FOR A PICNIC.

SERVES SIX

INGREDIENTS
5ml/1 tsp olive oil
1 garlic clove
5ml/1 tsp ground coriander
5ml/1 tsp garam masala
5ml/1 tsp hot chilli powder
120ml/4fl oz/½ cup tomato juice
30ml/2 tbsp balsamic vinegar
dash of Tabasco sauce
½ cucumber
675g/1½lb cherry tomatoes
1 bunch radishes
1 bunch spring onions (scallions)
50g/2oz watercress or American cress
2–3 fresh parsley sprigs
1 small bunch fresh chives
2 x 400g/14oz cans chickpeas,
    rinsed and drained
400g/14oz can tuna in brine or
    water, drained and flaked
salt and ground black pepper

1 Heat the oil in a small pan. Crush the garlic in a garlic press, add it and the spices to the pan and cook gently for 1 minute, stirring constantly with a wooden spoon.

2 Stir the tomato juice, vinegar and Tabasco sauce into the oil mixture and heat until it bubbles gently. Remove the pan from the heat and set aside to cool slightly.

3 Leave the skin on the cucumber, or remove it, as you prefer. Slice the cucumber into thin rounds. If you prefer, you can slice the cucumber lengthways, take out the seeds and then slice it into rounds.

4 Halve the cherry tomatoes. Trim and slice the radishes and spring onions. Remove any tough stems from the watercress and chop it roughly.

5 Put the tomatoes and cucumber in a serving bowl. Add the radishes, spring onions and watercress to the salad bowl. Toss lightly to mix.

6 Chop the parsley finely and then bunch the chives and snip them into short sections, using kitchen scissors.

7 Stir the chickpeas, tuna and herbs into the salad. Pour the cooled tomato dressing over the salad and toss the ingredients together to mix well. Season to taste with salt and ground black pepper and serve.

Smoked Bacon ᴬᴺᴰ Tomato Salad
ᵂᴵᵀᴴ Pasta Twists

This tasty pasta salad is subtly flavoured with smoked bacon, which contrasts beautifully with the fresh flavour of the tomatoes and green beans.

SERVES FOUR

INGREDIENTS
    350g/12oz/3 cups wholemeal
      (wholewheat) pasta twists
    225g/8oz/1½ cups green beans
    8 strips of lean smoked back bacon,
      rind and fat removed
    350g/12oz cherry tomatoes, halved
    2 bunches spring onions
      (scallions), chopped
    400g/14oz can chickpeas, drained
    90ml/6 tbsp tomato juice
    30ml/2 tbsp balsamic vinegar
    5ml/1 tsp ground cumin
    5ml/1 tsp ground coriander
    30ml/2 tbsp chopped fresh
      coriander (cilantro)
    salt and ground black pepper

COOK'S TIP
Always rinse canned beans and pulses
before using to remove as much of the
brine as possible.

1 Cook the pasta in a large pan of
lightly salted, boiling water for 10–12
minutes until *al dente.* Meanwhile,
trim and halve the green beans and
cook them in boiling water for about
5 minutes, until tender. Drain thoroughly
and keep warm.

2 Preheat the grill (broiler) to high and
cook the bacon for 2–3 minutes. Using
tongs, turn the bacon over and cook for
2–3 minutes on the other side, until
lightly done. Dice the bacon and add to
the green beans.

3 Put the tomatoes, spring onions and
chickpeas in a bowl and mix together.
In a small bowl, combine the tomato
juice, vinegar, spices, fresh coriander
and seasoning, and pour over the
tomato mixture.

4 Using a sieve, or pan lid, drain the
pasta thoroughly and add to the tomato
mixture with the green beans and
chopped bacon. Toss all the ingredients
together to mix. Serve the meal warm
or cold.

ROASTED CHERRY TOMATO <u>AND</u> PEPPERY GREEN SALAD

THIS IS A GOOD SIDE SALAD TO ACCOMPANY FLAME-GRILLED CHICKEN, STEAKS OR CHOPS. ROASTED TOMATOES ARE VERY JUICY, WITH AN INTENSE, SMOKY-SWEET FLAVOUR.

SERVES FOUR

INGREDIENTS

450g/1lb ripe baby Italian plum
   tomatoes, halved lengthways
75ml/5 tbsp extra virgin olive oil
2 garlic cloves, cut into thin slivers
225g/8oz/2 cups dried pasta shapes
30ml/2 tbsp balsamic vinegar
2 pieces sun-dried tomato in olive
   oil, drained and chopped
large pinch of granulated sugar
1 handful rocket (arugula),
   about 65g/2½oz
salt and ground black pepper

VARIATIONS
• If you are in a hurry and don't have
time to roast the tomatoes, you can
make the salad with halved raw
tomatoes instead.
• If you like, add 150g/5oz mozzarella
cheese, drained and diced, with the
rocket in Step 4.

1 Preheat the oven to 190°C/375°F/
Gas 5. Arrange the halved tomatoes cut
side up in a roasting tin, drizzle 30ml/
2 tbsp of the oil over them and sprinkle
with the slivers of garlic and salt and
pepper to taste. Roast in the oven for
20 minutes, turning once.

2 Bring a pan of lightly salted water
to the boil and cook the dried pasta
shapes for 10–12 minutes, or according
to the instructions on the packet.

3 Put the remaining oil in a large bowl
with the vinegar, sun-dried tomatoes,
sugar and a little salt and pepper to
taste. Stir well to mix. Drain the pasta,
add it to the bowl of dressing and toss
to mix. Add the roasted tomatoes and
mix gently.

4 Before serving, add the rocket
leaves, toss lightly and taste for
seasoning. Serve either at room
temperature or chilled.

COUNTRY PASTA SALAD <u>WITH</u> FRESH CHERRY TOMATOES

COLOURFUL, TASTY AND NUTRITIOUS, THIS IS THE IDEAL PASTA SALAD FOR A SUMMER PICNIC, AND MAKES THE MOST OF THE DELICIOUSLY SWEET CHERRY TOMATOES AVAILABLE IN THE MARKETS.

SERVES SIX

INGREDIENTS
300g/11oz/2¾ cups dried fusilli or
   other pasta shapes
150g/5oz green beans, cut into
   5cm/2in lengths
1 potato, about 150g/5oz, diced into
   small pieces
200g/7oz cherry tomatoes, halved
2 spring onions (scallions), finely
   chopped or 90g/3½oz white of leek,
   finely chopped
90g/3½oz Parmesan cheese, diced or
   coarsely shaved
6–8 pitted black olives, cut
   into rings
15–30ml/1–2 tbsp capers, to taste
For the dressing
90ml/6 tbsp extra virgin olive oil
15ml/1 tbsp balsamic vinegar
15ml/1 tbsp chopped fresh flat
   leaf parsley
salt and ground black pepper

1 Bring a pan of lightly salted water to the boil and cook the dried fusilli for 10–12 minutes, or according to the instructions on the packet. Drain, cool and rinse under cold water, then shake the colander to remove as much water as possible. Leave to drain and dry.

2 Cook the beans and diced potato in a pan of salted boiling water for 5–6 minutes or until tender. Drain and leave the vegetables to cool.

3 Make the salad dressing. Put all the ingredients in a large serving bowl with salt and pepper to taste and whisk well to mix.

4 Add the cherry tomatoes, spring onions or leek, Parmesan, olive rings and capers to the dressing, then the cold pasta, beans and potato. Toss well to mix. Cover and leave to stand for about 30 minutes. Taste the salad and adjust the seasoning before serving.

ROASTED PLUM TOMATOES <u>WITH</u> GARLIC

*THESE ARE SO SIMPLE TO PREPARE YET TASTE ABSOLUTELY WONDERFUL. USE A LARGE, SHALLOW
EARTHENWARE DISH THAT WILL ALLOW THE TOMATOES TO SEAR AND CHAR IN A HOT OVEN.*

SERVES FOUR

INGREDIENTS
  60ml/4 tbsp extra virgin olive oil,
    plus extra for greasing
  8 plum tomatoes
  12 garlic cloves
  3 bay leaves
  salt and ground black pepper
  45ml/3 tbsp fresh oregano leaves,
    to garnish

COOK'S TIPS
• Use ripe plum tomatoes for this recipe
as they keep their shape and do not fall
apart when roasted at such a high
temperature. Leave the stalks on,
if possible.
• To give the tomatoes a bit of extra zing,
add a couple of dashes of hot pepper
sauce to the olive oil.

1 Preheat the oven to 230°C/450°F/
Gas 8. Select an ovenproof dish that will
hold all the tomatoes snugly in a single
layer. Grease it lightly with olive oil.

2 Cut the plum tomatoes in half
lengthways. Place them in the dish, cut
sides uppermost, and push the whole,
unpeeled garlic cloves between them.

3 Brush the tomatoes with the oil, add
the bay leaves and sprinkle black
pepper over the top. Roast for about
45 minutes until the tomatoes have
softened and are sizzling in the dish.
They should be charred around the
edges. Season with salt and a little more
black pepper, if needed. Garnish with
oregano and serve.

Green Beans WITH Tomatoes

THIS RECIPE IS FULL OF THE FLAVOURS OF SUMMER. IT RELIES ON FIRST-CLASS INGREDIENTS, SO USE ONLY THE BEST RIPE PLUM TOMATOES AND GREEN BEANS THAT YOU CAN BUY.

SERVES FOUR

INGREDIENTS
30ml/2 tbsp olive oil
1 large onion, finely sliced
2 garlic cloves, finely chopped
6 large ripe plum tomatoes, peeled,
   seeded and coarsely chopped
150ml/¼ pint/⅔ cup dry white wine
450g/1lb green beans, sliced in
   half lengthways
16 pitted black olives
10ml/2 tsp lemon juice
salt and ground black pepper

COOK'S TIP
Green beans need little preparation, and now that they are grown without the string, you simply trim either end.

1 Heat the oil in a large frying pan. Add the finely sliced onion and chopped garlic. Cook over a medium heat for about 5 minutes, stirring frequently and lowering the heat if necessary, until the onion has softened but not browned.

2 Add the chopped tomatoes, white wine, beans, olives and lemon juice, and cook over a gentle heat for a further 20 minutes, stirring occasionally, until the sauce has thickened and the beans are tender. Season with salt and pepper to taste and serve immediately.

SPICY ROASTED VEGETABLES

OVEN ROASTING BRINGS OUT ALL THE FLAVOURS OF CHERRY TOMATOES, COURGETTES (ZUCCHINI), ONION AND RED PEPPERS. SERVE THEM HOT WITH MEAT OR FISH.

SERVES FOUR

INGREDIENTS

    2–3 courgettes (zucchini)
    1 Spanish onion
    2 red (bell) peppers
    16 cherry tomatoes
    2 garlic cloves, chopped
    pinch of cumin seeds
    5ml/1 tsp fresh thyme or 4–5 torn
      fresh basil leaves
    60ml/4 tbsp olive oil
    juice of ½ lemon
    5–10ml/1–2 tsp harissa or
      Tabasco sauce
    fresh thyme sprigs, to garnish

COOK'S TIP

Harissa is a chilli paste, popular in northern Africa. It can be bought in cans and contains pounded chillies, garlic, coriander, olive oil and seasoning.

1 Preheat the oven to 220°C/425°F/ Gas 7. Trim the courgettes and cut into long strips. Cut the onion into thin wedges. Cut the peppers into chunks, discarding the seeds and core.

2 Place these vegetables in a cast-iron dish or roasting tin (pan); add the tomatoes, chopped garlic, cumin seeds and thyme or torn basil leaves.

3 Sprinkle with the olive oil and toss to coat. Cook the mixture in the oven for 25–30 minutes until the vegetables are very soft and have begun to char slightly.

4 In a cup, mix the lemon juice with the harissa or Tabasco sauce. Stir into the vegetables, garnish with the thyme and serve immediately.

OKRA WITH CORIANDER AND TOMATOES

OKRA IS FREQUENTLY COMBINED WITH TOMATOES AND MILD SPICES IN MEDITERRANEAN COUNTRIES.
LOOK FOR FRESH OKRA THAT IS SOFT AND VELVETY, NOT DRY AND SHRIVELLED.

SERVES FOUR

INGREDIENTS
450g/1lb tomatoes or 400g/14oz can
  chopped tomatoes
450g/1lb okra
45ml/3 tbsp olive oil
2 onions, thinly sliced
10ml/2 tsp coriander seeds, crushed
3 garlic cloves, crushed
2.5ml/½ tsp sugar
finely grated (shredded) rind and
  juice of 1 lemon
salt and ground black pepper

COOK'S TIP
When okra pods are sliced, they ooze a
sticky, somewhat mucilaginous liquid
which, when cooked, acts as a thickener.
It gives dishes a very distinctive texture,
which not everyone appreciates. If the
pods are left whole, however, as here, all
you get is the delicious flavour.

1 If using fresh tomatoes, cut a cross
in the blossom ends, plunge them into
a bowl of boiling water for 30 seconds,
then refresh them in cold water.
Peel off the skins and chop the
tomatoes roughly.

2 Trim off any stalks from the okra and
leave whole. Heat the oil in a sauté pan
and fry the onions and coriander seeds
for 3–4 minutes until the onions are
beginning to colour.

3 Add the okra and garlic to the pan
and fry for 1 minute. Gently stir in the
chopped fresh or canned tomatoes.
Add the sugar, which will bring out the
flavour of the tomatoes. Simmer gently
for about 20 minutes, until the okra is
tender, stirring once or twice.

4 Stir in the lemon rind and juice, and
add salt and pepper to taste, adding a
little more sugar if necessary. Serve
warm or cold.

BRAISED FENNEL WITH TOMATOES

THE DISTINCTIVE ANISEED FLAVOUR OF FENNEL IS PERFECTLY PARTNERED BY TOMATOES IN THIS TASTY DISH, WHICH MAKES AN EXCELLENT ACCOMPANIMENT TO ROAST LAMB.

SERVES FOUR

INGREDIENTS
30–45ml/2–3 tbsp olive oil
5–6 shallots, sliced
2 garlic cloves, crushed
4 tomatoes, peeled and chopped
about 175ml/6fl oz/¾ cup dry
  white wine
15ml/1 tbsp chopped fresh basil or
  2.5ml/½ tsp dried basil
3 small fennel bulbs, trimmed and
  cut into 1cm/½in slices
40–50g/1½–2oz/¾–1 cup fresh
  white breadcrumbs
salt and ground black pepper

1 Preheat the oven to 150°C/300°F/Gas 2. Heat the olive oil in a large pan and fry the shallots and garlic for about 4–5 minutes over a medium heat.

2 Add the tomatoes, and then stir in 150ml/¼ pint/⅔ cup of the wine, the basil and seasoning. Bring to the boil.

3 Add the fennel, then cover and cook for 5 minutes. Use a slotted spoon to remove the fennel from the pan and arrange in layers in an ovenproof dish. Pour over the tomato mixture.

4 Sprinkle the top with half the breadcrumbs. Bake in the oven for about 1 hour. From time to time, press down on the breadcrumb crust with the back of a spoon and sprinkle over another layer of breadcrumbs and a little more of the wine. The crust will slowly become golden brown and very crunchy. Serve hot.

SPICED POTATOES AND TOMATOES

SUBSTANTIAL ENOUGH TO SERVE SOLO, THIS DISH CONSISTS OF DICED POTATOES COOKED GENTLY IN A FRESH TOMATO SAUCE, WHICH IS FLAVOURED WITH CURRY LEAVES AND GREEN CHILLIES.

SERVES FOUR

INGREDIENTS

2 medium potatoes
15ml/1 tbsp olive oil
2 medium onions, finely chopped
4 curry leaves
1.5ml/¼ tsp onion seeds
1 fresh green chilli, seeded and
  finely chopped
4 tomatoes, sliced
5ml/1 tsp grated fresh root ginger
1 garlic clove, crushed
5ml/1 tsp chilli powder
5ml/1 tsp ground coriander
5ml/1 tsp lemon juice
15ml/1 tbsp chopped fresh
  coriander (cilantro)
3 hard-boiled (hard-cooked) eggs

1 Peel and dice the potatoes. Heat the oil in a non-stick wok or frying pan and stir-fry the onions, curry leaves, onion seeds and chilli for about 1 minute.

2 Add the tomatoes and cook for about 2 minutes over a low heat, shaking the pan to prevent them from sticking.

3 Add the ginger, garlic, chilli powder, ground coriander and salt to taste. Continue to stir-fry for 1–2 minutes, then add the potatoes and cover the pan. Cook over a low heat for 5–7 minutes until the potatoes are tender.

4 Add the lemon juice and fresh coriander, and stir to mix together.

5 Shell the hard-boiled eggs, cut into quarters and add as a garnish to the finished dish.

POTATOES BAKED <u>WITH</u> TOMATOES

THIS SIMPLE, HEARTY DISH FROM THE SOUTH OF ITALY IS BEST WHEN TOMATOES ARE IN SEASON AND BURSTING WITH FLAVOUR, BUT IT CAN ALSO BE MADE WITH CANNED PLUM TOMATOES.

SERVES SIX

INGREDIENTS

90ml/6 tbsp olive oil, plus extra
  for greasing
2 large red or yellow onions,
  thinly sliced
1kg/2¼lb baking potatoes,
  thinly sliced
450g/1lb tomatoes, fresh or
  canned, sliced
115g/4oz/1–1⅓ cups freshly grated
  Cheddar or Parmesan cheese
a few fresh basil leaves
60ml/4 tbsp water
salt and ground black pepper

1 Preheat the oven to 180°C/350°F/
Gas 4. Brush a large ovenproof dish
generously with oil. Arrange some
onions in a layer on the base of the
dish, followed by a layer of potato and
tomato slices, alternating the three.

2 Pour a little of the oil over the
surface of the layered ingredients, and
sprinkle with some of the cheese.
Season with salt and add a generous
grinding of black pepper.

3 Continue to layer the ingredients in
the dish until they are used up, adding
oil, cheese and seasoning as before,
and ending with an overlapping layer of
potatoes and tomatoes.

4 Tear the basil leaves into small
pieces, and add them here and there
among the top layer, saving a few for
garnish. Sprinkle the top with the
remaining grated cheese and oil.

5 Pour the water over the dish. Bake in
the oven for 1 hour until the ingredients
are tender.

6 Check the potatoes towards the end
of cooking and if they are browning
too much, place a sheet of foil or
greaseproof (waxed) paper, or a flat
baking sheet, on top of the dish.
Garnish the dish with the remaining
fresh basil, and serve hot.

COOK'S TIP
If covered with foil, this is a very good-
tempered dish and will not spoil if it has
to be kept hot while other dishes
continue to be cooked in the oven.

MARQUIS POTATOES

*A VARIATION ON DUCHESSE POTATOES, THESE PIPED NESTS ARE FINISHED WITH A DELICIOUSLY TANGY
AND BRIGHTLY COLOURED TOMATO MIXTURE SET IN THE CENTRE.*

SERVES SIX

INGREDIENTS
   900g/2lb floury potatoes
   450g/1lb ripe tomatoes
   15ml/1 tbsp olive oil
   2 shallots, finely chopped
   25g/1oz/2 tbsp butter
   3 egg yolks
   60ml/4 tbsp milk
   sea salt and ground black pepper
   chopped fresh parsley, to garnish

1 Peel the potatoes and cut into small chunks. Boil in lightly salted water for 20 minutes or until very tender.

2 Meanwhile, cut a cross in the base of each tomato. Blanch them in a bowl of boiling water, then refresh them by plunging them into a bowl of cold water. Drain, peel off the skins, then cut in half and scoop out the seeds. Chop the tomato flesh.

3 Heat the olive oil in a large frying pan and fry the shallots for 2 minutes, stirring continuously. Add the chopped tomatoes to the pan and fry for a further 10 minutes, stirring frequently with a wooden spoon, until the moisture has evaporated. Set aside.

4 Drain the potatoes in a colander, then return them to the pan and allow the steam to dry off. Set aside to cool slightly.

5 Mash the potatoes with the butter, 2 of the egg yolks and the milk. Season.

6 Preheat the grill (broiler) to high. Spoon the potato into a piping (pastry) bag fitted with a medium star nozzle. Pipe six oval nests on to a greased baking sheet. Beat the remaining yolk with a little water and brush over the potato. Grill (broil) the nests until golden. Spoon the tomato mixture into the nests, sprinkle with parsley and serve.

Baked Cabbage ^{and} Tomatoes

This economical dish uses the whole cabbage, including the core where much of the flavour resides. The tomato topping keeps the cabbage beautifully moist.

SERVES FOUR

INGREDIENTS

   1 green or white cabbage, about
     675g/1½lb
   15ml/1 tbsp olive oil
   45–60ml/3–4 tbsp vegetable or
     chicken stock
   4 firm ripe tomatoes, peeled
     and chopped
   5ml/1 tsp mild chilli powder
   salt and ground black pepper
   15ml/1 tbsp chopped fresh parsley or
     fennel, to garnish (optional)
For the topping
   3 firm ripe tomatoes, thinly sliced
   15ml/1 tbsp extra virgin olive oil
     or nut oil

1 Preheat the oven to 180°C/350°F/ Gas 4. Finely shred the leaves and the core of the cabbage. Heat the oil in a frying pan with 30ml/2 tbsp water and add the cabbage. Cook over a very low heat, to allow the cabbage to sweat, for about 5–10 minutes with the lid on. Stir occasionally.

2 Add the stock and then stir in the chopped tomatoes. Cook for a further 10 minutes. Add the chilli powder and a little salt to season. Cook for 2–3 minutes, stirring occasionally.

3 Tip the cabbage mixture into the base of an ovenproof dish. Level the surface of the cabbage and arrange the sliced tomatoes on top. Season and brush with the oil to prevent them from drying out. Cook for 30–40 minutes, or until the tomatoes are just starting to brown. Serve hot, garnished with a little parsley or fennel sprinkled over the top, if you like.

VARIATION
• Add seeded, diced red or green (bell) peppers to the cabbage with the tomatoes.
• For those who do not like spicy food, this dish is just as delicious without chilli.

LECSÓ

THIS TRADITIONAL HUNGARIAN VEGETABLE DISH CAN BE EATEN AS A MAIN COURSE OR AS AN ACCOMPANIMENT. LECSÓ IN ITS MOST BASIC FORM IS A SIMPLE THICK TOMATO AND ONION PASTE.

SERVES SIX TO EIGHT

INGREDIENTS
5 green (bell) peppers, or red,
  if preferred
30ml/2 tbsp vegetable oil or
  melted lard (shortening)
1 onion, sliced
450g/1lb plum tomatoes, peeled
  and chopped
15ml/1 tbsp paprika
sugar and salt, to taste
cooked bacon strips, to garnish
crusty bread, to serve

VARIATION
Add 115g/4oz/1 cup sliced salami or
lightly scrambled eggs to the vegetables.

1 Wipe the green peppers, core and
seed them and slice into strips.

2 Heat the oil or lard in a frying pan.
Add the onion and cook over a low heat
for 5 minutes until just softened.

3 Add the strips of pepper to the pan
and cook gently for 10 minutes.

4 Add the chopped tomatoes and
paprika to the pan and season to taste
with a little sugar and salt.

5 Simmer the Lecsó over a low heat for
20–25 minutes. Serve immediately,
topped with the strips of grilled bacon
and accompanied by crusty bread.

COOK'S TIP
Although Lecsó is traditionally served
with grilled bacon strips, it is also
delicious with grilled sausages. Thanks to
its robust flavour, it can be partnered
with highly spiced varieties. Try it with
pork chops too, or simply spoon it over a
mound of mashed potato.

BAKED PEPPERS AND TOMATOES

SERVE THIS SIMPLY DELECTABLE DISH WITH LOTS OF WARM BREAD OR OVER COOKED RICE OR PASTA,
SO THAT NONE OF THE DELICIOUS TOMATO AND PEPPER JUICES ARE WASTED.

SERVES EIGHT

INGREDIENTS
  2 red (bell) peppers
  2 yellow (bell) peppers
  1 red onion, sliced
  2 garlic cloves, halved
  6 plum tomatoes, quartered
  50g/2oz/½ cup pitted black olives
  5ml/1 tsp soft light brown sugar
  45ml/3 tbsp sherry
  3–4 fresh rosemary sprigs
  30ml/2 tbsp olive oil
  salt and ground black pepper
  crusty bread, to serve

1 Cut the red and yellow peppers in half, remove the cores and seeds, then cut each into 12 strips.

2 Preheat the oven to 200°C/400°F/ Gas 6. Place the peppers, onion, garlic, tomatoes and olives in a large roasting tin (pan). Sprinkle over the sugar, then pour over the sherry. Season well, cover with foil and bake for 45 minutes.

3 Remove the foil from the tin and stir the vegetable and olive mixture well. Add the rosemary sprigs.

4 Drizzle over the olive oil. Return the tin to the oven for a further 30 minutes until the vegetables are tender and full of flavour. Serve hot, with warm bread for mopping up the juices.

RATATOUILLE

A HIGHLY VERSATILE TOMATO AND MIXED VEGETABLE STEW FROM PROVENCE, FRANCE, RATATOUILLE IS DELICIOUS WARM OR COLD, ON ITS OWN OR WITH EGGS, PASTA, FISH OR MEAT — PARTICULARLY LAMB.

SERVES SIX

INGREDIENTS
900g/2lb ripe tomatoes
120ml/4fl oz/½ cup olive oil
2 onions, thinly sliced
2 red and 1 yellow (bell) pepper,
  seeded and cut into chunks
1 large aubergine (eggplant), cut
  into chunks
2 courgettes (zucchini), sliced
4 garlic cloves, crushed
2 bay leaves
15ml/1 tbsp chopped thyme
salt and ground black pepper

1 Plunge the tomatoes into boiling water for 30 seconds, then refresh in cold water. Peel away the skins and chop the flesh roughly.

2 Heat a little of the olive oil in a large, heavy pan and gently fry the onions for 5 minutes. Stir them constantly so that they do not brown, as this will adversely affect their flavour and make them bitter, but cook them until they are just transparent.

3 Add the peppers to the fried onions and cook for a further 2 minutes. Using a slotted spoon, transfer the onions and peppers to a plate and set them aside.

4 Add more oil and the aubergine and fry gently for 5 minutes. Add the remaining oil and courgettes, and fry for 3 minutes. Lift out the courgettes and aubergine and set them aside.

5 Add the garlic and tomatoes to the pan with the bay leaves and thyme, and a little salt and pepper. Cook gently until the tomatoes have softened and are turning pulpy.

6 Return all the vegetables to the pan and cook gently, stirring frequently, for about 15 minutes, until fairly pulpy but retaining a little texture. Season to taste. Serve warm or cold.

COURGETTES IN TOMATO SAUCE

This richly flavoured Mediterranean dish can be served hot or cold as a side dish. Cut the courgettes into fairly thick slices, so that they stay slightly crunchy.

SERVES FOUR

INGREDIENTS

15ml/1 tbsp extra virgin olive oil or
    sunflower oil
1 onion, chopped
1 garlic clove, chopped
4 courgettes (zucchini),
    thickly sliced
400g/14oz can tomatoes
2 tomatoes, peeled, seeded
    and chopped
5ml/1 tsp vegetable bouillon powder
15ml/1 tbsp tomato purée (paste)
salt and ground black pepper

1 Heat the oil in a heavy pan, add the onion and garlic and sauté for 5 minutes or until the onion is softened, stirring occasionally. Add the courgettes and cook for a further 5 minutes, stirring occasionally.

2 Add the canned and fresh tomatoes, bouillon powder and tomato purée. Stir well, then simmer for 10–15 minutes until the sauce is thickened and the courgettes are just tender. Season to taste and serve.

SPICED TURNIPS <u>WITH</u> SPINACH <u>AND</u> TOMATOES

SWEET BABY TURNIPS, TENDER SPINACH AND RIPE TOMATOES MAKE TEMPTING PARTNERS IN THIS SIMPLE BUT VERY TASTY EASTERN MEDITERRANEAN VEGETABLE STEW.

SERVES SIX

INGREDIENTS
    450g/1lb plum tomatoes
    2 onions
    60ml/4 tbsp olive oil
    450g/1lb baby turnips, peeled
    5ml/1 tsp paprika
    2.5ml/½ tsp sugar
    60ml/4 tbsp chopped fresh
      coriander (cilantro)
    450g/1lb fresh young spinach
    salt and ground black pepper

VARIATION
Try this with celery hearts instead of baby turnips. It is also good with fennel or drained canned artichoke hearts.

1 Plunge the tomatoes into a bowl of boiling water for 30 seconds or so, then refresh in a bowl of cold water. Drain, peel away the tomato skins and chop the flesh roughly.

2 Slice the onions. Heat the olive oil in a large frying pan or sauté pan and gently fry the onion slices for about 5 minutes until golden. Ensure that they do not blacken.

3 Add the baby turnips, tomatoes and paprika to the pan with 60ml/4 tbsp water and cook until the tomatoes are pulpy. Cover the pan with a lid and continue cooking until the baby turnips have softened.

4 Stir in the sugar and coriander, then add the spinach and a little salt and ground black pepper. Cook the mixture for a further 2–3 minutes until the spinach has wilted. The dish can be served warm or cold.

TOMATO AND VEGETABLE BAKE

THIS DISH HAS BEEN MADE FOR CENTURIES IN THE SOUTH OF FRANCE – IN THE DAYS BEFORE HOME KITCHENS HAD OVENS, THE ASSEMBLED DISH WAS CARRIED TO THE BAKER'S TO MAKE USE OF THE HEAT REMAINING AFTER THE BREAD WAS BAKED.

SERVES FOUR

INGREDIENTS

15ml/1 tbsp olive oil, plus extra
    for drizzling
1 large onion, sliced
1 garlic clove, finely chopped
450g/1lb tomatoes
450g/1lb courgettes (zucchini)
5ml/1 tsp dried basil
30ml/2 tbsp freshly grated
    (shredded) Parmesan cheese
salt and ground black pepper

1 Preheat the oven to 180°C/350°F/
Gas 4. Heat the oil in a heavy pan over
a low heat and cook the onion and
garlic for about 20 minutes until soft
and golden.

2 Meanwhile, cut the tomatoes into
5mm/¼in thick slices. (If the tomatoes
are very large, cut the slices in half.)
Cut the courgettes diagonally into slices
about 1cm/½in thick. When the onions
are soft, spread the mixture over the
base of a shallow ovenproof dish.

3 Arrange alternate rows of courgettes
and tomatoes over the onion mixture and
sprinkle with the basil, cheese and
salt and pepper. Drizzle with olive oil,
then bake for 25 minutes until the
vegetables are tender. Serve the dish
hot or warm.

BAKED TOMATOES PROVENÇAL STYLE

THESE TOMATOES, EPITOMIZING THE FLAVOUR OF PROVENCE, FRANCE, ARE PERFECT WITH ROAST MEAT OR POULTRY. YOU CAN PREPARE THEM A FEW HOURS AHEAD, THEN COOK THEM WHILE CARVING THE ROAST. THEY ARE PARTICULARLY GOOD WITH ROAST LAMB OR BEEF.

SERVES FOUR

INGREDIENTS

2 large tomatoes
45ml/3 tbsp fresh white breadcrumbs
2 garlic cloves, very finely chopped
30ml/2 tbsp chopped fresh parsley
30–45ml/2–3 tbsp olive oil
salt and ground black pepper
fresh flat leaf parsley sprigs,
    to garnish

VARIATIONS
• This is a very versatile recipe. Use
wholemeal (whole-wheat) breadcrumbs,
if you like, and try adding finely chopped
hazelnuts or flaked (sliced) almonds.
• Alternatively, fry finely chopped
mushrooms and garlic in a little oil, bind
with breadcrumbs and use instead of the
dry crumb topping.

1 Preheat the oven to 220°C/425°F/
Gas 7. Cut the tomatoes in half and
arrange them cut-side up on a foil-lined
baking sheet.

2 In a bowl, mix together the
breadcrumbs, garlic and parsley. Stir in
salt and pepper to taste, then spoon the
mixture over the tomato halves.

3 Drizzle the tomatoes generously with
olive oil and bake them for about
8–10 minutes until lightly browned.
Serve immediately, garnished with the
parsley sprigs.

COOK'S TIP
If the tomato halves do not sit straight,
cut a thin slice from the bases.

The concentrated flavour of tomatoes adds a delicious richness to meat sauces and stews. Whether included in a main dish or as part of an accompanying sauce, their unique taste and texture is always popular. They have long been one of the most versatile ingredients to incorporate into meat dishes, and can be used in a variety of ways — whole, as in Romanian Kebabs; sliced, as in Polpettes with Mozzarella and Tomato; or peeled and chopped as in Tortiglioni with Spicy Sausage Sauce.

Meat and Poultry

MOUSSAKA

*THIS IS A TRADITIONAL EASTERN MEDITERRANEAN DISH, POPULAR IN BOTH GREECE AND TURKEY.
LAYERS OF MINCED LAMB, AUBERGINES, TOMATOES AND ONIONS ARE TOPPED WITH A CREAMY YOGURT
AND CHEESE SAUCE IN THIS DELICIOUS, AUTHENTIC RECIPE.*

SERVES FOUR

INGREDIENTS
   450g/1lb aubergines (eggplant)
   150ml/¼ pint/⅔ cup olive oil
   1 large onion, chopped
   2–3 garlic cloves, finely chopped
   675g/1½lb lean minced (ground) lamb
   15ml/1 tbsp plain (all-purpose) flour
   400g/14oz can chopped tomatoes
   30ml/2 tbsp chopped fresh herbs
   450g/1lb fresh tomatoes, sliced
   salt and ground black pepper
For the topping
   300ml/½ pint/1¼ cups natural yogurt
   2 eggs
   25g/1oz feta cheese, crumbled
   25g/1oz/⅓ cup freshly ground
      Parmesan cheese

1 Cut the aubergines into thin slices
and layer them in a colander, sprinkling
each layer with salt.

2 Cover the aubergines with a plate
and a weight, then leave for about
30 minutes. Pat dry with kitchen paper.

3 Heat 45ml/3 tbsp of the oil in a large,
heavy pan. Fry the onion and garlic
until softened, but not coloured. Add
the lamb and cook over a high heat,
stirring often, until browned.

4 Stir in the flour until mixed, then stir
in the canned tomatoes, herbs and
seasoning. Bring to the boil, reduce the
heat and simmer gently for 20 minutes.

5 Meanwhile, heat a little of the
remaining oil in a large frying pan. Add
as many aubergine slices as can be laid
in the pan, then cook until golden on
both sides. Set the cooked aubergines
aside. Heat more oil and continue frying
the aubergines in batches, adding oil
as necessary.

COOK'S TIP
Salting and drying the aubergines before
frying reduces the amount of fat that
they absorb and helps them to brown
more quickly.

6 Preheat the oven to 180°C/350°F/
Gas 4. Arrange half the aubergine slices
in a large, shallow ovenproof dish, then
add a layer of half the fresh tomatoes.

7 Top the slices with about half of the
meat and tomato sauce mixture, then
add a layer of the remaining aubergine
slices, followed by the remaining
tomato slices. Spread the remaining
meat mixture over the aubergines
and tomatoes.

8 Beat together the yogurt and eggs,
then mix in the feta and Parmesan
cheeses. Pour the mixture over the
meat and spread it evenly.

9 Transfer the moussaka to the oven
and bake for 35–40 minutes, or until
golden and bubbling.

VARIATION
Use large courgettes (zucchini) instead
of aubergines, if you like. Cut them
diagonally into fairly thick slices.

LAMB BURGERS ^{WITH} HOT, SPICY RED ONION AND TOMATO RELISH

A SHARP-SWEET RED ONION RELISH WORKS WELL WITH BURGERS BASED ON MIDDLE-EASTERN STYLE LAMB. SERVE WITH PITTA BREAD AND TABBOULEH OR WITH FRIES AND A CRISP GREEN SALAD.

SERVES FOUR

INGREDIENTS

25g/1oz/3 tbsp bulgur wheat
500g/1¼lb lean minced (ground) lamb
1 small red onion, finely chopped
2 garlic cloves, finely chopped
1 fresh green chilli, seeded and
  finely chopped
5ml/1 tsp ground toasted
  cumin seeds
2.5ml/½ tsp ground sumac
15g/½oz fresh flat leaf
  parsley, chopped
30ml/2 tbsp chopped fresh mint
olive oil, for frying
salt and ground black pepper
For the relish
2 red onions, cut into 5mm/¼in thick
  slices
75ml/5 tbsp extra virgin olive oil
2 red (bell) peppers, halved
  and seeded
350g/12oz cherry tomatoes, chopped
1 fresh red or green chilli, seeded
  and finely chopped
30ml/2 tbsp chopped fresh mint
30ml/2 tbsp chopped fresh parsley
15ml/1 tbsp chopped fresh oregano
2.5–5ml/½–1 tsp ground sumac
15ml/1 tbsp lemon juice
sugar, to taste

1 Pour 150ml/¼ pint/⅔ cup hot water over the bulgur wheat in a bowl and leave to stand for 15 minutes, then tip into a sieve lined with a clean dishtowel. Drain, then squeeze out the excess moisture.

2 Place the bulgur wheat in a bowl and add the lamb, onion, garlic, chilli, cumin, sumac, parsley and mint. Mix thoroughly together by hand, then season with 5ml/1 tsp salt and plenty of ground black pepper and mix again.

3 Using your hands, form the mixture into 8 burgers and set aside while you make the relish.

4 Brush the onions with 15ml/1 tbsp of the oil and grill (broil) for about 5 minutes on each side, until well browned. Cool, then chop.

5 Grill the peppers, skin-side up, until the skin chars and blisters. Place in a bowl, cover and leave to stand for 10 minutes. Peel off the skin, dice the peppers finely and place in a bowl.

6 Add the onions to the peppers in the bowl, with the tomatoes, chilli, herbs and sumac. Stir in the remaining oil and the lemon juice. Season with salt, pepper and sugar.

7 Heat a heavy frying pan or a ridged, cast-iron grill (broiling) pan over a high heat and grease lightly with olive oil. Cook the burgers for about 5–6 minutes on each side, or until just cooked at the centre.

8 While the burgers are cooking, taste the relish and adjust the seasoning. Serve the burgers as soon as they are cooked, with the relish.

COOK'S TIP
Sumac is a sweet-sour spice made from berries. Substitute grated (shredded) lemon rind, if you prefer.

ROMANIAN KEBABS

KEBABS ARE POPULAR WORLDWIDE, LARGELY BECAUSE THEY ARE SO EASILY ADAPTED TO SUIT EVERYONE'S TASTE. IN THIS RECIPE, LEAN LAMB IS MARINATED, THEN COOKED WITH CHUNKS OF VEGETABLES TO PRODUCE A DELICIOUS, COLOURFUL AND HEALTHY MEAL.

SERVES SIX

INGREDIENTS
    675g/1½lb lean lamb, cut into
        4cm/1½in cubes
    12 button (pearl) onions
    2 green (bell) peppers, seeded and
        cut into 12 pieces
    12 cherry tomatoes
    12 button (pearl) mushrooms
    lemon slices and rosemary sprigs,
        to garnish
    freshly cooked rice and crusty bread,
        to serve
For the marinade
    juice of 1 lemon
    120ml/4fl oz/½ cup red wine
    1 onion, finely chopped
    60ml/4 tbsp olive oil
    2.5ml/½ tsp dried sage
    2.5ml/½ tsp chopped fresh rosemary
    salt and ground black pepper

VARIATIONS
• Use rump (round) steak instead of lamb. Cut it into strips, marinate it as suggested, then interleave the strips on the skewers, with the onions, cherry tomatoes and mushrooms. Omit the green peppers.
• These kebabs are just as delicious cooked on a barbecue (grill).

1 For the marinade, combine the lemon juice, red wine, onion, olive oil, herbs and seasoning in a bowl. Stir the cubes of lamb into the marinade. Cover and chill in the refrigerator for 2–12 hours, stirring occasionally.

2 Remove the lamb pieces from the marinade and thread on 6 skewers with the onions, peppers, tomatoes and mushrooms. Preheat the grill (broiler).

3 Brush the kebabs with marinade and grill (broil) for 10–15 minutes, turning once. Arrange on cooked rice, with lemon and rosemary. Serve with crusty bread.

LAMB GOULASH WITH TOMATOES AND PEPPERS

GOULASH IS A POPULAR AND TRADITIONAL DISH THAT HAS TRAVELLED ACROSS THE WORLD FROM HUNGARY – THIS RECIPE HAS A WONDERFUL COMBINATION OF TOMATOES, PAPRIKA, GREEN PEPPERS, MARJORAM AND A HINT OF FRESH GARLIC.

SERVES FOUR TO SIX

INGREDIENTS
    30ml/2 tbsp vegetable oil
    900g/2lb lean lamb, trimmed and cut
      into cubes
    1 large onion, roughly chopped
    2 garlic cloves, crushed
    3 green (bell) peppers, seeded
      and diced
    30ml/2 tbsp paprika
    2 x 400g/14oz cans chopped tomatoes
    15ml/1 tbsp chopped fresh flat
      leaf parsley
    5ml/1 tsp chopped fresh marjoram
    30ml/2 tbsp plain (all-purpose) flour
    salt and ground black pepper
    green salad, to serve

COOK'S TIPS
• Lard (shortening) is traditionally used for frying the lamb cubes, and can be substituted for the vegetable oil.
• When frying the lamb cubes, it is important not to overload the pan. Cook them in batches if necessary.
• Sour cream is delicious with goulash. Offer a bowl at the table.

1 Heat the oil in a frying pan. Fry the pieces of lamb for 5–8 minutes, stirring frequently with a wooden spoon, or until browned on all sides. Season well.

2 Stir in the chopped onion and crushed garlic, and cook for a further 2 minutes. Add the diced green peppers, then sprinkle over the paprika and stir it in.

3 Pour in the tomatoes and enough water, if needed, to cover the meat in the pan. Stir in the herbs. Bring to the boil, reduce the heat, cover and simmer very gently for 1½ hours or until the lamb is tender.

4 Blend the flour with 60ml/4 tbsp water and pour into the stew. Bring back to the boil, then reduce the heat to a simmer and cook, stirring occasionally, until thickened. Serve with a crisp green salad.

GREEK LAMB SAUSAGES <u>WITH</u> TOMATO SAUCE

THE GREEK NAME FOR THESE SAUSAGES IS SOUDZOUKAKIA. THEY ARE MORE LIKE ELONGATED MEATBALLS THAN THE TYPE OF SAUSAGES THAT WE ARE ACCUSTOMED TO. PASSATA IS SIEVED TOMATO, BUT HOME-PURÉED FRESH TOMATOES CAN BE USED, IF PREFERRED.

SERVES FOUR TO SIX

INGREDIENTS

50g/2oz/1 cup fresh breadcrumbs
150ml/¼ pint/⅔ cup milk
675g/1½lb minced (ground) lamb
30ml/2 tbsp grated (shredded) onion
3 garlic cloves, crushed
10ml/2 tsp ground cumin
30ml/2 tbsp chopped fresh parsley
plain (all-purpose) flour, for dusting
olive oil, for frying
600ml/1 pint/2½ cups passata
   (bottled strained tomatoes)
5ml/1 tsp granulated sugar
2 bay leaves
1 small onion, peeled
salt and ground black pepper
flat leaf parsley, to garnish

VARIATION

• The sauce used here is based on passata, but you could substitute canned tomatoes, reduced to a purée in a blender or food processor.

• Smoked pork sausage could be used instead of the Greek sausages. Simply slice and heat in the sauce.

1 Mix together the breadcrumbs and milk. Add the lamb, onion, garlic, cumin and parsley, and season with salt and plenty of black pepper.

2 Shape the mixture with your hands into little fat sausages, each about 5cm/2in long, and roll them in flour. Heat about 60ml/4 tbsp olive oil in a large frying pan.

3 Fry the sausages for 8 minutes, turning them often. Drain. In another pan, simmer the passata, sugar, bay leaves and whole onion for 20 minutes.

4 Add the sausages to the sauce and cook for another 10 minutes. Remove the bay leaves and onion, and serve garnished with the parsley.

BEEF ROLLS ^{WITH} GARLIC ^{AND} TOMATO SAUCE

THIS TRADITIONAL ITALIAN RECIPE IS A CLASSIC WAY OF COOKING BEEF. THIN SLICES OF STEAK ARE WRAPPED AROUND A RICH CHEESE STUFFING AND BAKED IN A SIMPLE TOMATO AND RED WINE SAUCE. SERVE THE SAME WINE WITH THE MEAL.

SERVES FOUR

INGREDIENTS
   4 thin slices of rump (round) steak,
      about 115g/4oz each
   4 slices smoked ham
   2 eggs, soft-boiled (soft-cooked)
   150g/5oz Pecorino cheese,
      finely grated (shredded)
   2 garlic cloves, crushed or
      finely chopped
   75ml/5 tbsp chopped
      fresh parsley
   45ml/3 tbsp extra virgin olive oil, or
      grapeseed oil
   1 large onion, finely chopped
   150ml/¼ pint/⅔ cup passata
      (bottled strained tomatoes)
   75ml/5 tbsp red wine
   2 bay leaves
   150ml/¼ pint/⅔ cup beef stock
   salt and ground black pepper
   fresh flat leaf parsley sprigs,
      to garnish

3 Shell the soft-boiled eggs. Place on a plate and use a wooden spoon to mash them. Add salt and pepper to taste and mix well.

4 Put the grated cheese and egg in a bowl. Add the crushed garlic and chopped parsley, and mix well.

5 Use a spoon to pile the cheese stuffing on to the ham and beef slices. Fold two opposite sides of the meat over the stuffing, then roll up the meat to form neat parcels. Secure with string.

6 Heat the oil in a frying pan. Add the filled beef and ham parcels and fry quickly to brown on all sides, turning frequently with tongs. Transfer to an ovenproof dish.

7 Add the onion to the frying pan and fry for 3 minutes. Stir in the passata, red wine, bay leaves and stock. Season with salt and plenty of ground black pepper. Bring to the boil, then pour the sauce over the meat.

8 Cover the dish and bake in the oven for 1 hour. Lift out the beef rolls and remove the string. Transfer to warmed serving plates. Taste the sauce, adding extra salt and pepper if necessary, and spoon over the meat. Serve garnished with flat leaf parsley.

VARIATIONS
• Use skinless, boneless chicken or turkey instead of rump steak slices, if you prefer. Lay them between pieces of greaseproof paper and flatten them with the smooth side of a meat mallet. Use chicken stock instead of beef stock.
• The cheese does not have to be Pecorino. Use freshly grated Parmesan instead, or even a flavoursome, but not too mature, Cheddar.

COOK'S TIPS
• Use an even pressure when beating out the slices of rump steak. The aim is to thin the meat, but keep it as even as possible.
• When you cut the slices of ham to fit the steaks, save the trimmings. They can be chopped very finely and added to the stuffing for the rolls.
• If you prefer not to use soft-boiled eggs, which are not recommended for the very young, the elderly, pregnant women or anyone whose immune system is compromised, you can either boil the eggs hard, or leave them out of the recipe. Chopped raw mushrooms would be a good substitute.

1 Preheat the oven to 160°C/325°F/ Gas 3. Lay the beef slices on a sheet of greaseproof (waxed) paper. Cover the beef with another sheet of greaseproof paper or clear film and beat with a mallet or rolling pin until very thin.

2 Lay a ham slice over each slice of rump steak. Using a sharp knife or kitchen scissors, trim the ham slices, if necessary, so that they are more or less the same size as the rump steak slices.

PROVENÇAL BEEF <u>AND</u> OLIVE DAUBE

A DAUBE IS A FRENCH METHOD OF BRAISING MEAT WITH WINE AND HERBS. THIS VERSION FROM THE NICE AREA IN THE SOUTH OF FRANCE ALSO INCLUDES BLACK OLIVES AND TOMATOES.

SERVES SIX

INGREDIENTS
   1.3–1.6kg/3–3½lb topside (pot roast)
     of beef
   225g/8oz lardons, or thick
     streaky (fatty) bacon cut
     into strips
   225g/8oz carrots, sliced thickly
   1 bay leaf
   1 fresh thyme sprig
   2 fresh parsley stalks
   3 garlic cloves
   225g/8oz/2 cups pitted
     black olives
   400g/14oz can chopped tomatoes, or
     if not available, a can of whole
     tomatoes, chopped
   crusty bread, flageolet (small
     cannellini) beans or pasta, to serve
For the marinade
   120ml/4fl oz/½ cup extra
     virgin olive oil or other
     mild oil
   1 onion, sliced
   4 shallots, sliced
   1 celery stick, sliced
   1 carrot, sliced
   150ml/¼ pint/⅔ cup red wine
   6 whole black peppercorns
   2 garlic cloves, sliced
   1 bay leaf
   1 fresh thyme sprig
   2 fresh parsley stalks
   salt and ground black pepper

VARIATIONS
• This dish can be varied quite easily, simply keep the main ingredients the same and change the herbs: instead of thyme and parsley, try rosemary.
• If you prefer, use chicken instead of beef and make the marinade with white wine.
• You could vary this dish further by choosing sweet white wine or adding some extra sugar, and leaving out the olives and herbs in favour of Chinese five-spice powder. This will give the dish a more oriental flavour.

1 To make the marinade, gently heat the oil in a large, shallow pan. Do not let it become too hot or it will smoke. Add the sliced onion, shallots, celery and carrot, then cook for 2 minutes.

2 Lower the heat and wait until the ingredients have cooled slightly, then add the red wine, peppercorns, garlic, bay leaf, thyme and parsley stalks.

3 Season with salt, then cover and leave to simmer on a gentle heat for 15–20 minutes, stirring occasionally. Set the pan aside.

4 Place the beef in a large glass or earthenware dish and pour over the cooled marinade from the frying pan.

5 Cover the dish with a cloth or greaseproof (waxed) paper and let the beef marinate in a cool place or in the fridge for 12 hours. Turn the meat every few hours if possible, but at least once during this time.

6 Preheat the oven to 160°C/325°F/ Gas 3. Lift the meat out of the marinade and fit snugly into a casserole. Add the lardons or bacon and carrots, along with the herbs and garlic.

7 Strain in all the marinade. Cover the casserole with greaseproof paper, then the lid and cook in the oven for 2½ hours.

8 Remove the casserole from the oven, blot the surface of the liquid with kitchen paper to remove the surplus fat, or use a spoon to skim it off, then stir in the olives and tomatoes.

9 Recover the casserole, return to the oven and cook for a further 30 minutes. Carve the meat into thick slices and serve it with chunky crusty bread, plain boiled flageolet beans or pasta.

COOK'S TIP
For those with an alcohol sensitivity, red grape juice and a squeeze of lemon or lime juice can be substituted for the red wine.

BEEF AND LENTIL BALLS WITH TOMATO SAUCE

MIXING LENTILS WITH THE BEEF NOT ONLY BOOSTS THE FIBRE CONTENT OF THESE DELICIOUS AND UNUSUAL MEATBALLS BUT ALSO ADDS TO THE FLAVOUR.

SERVES EIGHT

INGREDIENTS

   15ml/1 tbsp olive oil
   2 onions, finely chopped
   2 celery sticks, finely chopped
   2 large carrots, finely chopped
   400g/14oz lean minced (ground) beef
   200g/7oz/scant 1 cup brown lentils
     or green lentils
   400g/14oz can chopped tomatoes or
     fresh plum tomatoes
   30ml/2 tbsp tomato purée (paste)
   2 bay leaves
   300ml/½ pint/1¼ cups vegetable
     stock
   175ml/6fl oz/¾ cup red wine
   30–45ml/2–3 tbsp Worcestershire
     sauce
   2 eggs
   2 large handfuls fresh
     parsley, chopped
   salt and ground black pepper
   mashed potatoes and green salad,
     to serve
For the tomato sauce
   4 onions, finely chopped
   2 x 400g/14oz cans tomatoes
   60ml/4 tbsp dry red wine
   3 fresh dill sprigs, finely chopped

1 To make the tomato sauce, combine the onions, tomatoes and red wine in a pan. Bring to the boil, lower the heat, cover the pan and simmer for 30 minutes, stirring occasionally.

2 Purée the mixture in a blender or food processor, then return it to a clean pan and set it aside.

3 To make the meatballs, heat the oil in a large heavy pan and fry the onions, celery and carrots for 5–10 minutes, or until the onions and carrots have softened.

4 Add the minced beef and cook over a high heat, stirring frequently, until the meat is lightly browned.

5 Stir in the lentils, tomatoes, tomato purée, bay leaves, vegetable stock and wine. Bring to the boil, then simmer for 20–30 minutes until the liquid has been absorbed. Remove the bay leaves and stir in the Worcestershire sauce.

6 Remove the pan from the heat and add the eggs and parsley. Season with salt and pepper, and mix well, then leave to cool. Meanwhile, preheat the oven to 180°C/350°F/Gas 4.

7 Shape the beef mixture into neat balls, rolling them in your hands. Arrange in an ovenproof dish and bake for 25 minutes.

8 While the meatballs are baking, reheat the tomato sauce. Just before serving, stir in the chopped dill. Pour the tomato sauce over the meatballs and serve with mashed potatoes and a green salad.

COOK'S TIP
It may not be necessary to add both eggs to bind the meatballs mixture. Much will depend upon how dry the lentils are after cooking. Start with one egg. If you think the mixture needs a little more, separate the second egg and add just the yolk at first. If you miscalculate, and the mixture is too sloppy to shape, put it in the refrigerator for about 1 hour to firm up.

BEEF STEW WITH RED WINE AND PEAS

THIS RICH, MEATY STEW IS PERFECT FOR A WINTER LUNCH OR DINNER. SERVE IT WITH BOILED OR MASHED POTATOES TO SOAK UP THE DELICIOUSLY TASTY WINE AND TOMATO SAUCE.

SERVES FOUR

INGREDIENTS
    30ml/2 tbsp plain (all-purpose) flour
    10ml/2 tsp chopped fresh or dried thyme
    1kg/2¼lb braising or stewing steak,
      cut into large cubes
    45ml/3 tbsp olive oil
    1 medium onion, roughly chopped
    450ml/¾ pint/scant 2 cups passata
      (bottled strained tomatoes)
    250ml/8fl oz/1 cup beef stock
    250ml/8fl oz/1 cup red wine
    2 garlic cloves, crushed
    30ml/2 tbsp tomato purée (paste)
    275g/10oz/2 cups shelled fresh peas
    5ml/1 tsp granulated sugar
    salt and ground black pepper
    fresh thyme, to garnish

1 Preheat the oven to 160°C/325°F/ Gas 3. Put the flour in a shallow dish and add the chopped fresh or dried thyme. Season with plenty of salt and pepper. Add the beef cubes and turn them in the seasoned flour until each cube is evenly coated on all sides.

2 Heat the oil in a large flameproof casserole, add the beef and brown on all sides over a medium to high heat. Remove with a slotted spoon and drain on kitchen paper.

3 Add the onion to the pan, scraping the base of the pan to mix in any residue. Cook gently for about 3 minutes, stirring frequently, until the onions have softened, then stir in the passata, stock, wine, garlic and tomato purée. Bring to the boil, stirring.

4 Return the beef to the pan and stir well to coat with the sauce. Cover and cook in the oven for 1½ hours.

5 Stir in the peas and sugar. Return the casserole to the oven and cook for 30 minutes more, or until the beef is tender. Season to taste and garnish with fresh thyme before serving.

VARIATION
Use frozen peas instead. Add them 10 minutes before the end of cooking.

TAGLIATELLE ^{WITH} BOLOGNESE SAUCE

MANY PEOPLE SERVE BOLOGNESE SAUCE WITH SPAGHETTI. TO BE ABSOLUTELY CORRECT, THIS RICH ITALIAN MEAT AND TOMATO RAGU SHOULD BE SERVED WITH TAGLIATELLE.

SERVES FOUR

INGREDIENTS
30ml/2 tbsp olive oil
1 onion, finely chopped
1 carrot, finely chopped
1 celery stick, finely chopped
1 garlic clove, crushed
350g/12oz minced (ground) beef
150ml/¼ pint/⅔ cup red wine
250ml/8fl oz/1 cup milk
400g/14oz can chopped tomatoes
450g/1lb tomatoes, peeled, seeded
   and finely chopped
15ml/1 tbsp sun-dried tomato
   purée (paste)
350g/12oz dried tagliatelle
salt and ground black pepper
shredded fresh basil, to garnish
grated Parmesan cheese, to serve

COOK'S TIPS
• When frying the meat, stir it constantly with a wooden spoon, making sure that any lumps are broken up.
• In winter, it is sometimes difficult to find tomatoes that are flavoursome. If the only ones you can locate taste rather dull, use an extra can of tomatoes instead.
• Don't skimp on the cooking time – it is essential for a full-flavoured Bolognese sauce. Some Italian cooks insist on cooking it for 3–4 hours, so the longer the better.

1 Heat the oil in a large pan. Add the onion, carrot, celery and garlic, and cook gently, stirring frequently, for about 10 minutes until softened.

2 Add the minced beef to the pan and cook over a medium heat until the meat changes colour.

3 Pour in the wine. Stir frequently until it has evaporated, then add the milk and continue cooking and stirring until this has evaporated, too.

4 Stir in all the tomatoes and tomato purée, and season. Simmer the sauce uncovered, over the lowest possible heat for at least 1 hour. Stir it once or twice during this time.

5 Boil the pasta for 10 minutes. Drain. Tip it into a warmed large bowl and pour over the sauce. Garnish with basil and serve with Parmesan cheese.

POLPETTES <u>WITH</u> MOZZARELLA <u>AND</u> TOMATO

THESE ITALIAN MEATBALLS ARE MADE WITH BEEF AND TOPPED WITH MOZZARELLA CHEESE AND TOMATO. THEY TASTE AS GOOD AS THEY LOOK.

SERVES SIX

INGREDIENTS

½ slice white bread, crusts removed
45ml/3 tbsp milk
675g/1½lb minced (ground) beef
1 egg, beaten
50g/2oz/⅔ cup dry breadcrumbs
vegetable oil, for frying
2 beefsteak or other large tomatoes,
   sliced to make 6 slices
15ml/1 tbsp chopped fresh oregano
6 slices mozzarella cheese
6 canned anchovies, drained and
   halved lengthways
salt and ground black pepper

1 Preheat the oven to 200°C/400°F/ Gas 6. Put the bread and milk into a small pan and heat very gently, until the bread absorbs all the milk. Transfer the mixture to a small bowl, mash it to a pulp and leave to cool.

2 Put the beef into a bowl with the bread mixture and the egg, and season with salt and pepper. Mix well, then shape the mixture into 6 patties. Sprinkle the breadcrumbs on to a plate and press the patties with the crumbs until they are thoroughly coated.

3 Heat oil to a depth of about 5mm/¼in in a large frying pan. Add the patties and fry for 2 minutes on each side, until brown. Transfer to a greased ovenproof dish, in a single layer.

4 Lay a slice of tomato on top of each patty, sprinkle with the oregano and season with salt and pepper. Place the mozzarella slices on top. Arrange two strips of anchovy, placed in a cross, on top of each slice of mozzarella. Bake for 10–15 minutes, until the mozzarella has melted. Serve the polpettes hot, straight from the oven.

VARIATION
Use strips of sun-dried tomato on the polpettes instead of anchovies.

Spanish Pork <u>and</u> Sausage Casserole

This dish is from the Catalan region of Spain, and combines pork chops with spicy butifarra sausages in a rich tomato sauce. You can find these sausages in some Spanish delicatessens but, if not, sweet Italian sausages will do.

SERVES FOUR

INGREDIENTS

   30ml/2 tbsp olive oil
   4 boneless pork chops, about
     175g/6oz each
   4 *butifarra* or sweet Italian sausages
   1 onion, chopped
   2 garlic cloves, chopped
   120ml/4fl oz/½ cup dry white wine
   6 plum tomatoes, chopped
   1 bay leaf
   30ml/2 tbsp chopped fresh parsley
   salt and ground black pepper
   baked potatoes and green salad,
    to serve

1 Heat the oil in a large, deep frying pan. Cook the pork chops over a high heat until browned on both sides, then transfer to a plate.

2 Add the sausages, onion and garlic to the pan and cook over a medium heat until the sausages are browned and the onion softened, turning the sausages two or three times during cooking. Return the chops to the pan.

3 Stir in the wine, tomatoes, bay leaf and parsley. Season. Cover the pan and cook for 30 minutes.

4 Remove the sausages and cut into thick slices. Return them to the pan and heat through. Serve with baked potatoes and a green salad.

ALBONDIGAS <u>WITH</u> SPICY TOMATO SAUCE

THESE TASTY MEXICAN MEATBALLS ARE ABSOLUTELY DELICIOUS, AND THE DRIED CHIPOTLE CHILLI
GIVES THE TOMATO SAUCE A DISTINCTIVE, SLIGHTLY SMOKY FLAVOUR.

SERVES FOUR

INGREDIENTS
225g/8oz minced (ground) pork
225g/8oz lean minced (ground) beef
1 medium onion, finely chopped
50g/2oz/1 cup fresh
   white breadcrumbs
5ml/1 tsp dried oregano
2.5ml/½ tsp ground cumin
2.5ml/½ tsp salt
2.5ml/½ tsp ground black pepper
1 egg, beaten
oil, for frying
fresh oregano sprigs, to garnish
For the sauce
1 chipotle chilli, seeded
15ml/1 tbsp vegetable oil
1 onion, finely chopped
2 garlic cloves, crushed
175ml/6fl oz/¾ cup beef stock
400g/14oz can chopped tomatoes
105ml/7 tbsp passata (bottled
   strained tomatoes)

COOK'S TIP
Dampen your hands before shaping the
meatballs so the mixture will be less
likely to stick.

1 Mix the minced pork and beef in a
bowl. Add the onion, breadcrumbs,
oregano, cumin, salt and pepper. Mix
with clean hands until all the
ingredients are well combined.

2 Mix the egg in well, then roll the
mixture into 4cm/1½in balls. Put these
on a baking sheet and chill while you
prepare the sauce.

3 Cover the dried chilli with hot water
and soak for 15 minutes. Heat the oil in
a pan and fry the onion and garlic for
3–4 minutes until softened.

4 Drain the chilli, reserving the soaking
water, then chop it and add it to the
onion mixture. Fry for 1 minute, then
stir in the beef stock, tomatoes, passata
and soaking water, with salt and pepper
to taste. Bring to the boil, lower the heat
and simmer, stirring occasionally, while
you cook the meatballs.

5 Heat the oil for frying in a flameproof
casserole and fry the meatballs in
batches for about 5 minutes, turning
them occasionally, until they have
browned all over. Drain off the oil and
return all the meatballs to the casserole.

6 Pour the tomato and chilli sauce
over the meatballs and simmer on a
hotplate (burner) for about 10 minutes,
occasionally stirring gently so that the
meatballs are coated. Be careful that
they do not disintegrate with stirring.
Garnish the dish with the oregano
and serve.

TORTILLA PIE ^{WITH} GREEN TOMATO SAUCE

THIS IS A POPULAR MEXICAN BREAKFAST DISH, KNOWN AS CHILAQUILES. THE FRIED TORTILLA STRIPS STAY CRISP IN THE TOMATO, CREAM AND CHEESE TOPPING.

<u>SERVES SIX</u>

INGREDIENTS
   30ml/2 tbsp vegetable oil
   500g/1¼lb minced (ground) pork
   3 garlic cloves, crushed
   10ml/2 tsp dried oregano
   5ml/1 tsp ground cinnamon
   2.5ml/½ tsp ground cloves
   2.5ml/½ tsp ground black pepper
   30ml/2 tbsp dry sherry
   5ml/1 tsp caster (superfine) sugar
   5ml/1 tsp salt
   12 corn tortillas
   oil, for frying
   350g/12oz/3 cups grated Monterey
      Jack or mild Cheddar cheese
   300ml/½ pint/1¼ cups crème fraîche
For the green tomato sauce
   300g/11oz/scant 2 cups canned
      green tomatoes, drained
   60ml/4 tbsp stock or water
   2 fresh chillies, seeded and chopped
   2 garlic cloves
   small bunch of fresh coriander
      (cilantro)
   120ml/4fl oz/½ cup sour cream

3 Cut the tortillas into 2cm/¾in strips. Pour oil into a frying pan to a depth of 2cm/¾in and heat to 190°C/375°F. Fry the tortilla strips in batches until crisp and golden brown all over.

4 Spread half the minced pork mixture in an ovenproof dish. Top with half the tortilla strips and grated cheese, then add dollops of crème fraîche. Repeat the layers. Bake for 20–25 minutes, or until bubbling.

5 To make the sauce, put all the ingredients except the sour cream in a food processor or blender (and reserve a little coriander for sprinkling). Process until smooth. Scrape into a pan, bring to the boil, then lower the heat and simmer for 5 minutes.

6 Stir the sour cream into the sauce, with salt and pepper to taste. Pour the mixture over the dish and serve immediately, sprinkled with coriander.

1 Preheat the oven to 180°C/350°F/ Gas 4. Heat the fat in a large pan. Add the minced pork and crushed garlic. Stir over a medium heat until the meat has browned, then stir in the oregano, cinnamon, cloves and pepper.

2 Cook for 3–4 minutes more, stirring constantly, then add the sherry, sugar and salt. Stir for 3–4 minutes until all the flavours are blended, then remove the pan from the heat.

TORTIGLIONI <u>WITH</u> SPICY SAUSAGE SAUCE

THIS HEADY PASTA DISH BASED ON PLUM TOMATOES AND CHILLI IS NOT FOR THE FAINT-HEARTED.
SERVE IT WITH A ROBUST SICILIAN RED WINE.

<u>SERVES FOUR</u>

INGREDIENTS

30ml/2 tbsp olive oil
1 onion, finely chopped
1 celery stick, finely chopped
2 large garlic cloves, crushed
1 fresh red chilli, seeded
   and chopped
450g/1lb ripe plum tomatoes, peeled
   and finely chopped
30ml/2 tbsp tomato purée (paste)
150ml/¼ pint/⅔ cup red wine
5ml/1 tsp granulated sugar
300g/11oz/2¾ cups dried tortiglioni,
   rigatoni or penne
175g/6oz spicy salami, rind removed
30ml/2 tbsp chopped fresh parsley
salt and ground black pepper
freshly grated Parmesan cheese,
   to serve

COOK'S TIP

Buy the salami for this dish in one piece
so that you can chop it into chunks.

1 Heat the oil in a medium pan, then add the onion, celery, garlic and chilli, and cook gently, stirring frequently with a wooden spoon for about 10 minutes until the onion has softened.

2 Add the tomatoes, tomato purée, wine, sugar, and salt and pepper to taste, and bring to the boil, stirring. Lower the heat, cover and simmer gently, stirring occasionally, for about 20 minutes. Add a few spoonfuls of water occasionally if the sauce becomes too thick.

3 Meanwhile, drop the pasta into a large pan of rapidly boiling salted water and simmer, uncovered, for 10–12 minutes, until *al dente*.

4 Chop the salami into bite-size chunks and add to the sauce. Heat through, then taste for seasoning.

5 Drain the pasta, tip it into a large bowl, then pour the sauce over and toss to mix. Sprinkle over the parsley and serve with the grated Parmesan.

HOT PEPPERONI PIZZA

THERE IS NOTHING MORE MOUTHWATERING THAN A FRESHLY BAKED PIZZA, ESPECIALLY WHEN THE TOPPING INCLUDES TOMATOES, PEPPERONI AND RED CHILLIES.

SERVES FOUR

INGREDIENTS

225g/8oz/2 cups strong white bread flour
10ml/2 tsp easy-blend (rapid-rise)
    dried yeast
5ml/1 tsp granulated sugar
2.5ml/½ tsp salt
15ml/1 tbsp olive oil
175ml/6fl oz/¾ cup mixed lukewarm
    milk and water
For the topping
400g/14oz can chopped tomatoes,
    strained
2 garlic cloves, crushed
5ml/1 tsp dried oregano
225g/8oz mozzarella cheese, grated
2 dried red chillies, crumbled
225g/8oz pepperoni, sliced
30ml/2 tbsp drained capers
fresh oregano, to garnish

1 Sift the flour into a bowl. Stir in the yeast, sugar and salt. Make a well in the centre. Stir the olive oil into the milk and water, then stir the mixture into the flour. Mix to a soft dough.

2 Knead the dough on a lightly floured surface for 10 minutes until it is smooth and elastic. Cover and leave in a warm place for about 30 minutes or until the dough has doubled in bulk.

3 Preheat the oven to 220°C/425°F/ Gas 7. Turn the dough out on to a lightly floured surface and knead lightly for 1 minute. Divide it in half and roll each piece out to a 25cm/10in circle. Place on lightly oiled pizza trays or baking sheets. To make the topping, mix the strained tomatoes, garlic and dried oregano in a bowl.

4 Spread half the tomato mixture over each base, leaving a border around the edge. Set half the mozzarella aside. Divide the rest between the pizzas, sprinkling it over evenly. Bake for 7–10 minutes until the dough rim on each pizza is pale golden.

5 Sprinkle the crumbled chillies over the pizzas, then arrange the pepperoni slices and capers on top. Sprinkle with the remaining mozzarella. Return the pizzas to the oven and bake for 7–10 minutes more. Scatter over the fresh oregano and serve at once.

VARNA-STYLE CHICKEN

*IN THIS TASTY DISH, CHICKEN PORTIONS ARE FIRST FRIED, THEN SMOTHERED IN A RICH, HERBY
TOMATO SAUCE AND BAKED IN THE OVEN.*

SERVES EIGHT

INGREDIENTS
    1 chicken, about 1.8kg/4lb cut into
        8 pieces, or 8 chicken portions
    1.5ml/¼ tsp chopped fresh thyme
    40g/1½oz/3 tbsp butter
    45ml/3 tbsp vegetable oil
    3–4 garlic cloves, crushed
    2 onions, finely chopped
    salt and ground black pepper
    fresh basil and thyme leaves,
        to garnish
    freshly cooked rice, to serve
For the sauce
    120ml/4fl oz/½ cup dry sherry
    45ml/3 tbsp tomato purée (paste)
    a few fresh basil leaves
    30ml/2 tbsp white wine vinegar
    generous pinch of granulated sugar
    5ml/1 tsp French mustard
    400g/14oz can chopped tomatoes
    225g/8oz/3 cups mushrooms, sliced

COOK'S TIP
To peel a clove of garlic, place it on a
board with the flat blade of a cook's knife
on top of it. Press down hard on the
knife blade until the garlic is sufficiently
crushed to allow you to remove the skin.

1 Preheat the oven to 180°C/350°F/
Gas 4. Season the chicken with salt,
pepper and thyme. In a large frying pan
heat the butter and oil, and cook the
chicken until golden brown. Remove
from the frying pan, place in an
ovenproof dish and keep hot. Add the
garlic and onions to the frying pan and
cook for 2–3 minutes, or until soft.

2 For the sauce, mix together the
sherry, tomato purée, salt and pepper,
basil, vinegar and sugar. Add the
mustard and tomatoes. Pour into the
frying pan and bring to the boil.

3 Reduce the heat and add the
mushrooms. Adjust the seasoning with
more sugar or vinegar to taste.

4 Pour the tomato sauce over the
chicken. Bake in the oven, covered, for
45–60 minutes, or until the chicken is
cooked right through. Serve on a bed of
rice, garnished with basil and thyme.

VARIATION
Replace the cultivated mushrooms with
wild mushrooms, if you like.

CHICKEN <u>WITH</u> CHORIZO

THE ADDITION OF CHORIZO SAUSAGE AND SHERRY GIVES A WARM, INTERESTING FLAVOUR TO THIS SIMPLE TRADITIONAL SPANISH DISH. SERVE WITH BOILED POTATOES OR RICE.

SERVES FOUR

INGREDIENTS

1 medium chicken, jointed, or
  4 chicken legs, halved
30ml/2 tbsp paprika
60ml/4 tbsp olive oil
2 small onions, sliced
6 garlic cloves, thinly sliced
150g/5oz chorizo sausage, sliced
400g/14oz can chopped tomatoes
12–16 fresh bay leaves
75ml/5 tbsp medium sherry
salt and ground black pepper
potatoes or rice, to serve

COOK'S TIP

Paprika is a mild spice, made from the powdered pods of the sweet red (bell) pepper. Rose or orange in colour, it gives dishes a delicious, slightly smoky flavour, and is particularly good with pork and chicken. It is also used as a garnish.

1 Preheat the oven to 190°C/375°F/ Gas 5. Coat the chicken pieces in the paprika, making sure they are evenly covered, then season with salt. Heat the olive oil in a frying pan and fry the chicken pieces until brown.

2 Transfer the chicken to an ovenproof dish. Add the onions to the pan and fry quickly. Add the garlic and sliced chorizo and fry for 2 minutes.

3 Add the tomatoes, two of the bay leaves and the sherry, and bring to the boil. Pour the sauce over the chicken and cover with a tight-fitting lid. Bake for 45 minutes.

4 Remove the lid and season to taste. Cook for a further 20 minutes until the chicken is tender and golden. Serve with potatoes or rice, garnished with the remaining bay leaves.

CASSOULET

CASSOULET IS A CLASSIC FRENCH DISH IN WHICH VARIOUS MEATS ARE BAKED SLOWLY WITH ROOT VEGETABLES AND FLAVOURSOME TOMATOES UNDER A GOLDEN CRUMB CRUST. IT IS HEARTY AND RICH.

SERVES SIX TO EIGHT

INGREDIENTS
675g/1½lb/3¾ cups dried haricot
   (navy) beans
900g/2lb salt belly pork
4 large duck breast portions
60ml/4 tbsp olive oil
2 onions, chopped
6 garlic cloves, crushed
2 bay leaves
1.5ml/¼ tsp ground cloves
60ml/4 tbsp tomato purée (paste)
8 good-quality sausages
12 large tomatoes
75g/3oz/¾ cup dried breadcrumbs
salt and ground black pepper

VARIATIONS
• You can easily alter the proportions and ingredients in a cassoulet. Turnips, carrots and celeriac make suitable vegetable substitutes, while cubed lamb and goose can replace the pork and duck.
• Try topping the cassoulet with a herby breadcrumb mixture. Crumb several pieces of bread in a food processor. Stir in 10ml/2 tsp of mixed dried herbs and sprinkle over the cassoulet.

1 Put the beans in a large bowl and cover with plenty of cold water. Leave to soak overnight. Put the salt belly pork in a separate bowl of cold water and soak it overnight too.

2 Next day, drain the beans in a colander. Rinse them under cold water, drain again and put them in a pan with fresh water to cover.

3 Bring the water to the boil and boil the beans hard for 10 minutes. Drain.

4 Drain the pork, then cut it into large pieces, discarding the rind. Halve the duck breasts. Heat 30ml/2 tbsp of the oil in a frying pan and fry the pork in batches, until browned.

5 Put the beans in a large, heavy pan with the onions, garlic, bay leaves, ground cloves and tomato purée. Stir in the browned pork and just cover with water. Bring to the boil, then cover and simmer for about 1½ hours until the beans are tender.

6 Preheat the oven to 180°C/350°F/ Gas 4. Heat the remaining oil in a frying pan and fry the duck breasts and sausages until browned. Cut the sausages into smaller pieces.

7 Plunge the tomatoes into boiling water for 30 seconds, then refresh in cold water. Peel off the skins and cut the tomatoes into quarters.

8 Transfer the bean mixture to a large earthenware pot or ovenproof dish and stir in the fried sausages and duck breasts and chopped tomatoes with salt and pepper to taste. Sprinkle with an even layer of breadcrumbs and bake in the oven for 45 minutes to 1 hour until the crust is golden. Serve hot.

COOK'S TIP
The best tomatoes to use for this dish are the delicious, meaty beefsteak type; if they are really large, you may only need about 8 of them. Use canned tomatoes only as a last resort.

Chicken <u>and</u> Tomato Curry

Tender pieces of chicken are lightly cooked with fresh vegetables and aromatic spices in this delicious dish. The tomatoes go in right at the end.

SERVES FOUR

INGREDIENTS

675g/1½lb chicken breast portions
30ml/2 tbsp oil
2.5ml/½ tsp cumin seeds
2.5ml/½ tsp fennel seeds
1 onion, thickly sliced
2 garlic cloves, crushed
2.5cm/1in piece fresh root ginger,
  finely chopped
15ml/1 tbsp curry paste
225g/8oz broccoli, broken into florets
12 tomatoes, cut into thick wedges
5ml/1 tsp garam masala
30ml/2 tbsp chopped fresh
  coriander (cilantro)
naan bread, to serve

VARIATION

This works just as well with turkey breasts.
Use thin turkey escalopes (scallops).

1 Pull the skin and any loose fat off the chicken breast portions. Use a knife to prise loose any remaining fat. Place each portion in turn between two sheets of clear film and pound with a meat mallet or pan to flatten evenly.

2 Using a sharp knife, cut the chicken fillets into cubes, each about the size of a walnut.

3 Heat the oil in a wok or large frying pan and fry the cumin and fennel seeds for 2 minutes until the seeds begin to splutter. Add the onion, garlic and ginger and cook for 5–7 minutes. Stir in the curry paste and cook for a further 2–3 minutes.

4 Add the broccoli florets and fry for about 5 minutes. Stir in the chicken cubes and fry for 5–8 minutes more.

5 Add the tomatoes, garam masala and chopped coriander. Cook for a further 5–10 minutes or until the chicken is tender. Serve with naan bread.

TURKEY <u>AND</u> TOMATO MEATBALLS

*A TASTY CHANGE FROM BEEF OR PORK MEATBALLS, THESE TURKEY MEATBALLS ARE SIMMERED WITH
RICE IN A SIMPLE, BUT DELICIOUS, TOMATO SAUCE.*

SERVES FOUR

INGREDIENTS

25g/1oz white bread, crusts removed
30ml/2 tbsp milk
1 garlic clove, crushed
2.5ml/½ tsp caraway seeds
225g/8oz minced (ground) turkey
1 egg white
350ml/12fl oz/1½ cups chicken stock
400g/14oz can tomatoes
15ml/1 tbsp tomato purée (paste)
90g/3½oz/½ cup easy-cook
  (converted) rice
salt and ground black pepper
15ml/1 tbsp chopped fresh basil
carrot and courgette (zucchini)
  ribbons, to serve

1 Cut the bread into small cubes, about
2.5cm/1in square. Put into a shallow
mixing bowl. Sprinkle over the milk and
leave to soak for about 5 minutes.

2 Add the garlic, caraway seeds and
turkey to the soaked bread in the bowl.
Season with plenty of salt and pepper.
Mix together well with a spatula.

3 Whisk the egg white until stiff, then
fold, half at a time, into the turkey
mixture. Chill the mixture for
10 minutes in the refrigerator.

4 Put the chicken stock, canned
tomatoes and tomato purée into a large,
heavy pan. Quickly bring to the boil,
add the rice, stir and cook briskly for
about 5 minutes. Turn the heat down to
a gentle simmer.

5 Shape the turkey mixture into
16 balls. Simmer them in the stock for
10 minutes, until the turkey balls and
rice are cooked. Garnish with basil.
Serve with carrot and courgette ribbons.

COOK'S TIP

To make carrot and courgette ribbons,
cut the vegetables lengthways into thin
strips using a vegetable peeler, and
blanch or steam until cooked through.

CHICKEN KHORESH

This tomato-flavoured stew originates from the Middle East. It is often served on festive occasions and is traditionally believed to have been a favourite of Persian kings.

SERVES FOUR

INGREDIENTS
    30ml/2 tbsp corn oil or extra virgin
    olive oil
    1 whole chicken or 4 large
    chicken pieces
    1 large onion, chopped
    2 garlic cloves, crushed
    400g/14oz can chopped tomatoes
    8 fresh tomatoes, peeled, seeded
    and chopped
    250ml/8fl oz/1 cup water
    3 small aubergines (eggplant), sliced
    3 (bell) peppers, red, green and
    yellow, seeded and sliced
    30ml/2 tbsp lemon juice
    15ml/1 tbsp ground cinnamon
    salt and ground black pepper
    boiled rice, to serve

1 Heat 15ml/1 tbsp of the oil in a large pan or flameproof casserole and fry the chicken or chicken pieces on both sides for about 8–10 minutes. Add the chopped onion and fry for a further 4–5 minutes, until the onion is golden brown. Ensure that the onion does not blacken, as this would change the flavour of the khoresh.

2 Add the garlic, the canned and fresh chopped tomatoes, the water and the seasoning. Bring to the boil, then reduce the heat and simmer slowly, covered, for 10 minutes.

3 Meanwhile, heat the remaining oil in a frying pan and fry the aubergines in batches until lightly golden. Transfer to a plate with a spatula or slotted spoon. Add the peppers to the pan and fry for a few minutes until they have softened slightly.

4 Arrange the aubergines over the chicken or chicken pieces and then add the peppers. Sprinkle over the lemon juice and cinnamon, then cover and continue cooking over a low heat for about 45 minutes, or until all the chicken pieces are cooked.

5 Transfer the chicken to a serving plate and spoon the aubergines and peppers around the edge. Reheat the sauce if necessary, adjust the seasoning and pour it over the chicken. Serve the khoresh with rice.

ENCHILADAS <u>WITH</u> HOT TOMATO <u>AND</u> GREEN CHILLI SAUCE

IN MEXICO, CHILLIES APPEAR IN ALMOST EVERY SAVOURY DISH, EITHER AS CHILLI POWDER OR CHOPPED, SLICED OR WHOLE. BY MEXICAN STANDARDS, THIS IS A MILD VERSION OF THE POPULAR CHICKEN ENCHILADAS. IF YOU LIKE YOUR FOOD HOT, ADD EXTRA CHILLIES TO THE TOMATO SAUCE.

SERVES FOUR

INGREDIENTS
   8 wheat tortillas
   175g/6oz Cheddar cheese, grated
   1 onion, finely chopped
   350g/12oz cooked chicken, cut into
     small chunks
   300ml/½ pint/1¼ cups sour cream
   1 avocado, sliced and tossed in
     lemon juice, to garnish
For the sauce
   1–2 fresh green chillies
   15ml/1 tbsp vegetable oil
   1 onion, chopped
   1 garlic clove, crushed
   400g/14oz can chopped tomatoes
   30ml/2 tbsp tomato purée (paste)
   salt and ground black pepper

1 To make the sauce, cut the chillies in half lengthways and carefully remove the cores and seeds. Slice the chillies very finely.

2 Heat the oil in a frying pan and fry the onion and garlic for about 3–4 minutes until softened. Stir in the tomatoes, tomato purée and chillies. Simmer gently, uncovered, for 12–15 minutes, stirring frequently.

3 Pour the sauce into a food processor or blender, and process until smooth. Return to the heat and cook very gently, uncovered, for a further 15 minutes. Season to taste, then set aside.

4 Preheat the oven to 180°C/350°F/ Gas 4. Butter a shallow ovenproof dish. Take one tortilla and sprinkle with some cheese and chopped onion, about 40g/1½oz of chicken and 15ml/1 tbsp of sauce. Pour over 15ml/1 tbsp of sour cream, roll up and place seam- side down in the dish.

5 Make 7 more enchiladas to fill the dish. Pour the remaining sauce over and sprinkle with the remaining cheese and onion. Bake for 25–30 minutes until the top is golden. Serve with the remaining sour cream, either poured over or in a separate container, and garnish with the sliced avocado.

Consider ripe tomatoes and fresh fish, and classic

Mediterranean combinations spring to mind in which

both raw ingredients are "home grown", from Black

Pasta with Squid and Tomato Sauce to Sea Bream with

Thyme and Tomatoes or Fresh Tuna and Tomato Stew.

These tasty partners aren't unique to Europe – think

spicy and aromatic, and be inspired by several

mouthwatering dishes from South America, such as

Chargrilled Swordfish with Spicy Tomato and Lime

Sauce or Red Snapper Burritos with Chilli and Cheese.

Fish and Shellfish

BAKED FISH ^{WITH} TAHINI SAUCE

THIS AFRICAN RECIPE EVOKES ALL THE COLOUR AND RICH FLAVOURS OF THE SUN. ALTHOUGH THE
TOMATOES ARE PRESENTED VERY SIMPLY HERE, THEY ARE AN ESSENTIAL ADDITION.

SERVES FOUR

INGREDIENTS
   1 whole white fish, about
      1.2kg/2½lb, scaled and cleaned
   10ml/2 tsp coriander seeds
   4 garlic cloves, sliced
   10ml/2 tsp harissa
   90ml/6 tbsp olive oil
   18 plum tomatoes, sliced
   1 onion, sliced
   3 preserved lemons or 1 fresh lemon
   plenty of fresh herbs, such as bay
      leaves, thyme and rosemary
   salt and ground black pepper
For the sauce
   75ml/5 tbsp light tahini sauce
   juice of 1 lemon
   1 garlic clove, crushed
   45ml/3 tbsp finely chopped fresh
      parsley or coriander (cilantro)
   extra herbs, to garnish

1 Preheat the oven to 200°C/400°F/
Gas 6. Grease the base and sides of a
large shallow ovenproof dish or roasting
tin (pan) that will hold the fish.

2 Slash the fish diagonally on both
sides with a sharp knife. Finely crush
the coriander seeds and garlic with a
pestle and mortar. Mix with the harissa
and about 60ml/4 tbsp of the olive oil.

3 Spread a little of the harissa,
coriander and garlic paste inside the
cavity of the fish, then spread the
remainder over each side of the fish
and set aside.

4 Scatter the tomatoes, onion and
preserved or fresh lemon into the dish
or tin. (Thinly slice the lemon if using
fresh.) Sprinkle with the remaining oil
and season with salt and pepper. Lay
the fish on top and tuck plenty of herbs
around it. Bake, uncovered, for about
25 minutes, or until the flesh of the fish
has turned opaque – test by piercing
the thickest part with a knife.

5 Meanwhile, make the sauce. Put the
tahini, lemon juice, garlic and parsley
or coriander in a small pan with 120ml/
4fl oz/½ cup water. Stir in a little salt
and pepper. Heat through gently and
serve in a separate dish.

COOK'S TIP
If you can't get a suitable large fish, use
several small fish, such as red mullet
(snapper). Reduce the cooking time slightly.

TURKISH COLD FISH WITH TOMATOES

COLD FISH DISHES ARE MUCH APPRECIATED IN THE MIDDLE EAST AND FOR GOOD REASON — THEY ARE DELICIOUS! THE TOMATO TOPPING GIVES A WONDERFUL COLOUR TO AN OTHERWISE GREY-LOOKING MEAL. THIS PARTICULAR VERSION CAN BE MADE USING MACKEREL IF PREFERRED.

SERVES FOUR

INGREDIENTS

60ml/4 tbsp olive oil
900g/2lb red mullet or snapper
2 onions, sliced
1 green (bell) pepper, seeded and sliced
1 red (bell) pepper, seeded and sliced
3 garlic cloves, crushed
15ml/1 tbsp tomato purée (paste)
60ml/4 tbsp fish stock or water
5–6 tomatoes, peeled and sliced
400g/14oz can tomatoes
30ml/2 tbsp chopped fresh parsley
30ml/2 tbsp lemon juice
5ml/1 tsp paprika
15–20 green and black olives
salt and ground black pepper
bread and salad, to serve

VARIATION

One large fish looks spectacular, but it is tricky to both cook and serve. If you prefer, buy 4 smaller fish or fish steaks and cook for a shorter time, until just tender. The flesh should flake when tested with the tip of a knife.

1 Heat half the oil in a large roasting tin (pan) and fry the fish on both sides until golden brown. Remove from the tin, cover and keep warm.

COOK'S TIP

The delicate flesh of red mullet is highly perishable, so it is important to buy fish that is absolutely fresh, and cook it as soon as possible after purchase. Ask the fishmonger to scale and gut it for you.

2 Heat the remaining oil in the tin and fry the onions for 2–3 minutes. Add the peppers and cook for 3–4 minutes, stirring occasionally, then add the garlic and stir-fry for 1 minute more.

3 Mix the tomato purée with the fish stock or water and stir into the tin with the fresh and canned tomatoes, parsley, lemon juice, paprika and seasoning. Simmer for 15 minutes.

4 Return the fish to the roasting tin and cover with the sauce. Cook for 10 minutes, then add the olives and cook for a further 5 minutes or until the fish is just cooked through.

5 Transfer the fish to a serving dish and pour the sauce over the top. Allow to cool, then cover and chill until completely cold. Serve cold, with chunks of bread and a mixed salad.

MARINATED MONKFISH WITH TOMATO COULIS

A LIGHT BUT WELL-FLAVOURED DISH, PERFECT FOR SUMMERTIME EATING AND ENJOYING AL FRESCO WITH A GLASS OR TWO OF CHILLED, FRUITY WINE, ROSÉ GOES WELL WITH THIS MEAL.

SERVES FOUR

INGREDIENTS
    30ml/2 tbsp olive oil
    finely grated rind and juice of 1 lime
    30ml/2 tbsp chopped fresh
      mixed herbs
    5ml/1 tsp Dijon mustard
    4 skinless, boneless monkfish fillets,
      about 175g/6oz each
    salt and ground black pepper
    fresh herb sprigs, to garnish
For the coulis
    4 plum tomatoes, peeled and chopped
    1 garlic clove, chopped
    15ml/1 tbsp olive oil
    15ml/1 tbsp tomato purée (paste)
    30ml/2 tbsp chopped fresh oregano
    5ml/1 tsp light soft brown sugar

COOK'S TIP

Monkfish may be hideous to look at, but the fish tastes wonderful, and is much sought after. Most of the flesh is to be found in the tail, which is the part that you will most often see at the fishmonger's. If you buy a whole tail, peel off the skin from the thick end towards the narrow section, then carefully pull off the pinkish membrane beneath. Fillet the fish by cutting through the flesh on either side of the backbone. This is very easy, as there are none of the usual side bones. The backbone can be used to make stock.

2 Place the monkfish fillets in a shallow, non-metallic container and pour over the lime mixture. Turn the fish several times in the marinade to coat it. Cover and chill for 1–2 hours.

3 Meanwhile, make the coulis. Place all the coulis ingredients in a blender or food processor and process until smooth. Season to taste, then cover and chill until required.

5 Spoon a little marinade over each piece of fish. Gather the paper loosely over the fish and fold over the edges to secure the parcel tightly. Place on a baking sheet. Bake for 20–30 minutes until the fish fillets are cooked, tender and just beginning to flake.

6 Carefully unwrap the parcels and serve the fish fillets immediately, with a little of the chilled coulis served alongside, garnished with a few fresh herb sprigs.

1 Place the oil, lime rind and juice, herbs, mustard and salt and pepper in a small bowl or jug and whisk together until thoroughly mixed.

4 Preheat the oven to 180°C/350°F/ Gas 4. Using a spatula, place each fillet on a sheet of greaseproof (waxed) paper big enough to hold it in a parcel.

VARIATION
The coulis can be served hot, if you prefer. Simply make as directed in the recipe and heat gently in a pan until almost boiling, before serving.

SEA BREAM <u>WITH</u> THYME, TOMATOES <u>AND</u> MEDITERRANEAN VEGETABLES

A WHOLE FISH COATED IN A TANGY MARINADE IS BAKED ON ROASTED VEGETABLES UNTIL TENDER AND FLAKY — AN IMPRESSIVE-LOOKING DISH THAT IS EASY TO MAKE AND SUITABLE FOR A DINNER PARTY.

<u>SERVES FOUR</u>

INGREDIENTS

1 or 2 whole sea bream or sea bass,
   total weight 1.3–1.6kg/3–3½lb,
   cleaned and scaled, with the head
   and tail left on
2 onions
2 courgettes (zucchini)
12 tomatoes
45ml/3 tbsp olive oil
5ml/1 tsp fresh chopped thyme
400g/14oz can artichoke hearts
lemon wedges and finely pared rind,
   black olives and fresh coriander
   (cilantro) leaves, to garnish
For the marinade
1 onion, chopped
2 garlic cloves, halved
½ bunch fresh parsley
3–4 fresh coriander (cilantro) sprigs
pinch of paprika
45ml/3 tbsp olive oil
30ml/2 tbsp white wine vinegar
15ml/1 tbsp lemon juice
salt and ground black pepper

1 First make the marinade. Place the ingredients in a food processor with 45ml/3 tbsp water and process until the onion is finely chopped and the ingredients are well combined.

2 Make 3–4 slashes on both sides of the fish. Place in a bowl and, using a palette knife (metal spatula), spread with the marinade, pressing it into both sides of the fish. Set aside for 2–3 hours, turning the fish occasionally.

3 Slice the onions. Trim the courgettes and cut into short julienne strips. Peel the tomatoes, discard the seeds and chop roughly.

4 Preheat the oven to 220°C/425°F/Gas 7. Place the onions, courgettes and tomatoes in a shallow ovenproof dish. Sprinkle with the olive oil, salt and thyme, and roast in the oven for 15–20 minutes, until softened and slightly charred, stirring occasionally.

5 Reduce the oven temperature to 180°C/350°F/Gas 4. Drain the artichokes and add them to the dish, spacing them evenly in the vegetable mixture. Place the fish, together with the marinade, on top of the vegetables. Pour over 150ml/¼ pint/⅔ cup water and cover with foil.

6 Bake for 30–35 minutes or until the fish is tender. (Exact timing will depend on whether you are cooking 1 large or 2 smaller fish.) For the last 5 minutes of cooking, remove the foil to allow the skin to brown slightly. Alternatively, if the dish is flameproof, place it under a hot grill (broiler) for 2–3 minutes.

7 Arrange the fish on a large, warmed serving platter and spoon the vegetables around the sides. Garnish with lemon wedges and finely pared strips of rind, black olives and fresh coriander leaves before serving.

CARIBBEAN FISH STEAKS

WEST INDIAN COOKS LOVE SPICES, AND USE THEM TO GOOD EFFECT. THIS QUICK AND EASY RECIPE IS A TYPICAL EXAMPLE OF HOW CHILLIES, CAYENNE AND ALLSPICE CAN BE USED WITH LIME TO ADD AN EXOTIC ACCENT TO A TOMATO SAUCE FOR FISH.

SERVES FOUR

INGREDIENTS
    45ml/3 tbsp sunflower oil
    6 shallots
    1 garlic clove
    1 fresh green chilli, seeded and
        finely chopped
    400g/14oz can chopped tomatoes
    2 bay leaves
    1.5ml/¼ tsp cayenne pepper
    5ml/1 tsp ground allspice
    juice of 2 limes
    4 cod steaks
    5ml/1 tsp muscovado (molasses) sugar
    10ml/2 tsp angostura bitters
    salt

VARIATION
This unusual and exotic sauce is also good over grilled (broiled) pork chops.

1 Slowly heat the oil in a frying pan. Finely chop the shallots and add them to the frying pan. Cook for 5 minutes until soft. Crush a peeled garlic clove into the frying pan and add the chilli. Cook for a further 2 minutes, then stir in the tomatoes, bay leaves, cayenne pepper, allspice and lime juice, with a little salt to taste.

2 Cook gently for 15 minutes, then add the cod steaks and baste with the tomato sauce. Cover and cook for 10 minutes. Transfer the steaks to a warmed dish and keep hot while you prepare the sauce. Stir the sugar and angostura bitters into the sauce, simmer for 2 minutes, then pour over the fish.

ROASTED COD <u>WITH</u> FRESH TOMATO SAUCE

REALLY FRESH COD HAS A SWEET, DELICATE FLAVOUR AND A PURE WHITE FLAKY FLESH. SERVED WITH AN AROMATIC TOMATO SAUCE, IT MAKES A DELICIOUS MEAL.

SERVES FOUR

INGREDIENTS

350g/12oz ripe plum tomatoes
75ml/5 tbsp olive oil
2.5ml/½ tsp sugar
2 strips of pared orange rind
1 fresh thyme sprig
6 fresh basil leaves
900g/2lb fresh cod fillet, skin on
salt and ground black pepper
steamed green beans, to serve

COOK'S TIP
Cod is becoming increasingly rare and expensive. You can substitute any firm white fish fillets in this dish. Try haddock, pollock, or that excellent and underrated fish, coley. When raw, coley flesh looks grey, but it turns white on cooking.

1 Preheat the oven to 230°C/450°F/ Gas 8. Roughly chop the tomatoes.

2 Heat 15ml/1 tbsp of the olive oil in a heavy pan, add the tomatoes, sugar, orange rind, thyme and basil, and simmer for 5 minutes until the tomatoes are soft.

3 Press the tomato mixture through a fine sieve, discarding the solids that remain in the sieve. Pour into a small pan and heat gently.

4 Scale the cod fillet and cut on the diagonal into 4 pieces. Season well.

5 Heat the remaining oil in a heavy frying pan and fry the cod, skin-side down, until the skin is crisp. Place the fish on a greased baking sheet, skin-side up, and roast in the oven for 8–10 minutes until the fish is cooked through. Serve the fish on the steamed green beans with the tomato sauce.

BAKED COD ^{WITH} TOMATOES ^{AND} PEPPERS

THE WONDERFUL SUN-DRENCHED FLAVOURS OF THE MEDITERRANEAN ARE BROUGHT TOGETHER IN THIS APPETIZING, POTATO-TOPPED BAKE. RED AND YELLOW PEPPERS ADD COLOUR TO THE DISH.

SERVES FOUR

INGREDIENTS

450g/1lb potatoes, peeled and
  thinly sliced
30ml/2 tbsp olive oil
1 red onion, chopped
1 garlic clove, crushed
1 red (bell) pepper, seeded
  and diced
1 yellow (bell) pepper, seeded
  and diced
225g/8oz/3 cups mushrooms, sliced
400g/14oz can chopped tomatoes
225g/8oz fresh tomatoes, chopped
150ml/¼ pint/⅔ cup dry white wine
450g/1lb skinless, boneless cod
  fillet, cut into 2cm/¾in cubes
50g/2oz/½ cup pitted black
  olives, chopped
15ml/1 tbsp chopped fresh basil
15ml/1 tbsp chopped fresh oregano
salt and ground black pepper
fresh oregano sprigs, to garnish
cooked courgettes (zucchini), to serve

1 Preheat the oven to 200°C/400°F/ Gas 6. Bring a large pan of lightly salted water to the boil. Add the potato slices and cook for 4 minutes. Tip into a colander, drain thoroughly, then put the potato slices into a bowl. Add 15ml/ 1 tbsp of the olive oil and toss gently to coat. Set aside.

3 Stir in the mushrooms, tomatoes and wine, bring to the boil and boil rapidly for a few minutes to reduce.

2 Heat the remaining olive oil in a large pan, add the chopped onion, crushed garlic and red and yellow peppers, and cook for 5 minutes, stirring occasionally.

4 Stir the fish cubes, olives and herbs into the tomato mixture, with salt and a generous grinding of black pepper. Stir well to combine.

5 Spoon the mixture into a lightly greased ovenproof dish and arrange the potato slices over the top, covering the fish mixture completely. Bake, uncovered, for about 45 minutes until the fish is cooked and tender and the potato topping is browned. Garnish with oregano and serve with courgettes.

FRESH TUNA AND TOMATO STEW

A DELICIOUSLY SIMPLE ITALIAN RECIPE THAT RELIES ON GOOD BASIC INGREDIENTS: FRESH FISH, TOMATOES AND HERBS. FOR AN AUTHENTIC FLAVOUR, SERVE WITH POLENTA OR PASTA.

SERVES FOUR

INGREDIENTS
    12 baby (pearl) onions, peeled
    900g/2lb ripe tomatoes
    675g/1½lb tuna
    45ml/3 tbsp olive oil
    2 garlic cloves, crushed
    45ml/3 tbsp chopped fresh herbs
    2 bay leaves
    2.5ml/½ tsp caster (superfine) sugar
    30ml/2 tbsp sun-dried tomato
        purée (paste)
    150ml/¼ pint/⅔ cup dry white wine
    salt and ground black pepper
    baby courgettes (zucchini) and fresh
        herbs, to garnish

VARIATION
Two large mackerel make a more readily available alternative to the tuna. Simply lay the whole fish over the sauce and cook, covered with a lid until the mackerel is cooked through.

1 Leave the onions whole and cook in a pan of boiling water for 4–5 minutes until softened. Drain. Plunge the tomatoes into boiling water for 30 seconds, then refresh in cold water. Peel off the skins and chop roughly.

2 Cut the tuna into 2.5cm/1in chunks. Heat the oil in a large frying or sauté pan and quickly fry the tuna until the surface has browned. Lift the chunks out of the pan and drain.

3 Stir in the onions, garlic, tomatoes, chopped herbs, bay leaves, sugar, tomato purée and wine, and bring to the boil, breaking up the tomatoes with a wooden spoon.

4 Reduce the heat and simmer the sauce gently for 5 minutes. Return the fish to the pan and cook for a further 5 minutes. Season, and serve hot, garnished with baby courgettes and fresh herbs.

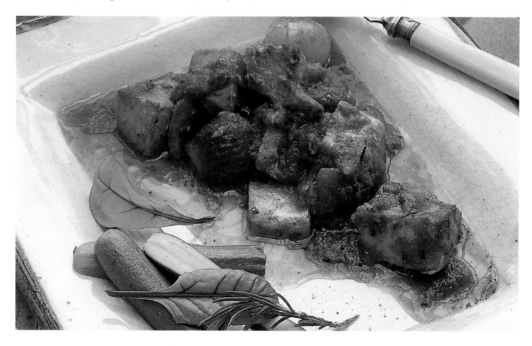

MONKFISH <u>WITH</u> TOMATOES

MONKFISH, ALSO KNOWN AS ANGLER FISH, WAS ONCE SCORNED BY FISHERMAN BECAUSE OF ITS HUGE, UGLY HEAD, YET NOW IT IS PRIZED FOR ITS RICH, MEATY TEXTURE. IT IS SOMETIMES CALLED "POOR MAN'S LOBSTER" AND IS SUBSTITUTED FOR LOBSTER OR SHRIMP IN SOME DISHES.

SERVES FOUR

INGREDIENTS
   800g/1¾lb monkfish tail, skinned
     and filleted
   plain (all-purpose) flour, for coating
   45–60ml/3–4 tbsp olive oil
   120ml/4fl oz/½ cup dry white wine or
     fish stock
   8 ripe tomatoes, peeled, seeded
     and chopped
   2.5ml/½ tsp dried thyme
   16 black olives, pitted
   15–30ml/1–2 tbsp capers, rinsed
   15ml/1 tbsp chopped fresh basil
   salt and ground black pepper
   pine nuts, to garnish

COOK'S TIP
The monkfish slices should only have a light dusting of seasoned flour. Drop each slice in turn into the flour, turn it until coated on all sides, then lightly jiggle it in your hand, holding the fingers slightly apart, until all the excess flour drops off. Alternatively, put the seasoned flour in a stout plastic bag, add the slices and shake gently to coat.

1 Using a thin, sharp knife, remove any pinkish membrane from the monkfish tail. Holding the knife at an angle, cut the fillets diagonally into 12 slices.

VARIATION
If monkfish is not available, try substituting any white fish, such as cod.

2 Season the flour and coat the fish in the mixture. Put a heavy frying pan on high heat and add the oil to coat. Add the monkfish slices and reduce the heat to medium–high. Cook the monkfish for 2 minutes on each side until the surface is lightly browned and the flesh is opaque. Transfer to a warmed plate while you make the sauce.

3 Add the wine or fish stock to the pan and boil for 1–2 minutes, stirring constantly. Add the tomatoes and thyme, and cook for 2 minutes, then stir in the olives, capers and basil, and cook for a further minute to heat through. Arrange three pieces of fish on each of 4 warmed plates. Spoon over the sauce and garnish with pine nuts.

SALMON <u>AND</u> TUNA PARCELS

YOU NEED FAIRLY LARGE SMOKED SALMON SLICES FOR THIS DISH, AS THEY ARE WRAPPED AROUND A
LIGHT TUNA MIXTURE BEFORE BEING SERVED ON A VIBRANT TOMATO SALAD.

SERVES FOUR

INGREDIENTS
    30ml/2 tbsp natural (plain) yogurt
    15ml/1 tbsp tomato purée (paste)
    5ml/1 tsp wholegrain honey mustard
    grated rind and juice of 1 lime
    200g/7oz can tuna in brine, drained
    12–16 large slices of smoked salmon
    salt and ground black pepper
    fresh mint leaves, to garnish
For the salad
    3 ripe vine tomatoes, sliced
    2 kiwi fruit, peeled and sliced
    ¼ cucumber, cut into julienne sticks
    15ml/1 tbsp chopped fresh mint
    7.5ml/1½ tsp white wine vinegar
    45ml/3 tbsp olive oil
    2.5ml/½ tsp mustard

1 Mix the yogurt, tomato purée and
mustard in a bowl. Stir in the grated
lime rind and juice. Add the tuna, with
black pepper to taste, and mix well.

2 Spread out the salmon slices on a
chopping board and spoon some of the
tuna mixture on to each piece.

3 Roll up or fold the smoked salmon
into neat parcels. Carefully press the
edges together to seal.

COOK'S TIP
Whole sides of smoked salmon are often
on sale quite cheaply around Christmas
time, and would be ideal. As the filling is
strongly flavoured, it is quite all right to
use farmed salmon. The parcels would
make a welcome change from turkey.

4 Make the salad. Arrange the tomato
and kiwi slices on 4 serving plates.
Sprinkle over the cucumber sticks. In
a bowl, whisk the chopped mint, white
wine vinegar, oil, mustard and a little
seasoning together and spoon some
over each salad.

5 Arrange 3–4 salmon parcels on each
plate, garnish with the fresh mint leaves
and serve immediately.

MEDITERRANEAN FISH CUTLETS
WITH ANISEED TOMATO SAUCE

THIS DELICIOUS DISH IS PERFECT FOR A DINNER PARTY, AS THE WHITE FLESH OF THE FISH CONTRASTS WITH THE STRIKING RED OF THE SAUCE. THE PASTIS IN THE SAUCE ADDS A SURPRISE TO THE RANGE OF FLAVOURS, AND WILL GIVE YOUR GUESTS A MEAL TO REMEMBER.

SERVES FOUR

INGREDIENTS

4 white fish cutlets, about 150g/
   5oz each
150ml/¼ pint/⅔ cup fish stock and/
   or dry white wine, for poaching
1 bay leaf
a few black peppercorns
a strip of pared lemon rind
fresh parsley and lemon wedges,
   to garnish
For the tomato sauce
400g/14oz can chopped tomatoes
1 garlic clove
15ml/1 tbsp sun-dried tomato
   purée (paste)
15ml/1 tbsp pastis or other aniseed
   (anise seed) flavoured liqueur
15ml/1 tbsp drained capers
12–16 pitted black olives
salt and ground black pepper

1 Make the sauce. Heat the chopped tomatoes in a pan with the whole garlic clove. Stir in the sun-dried tomato paste or tomato purée.

2 Measure the pastis or other liqueur into the pan, then add the capers and olives. Season with salt and black pepper. Heat all the ingredients together for 5 minutes, stirring occasionally, to blend the flavours.

3 Place the fish in a frying pan, pour over the stock and/or wine and add the flavourings. Cover and simmer for 10 minutes or until the fish flakes easily.

4 Using a slotted spoon, transfer the fish to a heated dish. Strain the stock into the sauce and boil to reduce slightly. Season the sauce, pour it over the fish and serve immediately, with parsley and lemon wedges.

FISH BOULETTES ᴼᴺ HOT TOMATO SAUCE

THIS IS AN UNUSUAL AND TASTY DISH THAT NEEDS SCARCELY ANY PREPARATION AND LEAVES VERY FEW DISHES TO WASH, AS IT IS ALL COOKED IN ONE PAN. IT SERVES FOUR PEOPLE AS A MAIN COURSE, BUT ALSO MAKES A GREAT APPETIZER FOR EIGHT.

SERVES FOUR TO EIGHT

INGREDIENTS
  675g/1½lb white fish fillets
  pinch of saffron threads
  ½ bunch fresh flat leaf parsley
  1 egg
  25g/1oz/½ cup fresh white
    breadcrumbs
  25ml/1½ tbsp olive oil
  15ml/1 tbsp lemon juice
  salt and ground black pepper
  fresh flat leaf parsley and lemon
    wedges, to garnish
For the sauce
  1 onion, very finely chopped
  2 garlic cloves, crushed
  6 tomatoes, peeled and chopped
  1 fresh green or red chilli, seeded
    and finely sliced
  90ml/6 tbsp olive oil
  150ml/¼ pint/⅔ cup water
  15ml/1 tbsp lemon juice

1 Skin the fish, cut it into large chunks and place in a blender. Dissolve the saffron in 30ml/2 tbsp boiling water and pour into the blender with the parsley, egg, breadcrumbs, olive oil and lemon juice. Season well with salt and ground black pepper and process for 10–20 seconds until the fish is finely chopped and all the ingredients are combined.

2 Mould the mixture into small balls about the size of walnuts and place them in a single layer on a plate. Place in the refrigerator until ready to cook.

3 To make the sauce, place the onion, garlic, tomatoes, chilli, olive oil and water in a pan. Bring to the boil and then lower the heat and simmer, partially covered, for 10–15 minutes until the sauce is slightly reduced. Stir occasionally to prevent the mixture from sticking.

4 Stir in the lemon juice, then place the fish balls in the simmering sauce. Cover and simmer very gently for 12–15 minutes until the fish balls are cooked through, turning them over occasionally.

5 Serve the fish balls and sauce immediately from the pan, garnished with fresh flat leaf parsley and lemon wedges.

COD PLAKI

GENERALLY, FISH IS SERVED VERY SIMPLY IN GREECE, BUT THIS TRADITIONAL RECIPE IS A LITTLE MORE ELABORATE, AND INVOLVES BRAISING THE FISH WITH TOMATOES AND ONIONS.

SERVES SIX

INGREDIENTS
  300ml/½ pint/1¼ cups extra virgin
    olive oil
  2 onions, thinly sliced
  6 large well-flavoured tomatoes,
    roughly chopped
  3 garlic cloves, thinly sliced
  5ml/1 tsp granulated sugar
  5ml/1 tsp chopped fresh dill
  5ml/1 tsp chopped fresh mint
  5ml/1 tsp chopped fresh
    celery leaves
  15ml/1 tbsp chopped fresh parsley
  6 cod steaks, about 175g/6oz each
  juice of 1 lemon
  salt and ground black pepper
  extra dill, mint or parsley, or other
    fresh herbs, to garnish

1 Heat the oil in a large sauté pan or flameproof casserole. Add the onions and cook until pale golden. Add the tomatoes, garlic, sugar, chopped dill, mint, celery leaves and parsley with 300ml/ ½ pint/1¼ cups water. Season with salt and pepper, then simmer, uncovered, for 25 minutes, until the liquid has reduced by one-third.

2 Add the fish steaks to the pan or casserole and braise gently for 10–12 minutes, until the fish is just cooked. Remove from the heat and add the lemon juice. Cover and leave to stand for about 20 minutes before serving. Arrange the cod in a dish and spoon the sauce over. Garnish with herbs and serve warm or cold.

MEXICAN-STYLE SALT COD

THIS TRADITIONAL RECIPE IS MILDER THAN THE SIMILAR SPANISH DISH, BACALDO A LA VIZCAINA, BUT IS JUST AS FULL OF TOMATOES. IT IS EATEN ON CHRISTMAS EVE THROUGHOUT MEXICO.

SERVES SIX

INGREDIENTS

450g/1lb dried salt cod
105ml/7 tbsp extra virgin olive oil
1 onion, halved and thinly sliced
4 garlic cloves, crushed
2 x 400g/14oz can chopped tomatoes
450g/½ lb fresh tomatoes, chopped
75g/3oz/¾ cup flaked (sliced)
    almonds
75g/3oz/½ cup pickled chilli slices
115g/4oz/1 cup green olives stuffed
    with pimiento
small bunch of fresh parsley,
    finely chopped
salt and ground black pepper
fresh flat leaf parsley, to garnish
crusty bread, to serve

1 Put the cod in a large bowl and pour over enough cold water to cover. Soak for 24 hours, changing the water at least 5 times during this period.

2 Drain the cod and remove the skin. Shred the flesh finely using two forks, and put it into a bowl. Set it aside.

3 Heat half the oil in a large frying pan. Add the onion slices and fry over a medium heat, stirring often with a wooden spoon, until the onion has softened and is translucent. Do not let the onion slices burn.

4 Remove the onion from the pan and set aside. Make sure you transfer the oil with the onion as it is an important flavouring in this dish and must not be discarded.

5 Add the remaining olive oil to the frying pan. When it is hot but not smoking, add the crushed garlic and fry gently for 2 minutes, stirring constantly with the wooden spoon.

6 Add the tomatoes and their juice to the pan and stir to mix. Cook over a medium–high heat for about 20 minutes, stirring occasionally with the wooden spoon, until the mixture has reduced and thickened. Towards the end of the cooking time, stir the sauce more frequently to make sure it does not stick on the base of the pan.

7 Meanwhile, spread out the flaked almonds in a single layer in a large heavy frying pan. Toast them over a medium heat for a few minutes, shaking the pan lightly throughout the process so that they turn golden brown all over. Do not let them burn.

8 Add the chilli slices and stuffed olives to the toasted almonds.

9 Stir in the shredded fish, mixing it in thoroughly, and cook for 20 minutes more, stirring occasionally, until the mixture is almost dry.

10 Season to taste, add the parsley and cook for a further 2–3 minutes. Garnish with parsley leaves and serve in heated bowls, with crusty bread.

COOK'S TIPS

• Salt cod is available in specialist fishmongers, Spanish delicatessens and West Indian stores.
• Any leftovers can be used to fill burritos or empanadas.

CHARGRILLED SWORDFISH <u>WITH</u> SPICY, TOMATO <u>AND</u> LIME SAUCE

SWORDFISH IS A PRIME CANDIDATE FOR THE BARBECUE, AS LONG AS IT IS NOT OVERCOOKED. IT TASTES WONDERFUL WITH A SPICY TOMATO SAUCE WHOSE FIRE IS TEMPERED WITH CRÈME FRAÎCHE.

SERVES FOUR

INGREDIENTS
  2 fresh chillies
  4 tomatoes
  45ml/3 tbsp olive oil
  grated rind and juice of 1 lime
  4 swordfish steaks, about
    225g/8oz each
  2.5ml/½ tsp salt
  2.5ml/½ tsp ground black pepper
  175ml/6fl oz/¾ cup crème fraîche
  fresh flat leaf parsley, to garnish
  chargrilled vegetables, to serve

1 Roast the chillies in a dry griddle pan until the skins are blistered. Put in a plastic bag and tie the top. Set aside for 20 minutes, then peel off the skins. Cut off the stalks, then slit the chillies, take out the seeds and slice the flesh.

2 Cut a cross in the base of each tomato. Place them in a heatproof bowl and pour over boiling water to cover. After 30 seconds, lift the tomatoes out on a slotted spoon and plunge them into a bowl of cold water. Drain. The skins will have begun to peel back from the crosses.

3 Remove all the skin from the tomatoes, then cut them in half and squeeze out the seeds. Using a serrated knife, chop tomato flesh into 1cm/½in pieces.

4 Heat 15ml/1 tbsp of the oil in a small pan and add the strips of chilli, with the lime rind and juice. Cook for 2–3 minutes, then stir in the tomatoes. Cook for 10 minutes, stirring the mixture occasionally, until the tomato is soft and pulpy.

5 Brush the swordfish steaks with the remaining olive oil and season them well. Barbecue or grill (broil) for 3–4 minutes or until just cooked, turning once. Meanwhile, stir the crème fraîche into the sauce, heat it through gently and pour over the swordfish steaks. Serve garnished with parsley and with chargrilled vegetables.

RED SNAPPER BURRITOS

FISH MAKES A GREAT FILLING FOR A TORTILLA, ESPECIALLY WHEN IT IS SUCCULENT RED SNAPPER MIXED WITH RICE, CHILLI AND TOMATOES.

SERVES EIGHT

INGREDIENTS
3 red snapper or any white
  fish fillets
90g/3½oz/½ cup long grain white rice
30ml/2 tbsp vegetable oil
1 small onion, finely chopped
5ml/1 tsp ground achiote seed
1 dried chilli, seeded and ground or
  2.5ml/½ tsp chilli powder
200g/7oz can chopped tomatoes
75g/3oz/¾ cup flaked (sliced) almonds
150g/5oz/1¼ cups grated Monterey
  Jack or mild Cheddar cheese
8 x 20cm/8in wheat flour tortillas

1 Grill (broil) the fish on an oiled rack for about 5 minutes, turning once. When cool, remove the skin and flake the fish into a bowl. Set it aside. Meanwhile, put the rice in a pan, pour over cold water, cover and bring to the boil. Drain, rinse and drain again.

2 Heat the oil and fry the onion until soft. Stir in the ground achiote and the chilli, and cook for 5 minutes.

3 Add the rice, stir to coat all the grains in the flavoured oil, then stir in the tomatoes, flaked fish and almonds. Cook over a medium heat until the juice is absorbed and the rice is tender. Stir in the cheese and remove from the heat. Warm the tortillas.

4 Spread out the tortillas and divide the filling among them. Shape each burrito by folding the sides of the tortilla over the filling, then bringing the bottom up and the top down to form a neat parcel. Secure each burrito with a cocktail stick or toothpick until ready to serve.

RED SNAPPER WITH CHILLIES AND TOMATOES

THIS IS A CLASSIC MEXICAN DISH WHICH BORROWS BAY LEAVES AND OLIVES FROM SPAIN TO GO WITH THE NATIVE CHILLIES IN THE RICH TOMATO SAUCE.

SERVES FOUR

INGREDIENTS

    4 whole red snapper, cleaned
    juice of 2 limes
    4 garlic cloves, crushed
    5ml/1 tsp dried oregano
    2.5ml/½ tsp salt
    drained bottled capers, to garnish
    lime wedges, to serve (optional)
For the sauce
    120ml/4fl oz/½ cup olive oil
    2 bay leaves
    2 garlic cloves, sliced
    4 fresh chillies, seeded and cut
      in strips
    1 onion, thinly sliced
    450g/1lb fresh tomatoes
    75g/3oz/½ cup pickled jalapeño
      chilli slices
    15ml/1 tbsp soft dark brown sugar
    2.5ml/½ tsp ground cloves
    2.5ml/½ tsp ground cinnamon
    150g/5oz/1¼ cups green olives
      stuffed with pimiento
    lime rind, to garnish

4 Add the onion slices to the flavoured oil in the pan and cook for 3–4 minutes more, until all the onion is softened and translucent. Keep the heat low and stir the onions often so that they do not brown.

5 Cut a cross in the base of each tomato. Place them in a heatproof bowl and pour over boiling water to cover. After 30 seconds, lift the tomatoes out on a slotted spoon and plunge them into a bowl of cold water. Drain. The skins will have begun to peel back from the crosses.

6 Skin the tomatoes completely, then cut them in half and squeeze out the seeds. Chop the flesh finely and add it to the onion. Cook for 3–4 minutes, until the tomato is starting to soften.

7 Add the pickled jalapeños, brown sugar, ground cloves and cinnamon to the sauce. Cook for 10 minutes, stirring frequently, then stir the olives into the sauce and pour a little over each fish. Garnish with the capers and serve with lime wedges for squeezing over the fish, if you like. A rice dish would make a good accompaniment.

1 Preheat the oven to 180°C/350°F/Gas 4. Rinse the fish inside and out. Pat dry with kitchen paper. Place in a large roasting tin (pan) in a single layer.

2 Mix the lime juice, garlic, oregano and salt. Pour the mixture over the fish. Bake for about 30 minutes, or until the flesh flakes easily.

3 Make the sauce. Heat the oil in a pan, add the bay leaves, garlic and chilli strips; fry for 3–4 minutes.

CEVICHE

*THIS FAMOUS DISH IS PARTICULARLY POPULAR ALONG MEXICO'S WESTERN SEABOARD, IN PLACES SUCH
AS ACAPULCO. IT CONSISTS OF VERY FRESH RAW SHELLFISH, "COOKED" BY THE ACTION OF LIME JUICE.*

<u>SERVES SIX</u>

INGREDIENTS

200g/7oz raw peeled prawns (shrimp)
200g/7oz shelled scallops
200g/7oz squid, cleaned and cut into
    serving pieces
7 limes
12 plum tomatoes
1 small onion
1 ripe avocado
20ml/4 tsp chopped fresh oregano,
    or 10ml/2 tsp dried oregano
5ml/1 tsp salt
ground black pepper
fresh oregano sprigs, to garnish
crusty bread and lime wedges, to
    serve (optional)

1 Spread out the shellfish in a non-metallic dish. Squeeze 6 limes and pour the juice over. Cover and chill for 8 hours or overnight.

2 Drain the shellfish in a colander to remove the excess lime juice, then pat it dry with kitchen paper. Place the shellfish in a bowl.

3 Cut the tomatoes in half, squeeze out the seeds, then dice the flesh. Cut the onion in half, then slice it thinly. Cut the avocado in half lengthways, remove the stone (pit) and peel, then cut the flesh into 1cm/½in dice.

4 Add the tomatoes, onion and avocado to the shellfish with the oregano and seasoning. Squeeze the remaining lime and pour over the juice. Garnish with oregano and serve, with crusty bread and lime wedges, if you like.

PRAWNS <u>WITH</u> ALMOND <u>AND</u> TOMATO SAUCE

GROUND ALMONDS ADD AN INTERESTING TEXTURE TO THE CREAMY, PIQUANT SAUCE THAT
ACCOMPANIES THESE SUCCULENT SHELLFISH.

SERVES SIX

INGREDIENTS
  1 dried chilli
  1 onion
  3 garlic cloves
  30ml/2 tbsp vegetable oil
  8 plum tomatoes
  5ml/1 tsp ground cumin
  120ml/4fl oz/½ cup chicken stock
  130g/4½oz/generous 1 cup
    ground almonds
  175ml/6fl oz/¾ cup crème fraîche
  ½ lime
  900g/2lb cooked, peeled
    prawns (shrimp)
  salt
  fresh coriander (cilantro) and spring
    onion (scallion) strips, to garnish
  cooked rice and warm tortillas,
    to serve

VARIATION
Try this sauce with other types of fish.
Adding just a few prawns and serving
it over steamed sole makes a very
luxurious dish.

1 Place the dried chilli in a heatproof
bowl and pour over boiling water to
cover. Leave to soak for 30 minutes
until softened. Drain, remove the stalk,
then slit the chilli and scrape out the
seeds with a small sharp knife. Chop
the flesh roughly and set it aside.

2 Chop the onion finely and then crush
the cloves of garlic. Heat the oil in a
frying pan and fry the onion and garlic
over a low heat until soft.

3 Cut a cross in the base of each
tomato. Place them in a heatproof bowl
and cover with boiling water. After 30
seconds, lift them out and plunge them
into a bowl of cold water. Drain.

4 Skin and seed the tomatoes. Chop
the flesh into 1cm/½in cubes and add
them to the onion mixture in the frying
pan, with the chopped chilli. Stir in the
ground cumin and cook for 10 minutes,
stirring occasionally.

5 Tip the mixture into a food processor
or blender. Add the stock and process
on high speed until smooth.

6 Pour the mixture into a large pan,
then add the ground almonds and stir
over a low heat for 2–3 minutes. Stir in
the crème fraîche until it has been
incorporated completely.

7 Squeeze the juice from the lime into
the sauce and stir it in. Season with salt
to taste, then increase the heat and
bring the sauce to simmering point.

8 Add the prawns to the sauce and
heat until warmed through. Serve on a
bed of hot rice garnished with the
coriander and spring onion strips. Offer
warm tortillas separately.

GRILLED KING PRAWNS WITH ROMESCO SAUCE

THIS SAUCE, FROM THE CATALAN REGION OF SPAIN, IS SERVED WITH FISH AND SHELLFISH. ITS MAIN INGREDIENTS ARE TOMATOES, CANNED PIMIENTO, GARLIC AND ALMONDS.

SERVES FOUR

INGREDIENTS
    24 raw king prawns (jumbo shrimp)
    30–45ml/2–3 tbsp extra virgin
      olive oil
    fresh flat leaf parsley sprigs,
      to garnish
    lemon wedges, to serve
For the sauce
    8 ripe tomatoes, preferably
      plum tomatoes
    60ml/4 tbsp olive oil
    1 onion, chopped
    4 garlic cloves, chopped
    1 canned pimiento, drained
      and chopped
    2.5ml/½ tsp dried chilli flakes or
      chilli powder
    75ml/5 tbsp fish stock or half white
      wine and half fish stock
    30ml/2 tbsp white wine
    10 blanched almonds
    15ml/1 tbsp red wine vinegar
    salt and ground black pepper

COOK'S TIP
A grilled red (bell) pepper, skinned and seeded, can be substituted for the canned pimiento, but don't be tempted to use a raw red pepper; it will not have the essential, smoky flavour.

1 Prepare the tomatoes. Cut a cross in the base of each tomato with a sharp knife. Place them in a heatproof bowl and cover with boiling water. After 30 seconds, lift them out with a slotted spoon and plunge them into a bowl of cold water. Drain.

2 The tomato skins will have begun to peel back. Using a very sharp knife, remove the skins, then cut each tomato in half and scoop out the seeds.

3 With a knife, chop the skinned tomato halves into pieces.

4 To make the sauce, heat 30ml/ 2 tbsp of the oil in a large pan, add the onion and three of the garlic cloves and cook until soft. Stir in the pimiento, tomatoes, chilli flakes or powder, fish stock (or mixture) and wine. Cover the pan and simmer the sauce for 30 minutes.

5 Toast the almonds under the grill (broiler) until golden. Transfer to a blender or food processor and grind coarsely.

6 Add the remaining 30ml/2 tbsp of oil, the vinegar and the last garlic clove, and process until evenly combined. Add the tomato and pimiento sauce and process until smooth. Season with salt and ground black pepper.

7 Remove the heads from the prawns, leaving them otherwise unshelled. Using a sharp knife, slit each one down the back and remove the dark vein. Rinse under cold running water, drain and pat dry on kitchen paper.

8 Preheat the grill. Toss the prawns in olive oil, then spread them out in the grill pan. Grill for about 2 minutes on each side, until they are pink.

9 Arrange on a serving platter and garnish with the parsley sprigs. Add the lemon wedges, and offer the sauce separately in a small bowl or jug. Serve immediately.

ZARZUELA

TOMATOES ARE AN IMPORTANT INGREDIENT IN ZARZUELA. THE NAME MEANS "LIGHT OPERA" OR
"MUSICAL COMEDY" IN SPANISH, AND THIS CLASSIC FISH STEW SHOULD BE AS LIVELY AND COLOURFUL
AS THE ZARZUELA ITSELF. THIS FEAST OF FISH INCLUDES LOBSTER AND OTHER SHELLFISH, BUT YOU
CAN MODIFY THE INGREDIENTS TO SUIT THE OCCASION AND AVAILABILITY.

SERVES SIX

INGREDIENTS
   1 cooked lobster
   24 fresh mussels
   1 large monkfish tail
   225g/8oz squid rings
   45ml/3 tbsp plain (all-purpose) flour
   90ml/6 tbsp olive oil
   12 large raw prawns (shrimp)
   450g/1lb ripe tomatoes
   2 large mild onions, chopped
   4 garlic cloves, crushed
   30ml/2 tbsp brandy
   2 bay leaves
   5ml/1 tsp paprika
   1 fresh red chilli, seeded
    and chopped
   300ml/½ pint/1¼ cups fish stock
   15g/½oz/2 tbsp ground almonds
   30ml/2 tbsp chopped fresh parsley
   salt and ground black pepper
   green salad and warm bread,
    to serve

VARIATION
Zarzuela de Mariscos is a variation that
is made solely with shellfish. In addition
to lobster and prawns, langoustines and
scallops are used, and clams are added
as well as the mussels.

1 Using a large knife, cut the lobster in
half lengthways. Remove the dark
intestine that runs down the length of
the tail. Crack the claws using a
hammer, so that their delicious meat
can be extracted.

2 Scrub the mussel shells with a
scouring pad and rinse well. This is
easiest under cold running water.

3 Pull off the "beards" (the anchor
threads) from the mussels with the help
of a small knife. Discard any open
mussels that fail to close when tapped
with a knife. Also throw away any
mussels with damaged shells.

4 Skin the monkfish tail, if necessary,
and carefully pull off the pinkish
membrane beneath. Fillet the tail by
cutting through the flesh on either
side of the backbone. Cut each fillet
into three.

5 Toss the monkfish pieces and squid
rings in the flour, seasoned with salt
and pepper. Shake off any excess. Heat
the oil in a large frying pan. Add the
monkfish and squid, and fry quickly
until just cooked. Remove from the pan.
Fry the prawns on both sides, then
remove from the pan.

6 Skewer each tomato on a metal fork
and hold in a gas flame for a minute,
turning it until the skin splits and
wrinkles. Peel and chop the tomatoes.

7 Add the onions and two-thirds of the
garlic to the frying pan and fry for
3 minutes. Pour over the brandy and
ignite it with a match. When the flames
die down, add the tomatoes, bay leaves,
paprika, chilli and stock. Bring to the
boil, reduce the heat and simmer for
5 minutes. Add the mussels, cover
and cook for 3 minutes, until the
shells have opened. Remove any that
remain closed.

8 Arrange all the shellfish in a large
flameproof serving dish. Mix the ground
almonds with the remaining garlic and
the parsley, and stir into the sauce.
Season with salt and pepper. Pour the
sauce into the dish and cook gently for
about 5 minutes until hot. Serve
immediately, with a green salad and
plenty of warm bread.

BRODETTO

*THIS ROBUST FISH AND TOMATO STEW COMES FROM ITALY. THERE ARE MANY VERSIONS, BUT ALL
REQUIRE FLAVOURSOME SUN-RIPENED TOMATOES AND A GOOD FISH STOCK. MAKE SURE YOU BUY
SOME OF THE FISH WHOLE SO THAT YOU CAN SIMPLY SIMMER THEM, REMOVE THE COOKED FLESH
AND STRAIN THE DELICIOUSLY FLAVOURED JUICES TO MAKE THE STOCK.*

SERVES FOUR TO FIVE

INGREDIENTS

900g/2lb mixture of fish fillets or
   steaks, such as monkfish, cod,
   haddock, halibut or hake
900g/2lb mixture of conger eel, red or
   grey mullet, snapper or small white
   fish, prepared according to type
1 onion, halved
1 celery stick, roughly chopped
225g/8oz squid
225g/8oz fresh mussels
675g/1½lb ripe tomatoes
60ml/4 tbsp olive oil
1 large onion, thinly sliced
3 garlic cloves, crushed
5ml/1 tsp saffron threads
150ml/¼ pint/⅔ cup dry white wine
90ml/6 tbsp chopped fresh parsley
salt and ground black pepper
croûtons, to serve

1 Remove any skin and bones from the
fish fillets or steaks, cut the fish into large
pieces and reserve. Place the bones in a
pan with all the remaining fish.

2 Add the halved onion and the celery
and just cover with water. Bring almost
to the boil, then reduce the heat and
simmer gently for about 30 minutes. Lift
out the fish and remove the flesh from
the bones. Strain the stock.

3 To prepare the squid, twist the head
and tentacles away from the body. Cut
the head from the tentacles. Discard the
body contents and peel away the
mottled skin. Wash the tentacles and
bodies and dry on kitchen paper.

4 Scrub the mussels, discarding any
that are damaged or open ones that do
not close when sharply tapped.

5 Plunge the tomatoes into boiling
water for 30 seconds, then refresh in
cold water. Peel off the skins and chop
the flesh roughly.

6 Heat the oil in a large sauté pan. Add
the sliced onion and the garlic, and fry
gently for 3 minutes. Add the squid and
the uncooked white fish, which you
reserved earlier, and fry quickly on all
sides. Remove the fish from the pan
using a slotted spoon.

7 Add 475ml/16fl oz/2 cups strained
reserved fish stock, the saffron and
tomatoes to the pan. Pour in the wine.
Bring to the boil, then reduce the heat
and simmer for about 5 minutes. Add
the mussels, cover, and cook for
3–4 minutes until the mussels have
opened. Discard any mussels that
remain closed.

8 Season the sauce with salt and
pepper and put all the fish in the pan.
Cook gently for 5 minutes. Sprinkle with
the parsley and serve with the croûtons.

BLACK PASTA WITH SQUID AND TOMATO SAUCE

TAGLIATELLE FLAVOURED WITH SQUID INK LOOKS AMAZING AND TASTES DELICIOUSLY OF THE SEA.
YOU'LL FIND IT IN GOOD ITALIAN DELICATESSENS AND SOME OF THE LARGER SUPERMARKETS.

SERVES FOUR

INGREDIENTS
105ml/7 tbsp olive oil
2 shallots, chopped
3 garlic cloves, crushed
45ml/3 tbsp chopped fresh parsley
675g/1½lb cleaned squid, cut into
  rings and rinsed
150ml/¼ pint/⅔ cup dry white wine
400g/14oz can chopped tomatoes
2.5ml/½ tsp dried chilli flakes
450g/1lb squid ink tagliatelle
salt and ground black pepper

1 Heat the oil in a pan and add the shallots. Cook until pale golden, then add the garlic. When the garlic colours a little, add 30ml/2 tbsp of the parsley, stir, then add the squid and stir again. Cook for 3–4 minutes, then pour in the wine and mix well.

2 Simmer for a few seconds, then add the tomatoes and chilli flakes, and season with salt and pepper. Cover and simmer gently for about 1 hour, until the squid is tender.

3 Fill a pan with water, add salt and bring to the boil. Cook the pasta according to the packet instructions, until *al dente*. A little oil can be added to the water to stop the pasta from sticking.

4 Remove the tagliatelle from the heat and, using a colander, drain it well, then return it to the pan. Add the squid sauce and toss over the heat with two spatulas or wooden spoons until all the strands are coated in sauce.

5 Serve in heated bowls, sprinkling each serving with a little of the remaining chopped parsley.

COOK'S TIP
The cooking time for the pasta will depend on what type you use. Dried tagliatelle generally takes 10–12 minutes; fresh pasta cooks in 2–3 minutes.

CLAMS <u>WITH</u> NEAPOLITAN TOMATO SAUCE

THIS RECIPE TAKES ITS NAME FROM THE CITY OF NAPLES, WHERE BOTH FRESH TOMATO SAUCE AND SHELLFISH ARE TRADITIONALLY SERVED WITH VERMICELLI. HERE THE TWO ARE COMBINED TO MAKE A VERY TASTY DISH THAT IS PERFECT FOR A COLD WINTER'S EVENING.

<u>SERVES FOUR</u>

INGREDIENTS

1kg/2¼lb fresh clams
250ml/8fl oz/1 cup dry white wine,
  or vegetable stock
2 garlic cloves, bruised
1 large handful fresh flat leaf parsley
30ml/2 tbsp extra virgin olive oil or
  sunflower oil
1 small onion, finely chopped
8 ripe plum tomatoes, peeled seeded
  and finely chopped
½–1 fresh red chilli, seeded and
  finely chopped
350g/12oz dried vermicelli
salt and ground black pepper

1 Scrub the clams thoroughly with a brush under cold running water and discard any that are open or do not close their shells when sharply tapped against the work surface.

2 Pour the white wine or vegetable stock into a large, heavy pan and add the bruised garlic cloves. Shred half the parsley finely, then add to the wine or stock, then add the clams.

3 Cover the pan tightly with the lid and bring to the boil over a high heat. Cook for about 5 minutes, shaking the pan frequently, until all the clams have re-opened.

4 Tip the clams into a large colander set over a bowl and let the liquid drain through. Leave the clams until cool enough to handle, then remove about two-thirds of them from their shells, tipping the clam liquor into the bowl of cooking liquid.

5 Discard any clams that have failed to open. Set both shelled and unshelled clams aside, keeping the unshelled clams warm in a bowl covered with a lid or thick cloth.

6 Heat the oil in a pan, add the onion and cook gently, stirring frequently, for about 5 minutes until softened and lightly coloured. Add the tomatoes, then strain in the clam cooking liquid. Add the chilli, and salt and pepper to taste.

7 Bring to the boil, half cover the pan and simmer gently for 15–20 minutes. Meanwhile, cook the pasta according to the packet instructions. Chop the remaining parsley finely.

8 Add the shelled clams to the tomato sauce, stir well and heat through very gently for 2–3 minutes.

9 Drain the cooked pasta well and tip it into a warmed bowl. Taste the sauce for seasoning, then pour the sauce over the pasta and toss everything together well. Garnish with the reserved clams, sprinkle the parsley over the pasta and serve immediately.

PASTA <u>WITH</u> TOMATOES <u>AND</u> SHELLFISH

COLOURFUL AND DELICIOUS, THIS TYPICAL GENOESE DISH IS IDEAL FOR A DINNER PARTY. THE TOMATO SAUCE IS QUITE RUNNY, SO SERVE IT WITH CRUSTY BREAD AND SPOONS AS WELL AS FORKS. FOR A REAL TASTE OF ITALY, CHOOSE A DRY WHITE ITALIAN WINE TO SERVE WITH THE MEAL.

SERVES FOUR

INGREDIENTS
45ml/3 tbsp olive oil
1 small onion, chopped
1 garlic clove, crushed
½ fresh red chilli, seeded
   and chopped
200g/7oz can chopped
   plum tomatoes
30ml/2 tbsp chopped fresh flat
   leaf parsley
400g/14oz fresh clams
400g/14oz fresh mussels
60ml/4 tbsp dry white wine
400g/14oz/3½ cups dried trenette
   or spaghetti
a few fresh basil leaves
90g/3½oz/⅔ cup cooked, peeled
   prawns (shrimp), thawed and
   thoroughly dried if frozen
salt and ground black pepper
lemon wedges and chopped fresh herbs,
   such as parsley or thyme, to garnish

1 Heat 30ml/2tbsp of the oil in a frying pan or medium pan. Add the onion, garlic and chilli, and cook over a medium heat for 1–2 minutes, stirring constantly. Stir in the tomatoes, half the parsley and pepper to taste. Bring to the boil, lower the heat, cover and simmer for 15 minutes.

2 Meanwhile, scrub the clams and mussels under cold running water. Discard any that are open and that do not close when sharply tapped against the work surface.

3 In a large pan, heat the remaining oil. Add the clams and mussels, with the rest of the parsley and toss over a high heat for a few seconds. Pour in the wine, then cover tightly. Cook for about 5 minutes, shaking the pan frequently, until the clams and mussels have opened.

4 Transfer the clams and mussels to a bowl, discarding any shellfish that have failed to open. Strain the cooking liquid and set aside. Reserve 8 clams and 4 mussels for the garnish, then remove the rest from their shells.

5 Cook the pasta according to the instructions on the packet. Meanwhile, add 120ml/4fl oz/½ cup of the reserved shellfish liquid to the tomato sauce. Add the basil, prawns, shelled clams and mussels to the sauce. Season.

6 Drain the pasta and tip it into a warmed bowl. Add the sauce and toss well to combine. Serve in individual bowls, sprinkle with herbs and garnish each portion with lemon, 2 clams and 1 mussel in their shells.

An essential ingredient in so many vegetarian dishes, tomatoes are often used as the basis for sauces — try Couscous with Eggs and Tomato Sauce or Pasta with Tomato and Chilli Sauce. They play an important role in one-pot dishes, such as warming Harvest Vegetable and Lentil Casserole or Tomato, Pistachio and Sesame Pilau, but it is in treats like Spicy Tomato Tart with Tomato Roses or Classic Margherita Pizza that they really take centre stage.

Vegetarian
Main Meals

BEAN <u>AND</u> TOMATO CASSEROLE

JUICY TOMATOES AND FILLING CANNELLINI BEANS BAKED — A GREAT DISH FOR A COLD DAY.

SERVES FOUR

INGREDIENTS
  45ml/3 tbsp extra virgin olive oil or
    sunflower oil
  45ml/3 tbsp chopped fresh flat
    leaf parsley
  400g/14oz can cannellini beans,
    rinsed and drained
  1kg/2¼lb firm ripe tomatoes
  5ml/1 tsp caster (superfine) sugar
  40g/1½oz/scant 1 cup
    day-old breadcrumbs
  2.5ml/½ tsp chilli powder or paprika
  salt
  chopped fresh parsley, to garnish
  rye bread, to serve

1 Preheat the oven to 200°C/400°F/
Gas 6. Brush a large ovenproof dish
with 15ml/1 tbsp of the oil.

2 Sprinkle the chopped flat leaf parsley
over the base of the dish and cover with
the beans. Cut the tomatoes into even
slices, discarding the two end slices of
each. Arrange the slices of tomato in
the dish over the beans so that they
overlap slightly. Sprinkle them with a
little salt and the sugar.

3 In a mixing bowl, stir together the
breadcrumbs, the remaining olive or
sunflower oil and chilli powder or
paprika, whichever you are using.

4 Sprinkle the crumb mixture over the
tomatoes, and bake in the oven for
50 minutes. Serve hot or cold,
garnished with chopped parsley and
accompanied by rye bread.

MIXED VEGETABLE CASSEROLE

THE VEGETABLES IN THIS RICH TOMATO SAUCE CAN BE VARIED ACCORDING TO SEASON.

SERVES FOUR

INGREDIENTS
  1 aubergine (eggplant), diced into
    2.5cm/1in pieces
  115g/4oz/½ cup okra, halved
    lengthways
  115g/4oz/1 cup frozen or fresh peas
    or petits pois (baby peas)
  115g/4oz/¾ cup green beans, cut
    into 2.5cm/1in pieces
  400g/14oz can flageolet (small
    cannellini) beans, rinsed and drained
  4 courgettes (zucchini), cut into
    1cm/½in pieces
  2 onions, finely chopped
  450g/1lb maincrop potatoes, diced
    into 2.5cm/1in pieces
  1 red (bell) pepper, seeded and sliced
  400g/14oz can chopped tomatoes
  150ml/¼ pint/⅔ cup vegetable stock
  60ml/4 tbsp olive oil
  75ml/5 tbsp chopped fresh parsley
  5ml/1 tsp paprika
  salt
  crusty bread, to serve
For the topping
  6 tomatoes, sliced
  1 courgette (zucchini), sliced

1 Slice the tomatoes and courgettes for
the topping.

2 Put all the other ingredients in an
ovenproof dish, combine them well.

3 Preheat the oven to 190°C/375°F/
Gas 5. Arrange alternate slices of
tomato and courgette attractively on the
top of the other vegetables.

4 Put the lid on or cover the casserole
tightly with foil. Bake in the oven for
60–70 minutes until all the vegetables
are tender. Remove the lid or foil for the
last 15 minutes to brown the topping
slightly, if you like. Serve either hot or
cold with wedges of crusty bread.

COOK'S TIP
For the finest flavour, use extra virgin
olive oil in the bake and vine-ripened or
home-grown tomatoes for the topping.

BAKED CHEESE POLENTA WITH TOMATO SAUCE

POLENTA, OR CORNMEAL, IS A STAPLE FOOD IN ITALY. IT IS PREPARED LIKE A SORT OF OATMEAL, AND EATEN SOFT, OR LEFT TO SET, CUT INTO SHAPES THEN COOKED.

SERVES FOUR

INGREDIENTS
  5ml/1 tsp salt
  250g/9oz/1½ cups quick-cook
    polenta
  5ml/1 tsp paprika
  2.5ml/½ tsp ground nutmeg
  30ml/2 tbsp extra virgin
    olive oil
  1 large onion, finely chopped
  2 garlic cloves, crushed
  2 x 400g/14oz cans chopped
    tomatoes, or 450g/1lb
    fresh tomatoes
  15ml/1 tbsp tomato purée (paste), or
    30ml/2 tbsp if using fresh tomatoes
  5ml/1 tsp granulated sugar
  salt and ground black pepper
  75g/3oz Gruyère cheese or other mild
    cheese, grated

1 Preheat the oven to 200°C/400°F/ Gas 6. Line a 28 x 18cm/11 x 7in baking tin (pan) with clear film. Boil 1 litre/ 1¾ pints/4 cups water with the salt.

2 Pour in the polenta in a steady stream and cook, stirring continuously, for 5 minutes. Beat in the paprika and nutmeg, then pour into the prepared tin and smooth the surface. Leave to cool.

3 Heat the oil in a pan and cook the onion and garlic until soft. Add the tomatoes, purée and sugar. Season. Simmer for 20 minutes.

4 Cut the polenta into 5cm/2in squares. Layer the polenta and tomato sauce in an ovenproof dish. Sprinkle with the cheese and bake for 25 minutes, until golden. Serve immediately.

LEEK, SQUASH AND TOMATO GRATIN

COLOURFUL AND SUCCULENT, YOU CAN USE VIRTUALLY ANY KIND OF SQUASH FOR THIS AUTUMN GRATIN, FROM PATTY PANS AND ACORN SQUASH TO PUMPKINS.

SERVES FOUR TO SIX

INGREDIENTS
- 450g/1lb peeled and seeded squash, cut into 1cm/½in slices
- 60ml/4 tbsp olive oil
- 450g/1lb leeks, cut into thick, diagonal slices
- 675g/1½lb tomatoes, peeled and thickly sliced
- 2.5ml/½ tsp ground toasted cumin seeds
- 300ml/½ pint/1¼ cups single (light) cream
- 1 fresh red chilli, seeded and sliced
- 1 garlic clove, finely chopped
- 15ml/1 tbsp chopped fresh mint
- 30ml/2 tbsp chopped fresh parsley
- 60ml/4 tbsp fine white breadcrumbs
- salt and ground black pepper

VARIATION
For a curried version of this dish, use ground coriander as well as cumin, and coconut milk instead of cream. Use fresh coriander (cilantro) instead of the mint and parsley.

1 Steam the squash over boiling salted water for 10 minutes.

2 Heat half the oil in a frying pan and cook the leeks gently for 5–6 minutes until lightly coloured. Try to keep the slices intact. Preheat the oven to 190°C/375°F/Gas 5.

3 Layer all the squash, leeks and tomatoes in a 2 litre/3½ pint/8 cup gratin dish, arranging them in rows. Season with salt, pepper and cumin.

4 Pour the cream into a small pan and add the sliced chilli and chopped garlic. Bring to the boil over a low heat then stir in the mint. Pour the mixture evenly over the layered vegetables, using a rubber spatula to scrape all the sauce out of the pan.

5 Cook for 50–55 minutes, or until the gratin is bubbling and tinged brown. Sprinkle the parsley and breadcrumbs on top and drizzle over the remaining oil. Bake for another 15–20 minutes until the breadcrumbs are browned and crisp. Serve immediately.

VEGETABLE MOUSSAKA

*THIS IS A REALLY FLAVOURSOME VEGETARIAN ALTERNATIVE TO CLASSIC MEAT MOUSSAKA. SERVE IT
WITH WARM BREAD AND A GLASS OR TWO OF RUSTIC RED WINE.*

SERVES SIX

INGREDIENTS
    450g/1lb aubergines (eggplant),
        sliced
    115g/4oz/½ cup whole green lentils
    600ml/1 pint/2½ cups vegetable stock
    1 bay leaf
    225g/8oz fresh tomatoes
    45ml/3 tbsp olive oil
    1 onion, sliced
    1 garlic clove, crushed
    225g/8oz/3 cups mushrooms, sliced
    400g/14oz can chickpeas, rinsed
        and drained
    400g/14oz can chopped tomatoes
    30ml/2 tbsp tomato purée (paste)
    10ml/2 tsp dried basil
    300ml/½ pint/1¼ cups natural
        (plain) yogurt
    3 eggs
    50g/2oz/½ cup grated mature (sharp)
        Cheddar cheese
    salt and ground black pepper
    fresh flat leaf parsley sprigs,
        to garnish

VARIATION
You can make various creamy toppings
for this moussaka by substituting cream
or white sauce for the yogurt. Or, if you
are short of time, you could consider
using a packet sauce – anything from
parsley sauce to béchamel sauce works
excellently with this recipe.

1 Sprinkle the aubergine slices with
salt and place in a colander. Cover and
leave for 30 minutes to allow any bitter
juices to be extracted.

2 Meanwhile, place the lentils, stock
and bay leaf in a pan. Cover, bring to
the boil and simmer for about
20 minutes until the lentils are just
tender. Drain well and keep warm.

3 If wished skin the fresh tomatoes
then cut them into pieces.

4 Heat 15ml/1 tbsp of the oil in a large
pan, add the onion and garlic, and cook
for 5 minutes, stirring. Stir in the lentils,
mushrooms, chickpeas, fresh and
canned tomatoes, tomato purée, basil
and 45ml/3 tbsp water. Bring to the boil,
cover and simmer gently for 10 minutes.

5 Preheat the oven to 180°C/350°F/
Gas 4. Rinse the aubergine slices, drain
and pat dry. Heat the remaining oil in a
frying pan and fry the slices in batches
for 3–4 minutes, turning once.

6 Season the lentil mixture. Layer the
aubergines and lentils in an ovenproof
dish, starting with aubergines and
finishing with the lentil mixture.

7 Beat together the yogurt, eggs and
salt and pepper, and pour the mixture
into the dish. Sprinkle the cheese on
top and bake for 45 minutes. Serve,
garnished with flat leaf parsley sprigs.

TOMATO BREAD AND BUTTER BAKE

THIS IS A GREAT FAMILY DISH AND IS IDEAL WHEN YOU DON'T HAVE TIME TO COOK ON THE DAY
BECAUSE IT CAN BE PREPARED IN ADVANCE. IT MAKES A WONDERFUL WARMING SUPPER.

SERVES FOUR

INGREDIENTS

50g/2oz/¼ cup butter, softened
15ml/1 tbsp red pesto sauce
1 garlic and herb focaccia
150g/5oz mozzarella cheese,
  thinly sliced
2 large ripe tomatoes, sliced
300ml/½ pint/1¼ cups milk
3 large eggs
5ml/1 tsp chopped fresh oregano,
  plus extra to garnish
50g/2oz Pecorino Romano or Fontina
  cheese, grated
salt and ground black pepper

VARIATIONS
If you like, you could use other cheeses,
such as Beaufort, Bel Paese or Taleggio,
in this recipe. A mild goat's cheese
would also work well.

1 Preheat the oven to 180°C/350°F/
Gas 4. Mix together the butter and
pesto sauce in a small bowl. Slice the
herb bread and spread one side of each
slice with the pesto mixture.

2 In an oval ovenproof dish, layer the
bread slices with the mozzarella and
tomatoes, overlapping each new layer
with the next.

3 Beat together the milk, eggs and
oregano, season well and pour over the
layers. Leave to stand for 5 minutes.

4 Sprinkle over the grated cheese and
bake for about 40 minutes or until
the top is golden brown and just set.
Serve immediately, straight from the
dish, sprinkled with more roughly
chopped oregano.

HARVEST VEGETABLE <u>AND</u> LENTIL CASSEROLE

THIS EASY-TO-PREPARE MEAL IS DELICIOUS SERVED WITH WARM GARLIC BREAD. IF YOU REALLY WANT TO MAKE THE MOST OF THE TOMATO FLAVOUR, ADD A FEW SUN-DRIED TOMATOES WITH THE LENTILS.

SERVES SIX

INGREDIENTS

15ml/1 tbsp sunflower oil or olive oil
2 leeks, sliced
1 garlic clove, crushed
4 celery sticks, chopped
2 carrots, sliced
2 parsnips, diced
1 sweet potato, diced
225g/8oz swede (rutabaga), diced
175g/6oz/¾ cup whole brown or
    green lentils
450g/1lb tomatoes, peeled, seeded
    and chopped
15ml/1 tbsp chopped fresh thyme
15ml/1 tbsp chopped fresh marjoram
900ml/1½ pints/3¾ cups vegetable
    stock
15ml/1 tbsp cornflour (cornstarch)
45ml/3 tbsp water
salt and ground black pepper
warm garlic bread, to serve

1 Preheat the oven to 180°C/350°F/ Gas 4. Heat the sunflower oil in a large flameproof casserole. Add the prepared leeks, garlic and celery, and cook over a gentle heat for 3 minutes, stirring the vegetables occasionally.

2 Add the carrots, parsnips, sweet potato, swede, lentils, tomatoes, herbs, stock and seasoning. Stir well. Bring to the boil, stirring occasionally to ensure that the vegetables are not sticking.

3 Cover and bake for about 50 minutes until the vegetables and lentils are cooked and tender, removing the casserole from the oven and stirring the vegetable mixture once or twice during the cooking time.

4 Remove the casserole from the oven. Mix the cornflour with 45ml/3 tbsp water in a small bowl. Stir it into the casserole and heat on the hob (stovetop), stirring until the mixture comes to the boil and thickens, then simmer gently for 2 minutes, stirring. Serve in warmed bowls. Hand round garlic bread.

COOK'S TIP
Green and brown lentils, unlike red lentils, keep their shape during cooking and are good for soups, salads and casseroles. Green lentils have a delicate flavour, while brown ones are more earthy in taste.

TOMATO, PISTACHIO <u>AND</u> SESAME PILAU

*FOR A SIMPLE YET REALLY TASTY DISH, YOU CAN'T GO WRONG WITH THIS NUTTY PILAU — THE
CARDAMOM SEEDS GIVE IT A REALLY EXOTIC FLAVOUR.*

<u>SERVES FOUR</u>

INGREDIENTS

12 fresh plum or
  round tomatoes
1 red (bell) pepper
225g/8oz/1⅓ cups brown
  basmati rice
pinch of saffron threads
600ml/1 pint/2½ cups vegetable
  stock or half white wine and
  half water
pinch of salt
4–5 cardamom pods
50g/2oz/½ cup pistachio nuts,
  shelled and roughly chopped,
  toasted if you like
30ml/2 tbsp sesame seeds or
  sunflower seeds, toasted

1 Plunge the tomatoes into boiling
water for 30 seconds, then refresh in
cold water. Peel off the skins and chop
the tomatoes.

2 Halve the pepper and remove the
seeds. Turn so that the cut side of the
pepper is flat on the chopping board
and cut into chunks.

3 Wash the rice in several changes of
cold water, then drain and tip into a
bowl. Pour over fresh cold water to
cover and soak for 30 minutes.

4 Meanwhile, soak the saffron threads
in the vegetable stock, or the wine and
water mixture.

5 Drain the rice, then tip it into a pan.
Add the saffron liquid and bring to the
boil. Lower the heat, cover and simmer
for 25 minutes. Meanwhile, break open
the cardamom pods, extract the seeds
and crush them finely.

6 Stir the tomato, peppers and crushed
seeds into the rice mixture. Cook for a
further 5–10 minutes until the rice is
tender and all the liquid has been
absorbed. If the liquid is absorbed
before the rice is cooked, add a little
more. It should not be necessary to
drain the rice.

7 Tip the rice into a serving dish and
sprinkle the pistachio nuts and sesame
or sunflower seeds over the top.

RED FRIED RICE

*THIS VIBRANT RICE DISH OWES AS MUCH OF ITS APPEAL TO THE BRIGHT COLOURS OF RED ONION,
RED PEPPER AND CHERRY TOMATOES AS IT DOES TO THEIR DISTINCTIVE FLAVOURS.*

SERVES TWO

INGREDIENTS
    115g/4oz basmati rice
    30ml/2 tbsp groundnut (peanut) oil
    1 small red onion, chopped
    1 red (bell) pepper, seeded and chopped
    225g/8oz cherry tomatoes, halved
    2 eggs, beaten
    salt and ground black pepper
    parsley, chopped, to garnish

VARIATION
For a nuttier flavour, substitute brown
basmati rice. It will take a little longer
to cook – about 25–30 minutes.

1 Wash the rice several times under
cold running water. Drain well. Bring
a large pan of salted water to the
boil, add the rice and cook for
10–12 minutes until tender.

3 Break the eggs into a bowl and beat
with a fork or a whisk until the texture
becomes uniform.

2 Meanwhile, heat the oil in a wok until
very hot. Add the onion and red pepper
and stir-fry for 2–3 minutes. Add the
cherry tomatoes and stir-fry for a further
2 minutes.

4 Add the eggs to the wok all at once.
Cook for 30 seconds without stirring, then
stir to break up the eggs as they set.

5 Drain the cooked rice thoroughly,
ensuring that no water remains. Add
it to the wok and toss it over the heat
to combine with the vegetable and
egg mixture for 3 minutes. Season with
salt and pepper. Sprinkle over the
parsley, to garnish.

PROVENÇAL RICE

ONE OF THE GLORIOUS THINGS ABOUT FOOD FROM THE SOUTH OF FRANCE IS ITS COLOUR — SWEET CHERRY TOMATOES, PURPLE AUBERGINES AND TENDER GREEN COURGETTES ARE A DELICIOUS COMBINATION.

SERVES FOUR

INGREDIENTS
2 onions
90ml/6 tbsp extra virgin olive oil or
  sunflower oil
225g/8oz/generous 1 cup long grain
  brown rice
10ml/2 tsp mustard seeds
600ml/1 pint/2½ cups vegetable stock
1 large or 2 small red (bell) peppers,
  seeded and cut into chunks
1 small aubergine (eggplant), cubed
2–3 courgettes (zucchini), sliced
about 12 cherry tomatoes
5–6 fresh basil leaves, torn into pieces
2 garlic cloves, finely chopped
60ml/4 tbsp white wine
60ml/4 tbsp passata (bottled strained
  tomatoes) or tomato juice
2 hard-boiled (hard-cooked) eggs,
  cut into wedges
8 stuffed green olives, sliced
15ml/1 tbsp capers
3 sun-dried tomatoes in oil, drained
  and sliced (optional)
sea salt and ground pepper

1 Preheat the oven to 200°C/400°F/ Gas 6. Roughly chop 1 onion. Heat 30ml/2 tbsp of the oil in a pan and fry the chopped onion over a low heat for 5–6 minutes until softened.

2 Add the rice and mustard seeds. Cook, stirring, for 2 minutes, then add the stock and a little salt. Bring to the boil, then lower the heat, cover and simmer for 35 minutes until the rice is tender and fairly dry.

3 Meanwhile, cut the remaining onion into wedges. Put these in a roasting pan (pan) with the peppers, aubergine, courgettes and cherry tomatoes. Sprinkle over the torn basil leaves and chopped garlic. Pour over the remaining olive oil and sprinkle with sea salt and black pepper. Roast for 15–20 minutes until the vegetables begin to char, stirring halfway through cooking. Remove from the oven, then reduce the temperature to 180°C/350°F/Gas 4.

4 Spoon the rice into an earthenware casserole. Put the roasted vegetables on top, together with any juices from the roasting pan, then pour over the combined wine and passata or tomato juice.

5 Arrange the egg wedges on top of the vegetables, with the sliced olives, capers and sun-dried tomatoes, if using. Dot with butter, cover and cook for 15–20 minutes until heated through. Serve immediately, in warmed bowls.

TOMATO RICE

PROOF POSITIVE THAT YOU DON'T NEED ELABORATE INGREDIENTS OR COMPLICATED COOKING METHODS TO MAKE A DELICIOUS DISH.

SERVES FOUR

INGREDIENTS

    30ml/2 tbsp sunflower oil
    2.5ml/½ tsp onion seeds
    1 onion, sliced
    4 tomatoes, sliced
    1 orange or yellow (bell) pepper,
        seeded and sliced
    5ml/1 tsp grated fresh root ginger
    1 garlic clove
    5ml/1 tsp chilli powder
    1 potato, diced
    7.5ml/1½ tsp salt
    400g/14oz/2 cups basmati
        rice, soaked
    750ml/1¼ pints/3 cups water
    30–45ml/2–3 tbsp chopped
        fresh coriander (cilantro)

3 Drain the rice and add it to the pan, then stir for about 1 minute until the grains are well coated. Pour in the water and bring the rice to the boil, then lower the heat, give the mixture a stir, cover the pan and cook the rice for 12–15 minutes.

4 Remove the pan from the heat, without lifting the lid, and leave the rice to stand for 5 minutes. Stir in the chopped coriander. Serve in warmed bowls, forking the rice over gently as you do so. If you like, sprinkle a little extra coriander on top of each portion.

1 Heat the oil and fry the onion seeds for about 30 seconds. Add the sliced onion and fry for about 5 minutes.

2 Stir in the tomatoes, pepper, ginger, garlic, chilli powder, diced potato and salt. Stir-fry over a medium heat for about 5 minutes more.

INDIAN RICE <u>WITH</u> TOMATOES <u>AND</u> SPINACH

THIS TASTY RICE DISH IS AN AROMATIC, RATHER THAN HOT INDIAN DISH. PERFECT FOR THOSE WITH DELICATE PALATES. IT CAN BE SERVED BY ITSELF OR AS ONE OF A NUMBER OF SMALLER DISHES.

SERVES FOUR

INGREDIENTS
30ml/2 tbsp sunflower oil
15g/½oz/1 tbsp ghee or butter
1 onion, chopped
2 garlic cloves, crushed
5 tomatoes, peeled, seeded
  and chopped
225g/8oz/generous 1 cup brown
  basmati rice, soaked
10ml/2 tsp *dhana jeera* powder or
  5ml/1 tsp ground coriander and
  5ml/1 tsp ground cumin
2 carrots, coarsely grated
900ml/1½ pints/3¾ cups vegetable
  stock
275g/10oz baby spinach
  leaves, washed
115g/4oz/1 cup unsalted cashew
  nuts, toasted
salt and ground black pepper

1 Heat the oil and ghee or butter in a flameproof casserole and fry the onion and garlic for 5 minutes. Add the chopped tomatoes and cook, stirring, until slightly thickened.

2 Drain the rice, add it to the casserole and cook gently for 1–2 minutes, stirring, until the rice is coated with the tomato and onion mixture.

3 Stir in the *dhana jeera* powder or the ground coriander and cumin, then add the grated carrots and season. Pour in the stock and mix well.

4 Bring to the boil, then cover tightly and simmer over a very low heat for 20–25 minutes until the rice is tender. Lay the baby spinach leaves on the surface of the rice, cover again and cook for 2–3 minutes until the spinach has wilted.

5 Fold the spinach into the rest of the rice and check the seasoning. Sprinkle with the toasted cashew nuts and serve in warmed bowls.

COOK'S TIP
If you can't get baby spinach leaves, use larger fresh spinach leaves. Remove any tough stalks and chop the leaves roughly. A sweeter and less acidic alternative is to use Swiss chard – again, the stalks will need to be removed before use.

MEXICAN RICE

VERSIONS OF THIS DISH — A RELATIVE OF SPANISH RICE — ARE POPULAR ALL OVER SOUTH AMERICA.
IT IS A DELICIOUS MEDLEY OF RICE, TOMATOES AND AROMATIC FLAVOURINGS.

SERVES SIX

INGREDIENTS
    200g/7oz/1 cup long grain rice
    400g/14oz can chopped tomatoes in
        tomato juice
    ½ onion, roughly chopped
    2 garlic cloves, roughly chopped
    30ml/2 tbsp vegetable oil, preferably
        olive oil
    225ml/½ pint/scant 1 cup vegetable
        stock
    2.5ml/½ tsp salt
    3 fresh chillies
    150g/5oz/1 cup frozen peas
    ground black pepper

1 Put the rice in a large heatproof bowl
and pour over boiling water to cover.
Stir once, then leave to stand for
10 minutes. Tip into a strainer over the
sink, rinse under cold water, then drain
again. Set aside to dry slightly.

2 Meanwhile, pour the tomatoes and
juice into a food processor or blender,
add the onion and garlic, and process
until smooth.

3 Heat the oil in a large, heavy pan,
add the rice and cook over a medium
heat until the rice becomes a delicate
golden brown colour. Stir occasionally
with a wooden spatula to ensure that
the rice does not stick to the base
of the pan.

4 Add the tomato mixture and stir over
a medium heat until all the liquid has
been absorbed. Stir in the stock, salt,
whole chillies and peas. Continue to
cook the mixture, stirring occasionally,
until all the liquid has been absorbed
and the rice is just tender.

5 Remove the pan from the heat, cover
it with a tight-fitting lid and leave it to
stand in a warm place for 5–10 minutes.
Remove the chillies, fluff up the rice
lightly with a fork, and serve in warmed
bowls, sprinkled with black pepper.
The chillies may be used as a garnish,
if you like.

COOK'S TIP
Do not stir the rice too often after adding
the stock or the grains will break down
and the mixture will become starchy.

TOMATO RICE AND BEANS WITH AVOCADO SALSA

MEXICAN-STYLE RICE AND BEANS MAKE A DELICIOUS SUPPER DISH. SPOON ON TO TORTILLAS AND SERVE WITH A TANGY SALSA. ALTERNATIVELY, SERVE AS AN ACCOMPANIMENT TO A SPICY STEW.

SERVES FOUR

INGREDIENTS
  40g/1½oz/¼ cup dried or
    75g/3oz/½ cup canned kidney
    beans, rinsed and drained
  8 tomatoes, halved and seeded
  2 garlic cloves, chopped
  1 onion, sliced
  45ml/3 tbsp olive oil
  225g/8oz/generous 1 cup long grain
    brown rice, rinsed
  600ml/1 pint/2½ cups vegetable stock
  2 carrots, diced
  75g/3oz/¾ cup green beans
  salt and ground black pepper
  4 wheat tortillas and sour cream,
    to serve
For the avocado salsa
  1 avocado
  juice of 1 lime
  1 small red onion, diced
  1 small fresh red chilli, seeded
    and chopped
  15ml/1 tbsp chopped fresh
    coriander (cilantro)

1 If using dried kidney beans, place in a bowl, cover with cold water and leave to soak overnight, then drain and rinse well. Place in a pan with enough water to cover and bring to the boil. Boil rapidly for 10 minutes, then reduce the heat. Simmer for 40–50 minutes until tender; drain and set aside.

2 Make the avocado salsa. Halve and stone (pit) the avocado. Peel and dice the flesh, then toss it in the lime juice. Add the onion, chilli and coriander. Mix well.

3 Preheat the grill (broiler) to high. Place the tomatoes, garlic and onion on a baking tray. Pour over 15ml/1 tbsp of the oil and toss to coat. Grill (broil) for 10 minutes or until the tomatoes and onions are softened, turning once. Set aside to cool. Heat the remaining oil in a pan, add the rice and cook for 2 minutes, stirring, until light golden.

4 Purée the cooled tomatoes and onion in a food processor or blender, then add the mixture to the rice and cook for a further 2 minutes, stirring frequently. Pour in the vegetable stock, then cover and cook gently for 20 minutes, stirring occasionally.

5 Stir 30ml/2 tbsp of the kidney beans into the salsa. Add the rest to the rice mixture with the carrots and green beans, and cook for 10 minutes until the vegetables are tender. Season well. Remove the pan from the heat and leave to stand, covered, for 15 minutes.

6 Warm the wheat tortillas and place one on each serving plate. Spoon the hot rice and bean mixture on top. Serve immediately, with the avocado salsa and a bowl of sour cream.

COUSCOUS WITH EGGS AND TOMATO SAUCE

MIDDLE EASTERN VEGETARIAN FOOD IS BOTH VARIED AND QUICK, ESPECIALLY WITH THE EASY-TO-USE, READY-PREPARED COUSCOUS THAT IS AVAILABLE TODAY.

SERVES FOUR

INGREDIENTS

675g/1½lb plum tomatoes,
  roughly chopped
4 garlic cloves, chopped
75ml/5 tbsp olive oil
½ fresh red chilli, seeded and chopped
10ml/2 tsp soft light brown sugar
4 eggs
1 large onion, chopped
2 celery sticks, finely sliced
50g/2oz/⅓ cup sultanas (golden raisins)
200g/7oz/generous 1 cup ready-to-
  use couscous
350ml/12fl oz/1½ cups hot
  vegetable stock
salt and ground black pepper

1 Preheat the oven to 200°C/400°F/ Gas 6. Spread out the tomatoes and garlic in a roasting tin (pan), drizzle with 30ml/2 tbsp of the oil, sprinkle with chopped chilli, sugar and salt and pepper, and roast for 20 minutes.

2 Cook the eggs in boiling water for 4 minutes, then plunge them straight into cold water and leave until cold. Carefully peel off the shells.

3 Heat 15–30ml/1–2 tbsp of the remaining olive oil in a large pan and fry the onion and celery until softened. Add the sultanas, couscous and hot stock, and set aside until all the liquid has been absorbed. Stir gently, adding extra hot stock if necessary, and season to taste. Tip the mixture into a large heated serving dish, bury the eggs in the couscous and cover with foil. Keep warm in the oven.

4 Remove the tomato mixture from the oven and press it through a sieve placed over a bowl. Add 15ml/1 tbsp boiling water and the rest of the olive oil and stir to make a smooth, rich sauce.

5 Remove the couscous mixture from the oven and locate the eggs. Spoon a little tomato sauce over the top of each egg. Serve immediately, with the rest of the sauce handed separately.

HOT VEGETABLE COUSCOUS WITH HARISSA

A NORTH AFRICAN FAVOURITE, THIS DELICIOUSLY SPICY DISH, MADE RICH WITH TOMATOES AND PRUNES, MAKES AN EXCELLENT AND UNUSUAL MEAL FOR VEGETARIANS.

SERVES FOUR

INGREDIENTS
    45ml/3 tbsp extra virgin olive oil or
      sunflower oil
    1 onion, chopped
    2 garlic cloves, crushed
    5ml/1 tsp ground cumin
    5ml/1 tsp paprika
    400g/14oz can chopped tomatoes
    300ml/½ pint/1¼ cups vegetable
      stock
    1 cinnamon stick
    generous pinch of saffron threads
    4 baby aubergines (eggplant),
      quartered
    8 baby courgettes (zucchini),
      trimmed
    8 baby carrots
    225g/8oz/1⅓ cups couscous, soaked
    400g/14oz can chickpeas, rinsed
      and drained
    175g/6oz/¾ cup prunes
    45ml/3 tbsp chopped fresh parsley
    45ml/3 tbsp chopped fresh
      coriander (cilantro)
    10–15ml/2–3 tsp harissa
    salt

COOK'S TIPS
• Harissa is a very hot chilli sauce from North Africa. It looks rather like puréed tomatoes but needs to be treated with a great deal more caution. Use it sparingly.
• When choosing a steamer, metal sieve or colander for steaming the couscous, check that it fits neatly over the pan in which you intend to cook the vegetables.

1 Heat the olive oil in a large pan. Add the onion and garlic, and cook gently for 5 minutes until soft. Add the cumin and paprika and cook, stirring, for 1 minute.

2 Add the tomatoes, stock, cinnamon stick, saffron, aubergines, courgettes and carrots, with water to cover. Season with salt. Bring to the boil, cover, lower the heat and cook for 20 minutes until the vegetables are just tender.

3 Line a steamer with muslin. Steam the couscous according to the instructions on the packet. Add the chickpeas and prunes to the vegetables and cook for 5 minutes.

4 Place the couscous on top of the vegetable pan, cover, and cook for 5 minutes until the couscous is hot.

5 Stir the parsley and coriander into the vegetables. Heap the couscous on to a serving plate. Using a slotted spoon, arrange the vegetables over the couscous. Spoon over a little of the remaining liquid and combine.

6 Stir the harissa into the remaining reserved liquor and serve separately.

PASTA WITH TOMATO AND CHILLI SAUCE

THIS DISH COMES FROM LAZIO, IN ITALY, WHERE IT IS DESCRIBED AS "ALL'ARRABBIATA" WHICH MEANS ANGRY — IT DESCRIBES THE HEAT THAT COMES FROM THE CHILLI.

SERVES FOUR

INGREDIENTS

500g/1¼lb sugocasa (see Cook's Tip)
2 garlic cloves, crushed
150ml/¼ pint/⅔ cup dry white wine
15ml/1 tbsp sun-dried tomato paste
1 fresh red chilli
300g/11oz/2¾ cups penne or tortiglioni
60ml/4 tbsp finely chopped fresh flat
leaf parsley
salt and ground black pepper
freshly grated (shredded) Pecorino
cheese, to serve

COOK'S TIP
Sugocasa resembles passata (bottled strained tomatoes), but is rougher.

3 Remove the chilli from the sauce and add 30ml/2 tbsp of the parsley. Taste for seasoning. If you prefer a hotter taste, chop some or all of the chilli and return it to the sauce.

4 Drain the pasta and tip it into a warmed large bowl. Pour the sauce over the pasta and toss to mix. Serve at once, sprinkled with grated Pecorino and the remaining parsley.

1 Mix the sugocasa, garlic, wine, sun-dried tomato paste and whole chilli in a pan and bring to the boil. Cover and simmer gently, stirring.

2 Drop the pasta into a large pan of rapidly boiling salted water. Lower the heat and simmer for 10–12 minutes or until *al dente*.

PAGLIA E FIENO <u>WITH</u> SUN-DRIED TOMATOES <u>AND</u> RADICCHIO

THIS IS A LIGHT, MODERN PASTA DISH OF THE KIND SERVED IN FASHIONABLE RESTAURANTS. IT IS THE PRESENTATION THAT SETS IT APART, THE CAREFUL DRIZZLING OF THE TOMATO SAUCE AND PLACING OF PASTA, NOT THE USUAL QUICK-AND-EASY PREPARATION.

SERVES FOUR TO SIX

INGREDIENTS
45ml/3 tbsp pine nuts
350g/12oz *paglia e fieno* (or two
   different colours of tagliatelle)
45ml/3 tbsp extra virgin olive oil or
   sunflower oil
30ml/2 tbsp sun-dried tomato paste
2 pieces drained sun-dried tomatoes
   in olive oil, cut into very
   thin slivers
40g/1½oz radicchio leaves,
   finely shredded
4–6 spring onions (scallions), thinly
   sliced into rings
salt and freshly ground black pepper

1 Put the pine nuts in a non-stick frying pan and toss over a low to medium heat for 1–2 minutes or until they are lightly toasted and golden. Remove and set aside.

2 Cook the pasta according to the packet instructions, keeping the colours separate by using two pans.

3 While the pasta is cooking, heat 15ml/1 tbsp of the oil in a medium pan or frying pan. Add the sun-dried tomato paste and the sun-dried tomatoes, then stir in 2 ladlefuls of the water used for cooking the pasta. Simmer until the sauce is slightly reduced, stirring constantly.

4 Mix in the shredded radicchio, then taste and season if necessary. Keep on a low heat. Drain the *paglia e fieno*, keeping the colours separate, and return the pasta to the pans. Add about 15ml/1 tbsp oil to each pan and toss over a medium to high heat until the pasta is glistening with the oil.

5 Arrange a portion of green and white pasta in each of 4–6 warmed bowls, then spoon the sun-dried tomato and radicchio mixture in the centre. Sprinkle the spring onions and pine nuts over the top and serve immediately. Before eating, each diner should toss the sauce ingredients with the pasta.

COOK'S TIP
If you find the presentation too fussy, you can toss the tomato and radicchio mixture with the pasta in a large bowl before serving, then sprinkle the spring onions and toasted pine nuts on top.

RIGATONI <u>WITH</u> TOMATOES, WILD MUSHROOMS <u>AND</u> FRESH HERBS

THIS IS A GOOD SAUCE TO MAKE FROM STORE-CUPBOARD INGREDIENTS BECAUSE IT DOESN'T RELY ON ANYTHING FRESH, APART FROM THE SHALLOTS AND HERBS. IT IS PERFECT FOR THE END-OF-WEEK MEAL WHEN YOU HAVE RUN OUT OF FOOD AND ENERGY FOR COOKING.

SERVES FOUR

INGREDIENTS
2 x 15g/½oz packets dried
  wild mushrooms
175ml/6fl oz/¾ cup warm water
30ml/2 tbsp olive oil
2 shallots, finely chopped
2 garlic cloves, crushed
a few sprigs of fresh marjoram,
  chopped, plus extra to garnish
1 handful fresh flat leaf
  parsley, chopped
25g/1oz/2 tbsp cold butter
400g/14oz can chopped tomatoes
400g/14oz/3½ cups dried rigatoni
25g/1oz/⅓ cup freshly grated
  Parmesan cheese, plus extra
  to serve
salt and ground black pepper

1 Put the dried mushrooms in a bowl, pour the warm water over to cover and soak for 15–20 minutes. Tip into a fine sieve set over a bowl and squeeze the mushrooms with your fingers to release as much liquid as possible. Reserve the mushrooms and the strained liquid.

2 Heat the oil in a medium frying pan and fry the shallots, garlic and herbs over a low heat, stirring frequently, for about 5 minutes. Add the mushrooms and butter, and stir until the butter has melted. Season well.

3 Stir in the tomatoes and the reserved liquid from the soaked mushrooms. Bring to the boil, then cover, lower the heat and simmer for about 20 minutes, stirring occasionally. Meanwhile, cook the pasta according to the instructions on the packet.

4 Taste the sauce for seasoning. Drain the pasta, reserving some of the cooking water, and tip it into a warmed large bowl. Add the sauce and the grated Parmesan and toss to mix. Add a little cooking water if you prefer a runnier sauce. Serve immediately, garnished with marjoram and with more Parmesan cheese, which can be handed around separately.

VARIATIONS
• If you have a bottle of wine open, red or white, add a splash when you add the canned tomatoes.
• For a richer sauce, add a few tablespoonfuls of cream or mascarpone to the sauce just before serving.

RIGATONI <u>WITH</u> TOMATOES <u>AND</u> FRESH HERBS

THIS PRETTY-COLOURED PASTA DISH RELIES FOR ITS SUCCESS ON THE BEST ITALIAN CANNED TOMATOES AND TENDER YOUNG HERBS, FRESHLY PICKED. FOR A REAL GOURMET TREAT, USE FRESH TOMATOES, SKINNED AND PURÉED. ADD A LITTLE SUGAR IF THE TOMATOES ARE NOT AT THE PEAK OF RIPENESS.

SERVES SIX TO EIGHT

INGREDIENTS
1 onion
1 carrot
1 celery stick
60ml/4 tbsp olive oil
1 garlic clove, thinly sliced
a few leaves each of fresh basil,
   thyme and oregano or marjoram
2 x 400g/14oz cans chopped Italian
   plum tomatoes
15ml/1 tbsp sun-dried tomato paste
5ml/1 tsp granulated sugar
about 90ml/6 tbsp dry red or white
   wine (optional)
350g/12oz/3 cups dried rigatoni
salt and ground black pepper
coarsely shaved Parmesan cheese,
   to serve

COOK'S TIP
Large pasta tubes are best for this recipe, as they capture the wonderful tomato and herb sauce. If you can't get rigatoni, try penne or penne rigate (ridged penne).

1 Chop the onion, carrot and celery stick finely, either in a food processor or by hand, with a sharp knife.

2 Heat the olive oil in a medium pan, add the garlic slices and stir over a very low heat for 1–2 minutes. Do not let the garlic burn.

3 Add the chopped vegetables and the fresh herbs, reserving a few to garnish. Cook over a low heat, stirring frequently, for 5–7 minutes until the vegetables have softened and are lightly coloured.

4 Add the canned tomatoes, tomato paste and sugar, then stir in the wine, if using. Add salt and pepper to taste. Bring to the boil, stirring, then lower the heat to a gentle simmer. Cook, stirring often, for about 45 minutes.

5 Cook the pasta in lightly salted boiling water for 10–12 minutes, drain and tip into a warmed bowl. Pour the sauce over the pasta and toss well. Garnish with the reserved herbs. Serve immediately, with shavings of Parmesan handed separately.

SPAGHETTI WITH FRESH TOMATO SAUCE

THE HEAT FROM THE PASTA WILL RELEASE THE DELICIOUS FLAVOURS OF THIS SAUCE. ONLY USE THE TRULY RED AND SOFT PLUM TOMATOES, AS THE AROMATIC QUALITY OF REALLY GOOD TOMATOES IMPROVES THE FLAVOUR OF THIS SAUCE — LARGE RIPE BEEFSTEAK TOMATOES ARE ALSO IDEAL.

SERVES FOUR

INGREDIENTS
675g/1½lb ripe Italian
    plum tomatoes or sweet
    cherry tomatoes
60ml/4 tbsp extra virgin olive oil or
    sunflower oil
1 onion, finely chopped
350g/12oz fresh or dried spaghetti
a small handful fresh basil leaves
salt and ground black pepper
coarsely shaved Parmesan cheese,
    to serve

COOK'S TIPS
• The Italian plum tomatoes called San Marzano are the best variety to use. When fully ripe, they have thin skins that peel off easily.
• In Italy, cooks often make this sauce in bulk in the summer months and freeze it for later use. Let it cool, then freeze in usable quantities in rigid containers. Thaw before reheating.

1 With a sharp knife, cut a cross in the base end of each tomato. Plunge the tomatoes, a few at a time, into a bowl of boiling water. Leave for 30 seconds or so, then lift them out with a slotted spoon and drop them into a bowl of cold water. Drain well. The skin will have begun to peel back from the crosses. Remove it entirely.

2 Place the tomatoes on a chopping board and cut into quarters, then eighths, and chop as finely as possible.

3 Heat the oil in a large pan, add the onion and cook over a low heat, stirring frequently, for about 5 minutes until softened and lightly coloured.

4 Add the tomatoes, season with salt and pepper to taste, bring to a simmer, then turn the heat down to low and cover the pan with a lid. Cook, stirring occasionally, for 30–40 minutes until the mixture is thick.

5 Meanwhile, cook the pasta according to the instructions on the packet. Shred the basil leaves finely, or tear them into small pieces.

6 Remove the sauce from the heat, stir in the basil and taste for seasoning again. Drain the pasta into a colander. Tip the spaghetti into a warmed bowl, pour the sauce over and toss the mixture well. Serve immediately, with shaved Parmesan handed around in a separate bowl.

POTATO GNOCCHI <u>WITH</u> SIMPLE TOMATO <u>AND</u> BUTTER SAUCE

GNOCCHI MAKE A SUBSTANTIAL AND TASTY ALTERNATIVE TO PASTA. IN THIS DISH THEY ARE SERVED WITH A VERY SIMPLE, BUT DELICIOUS, FRESH TOMATO SAUCE.

SERVES FOUR

INGREDIENTS
675g/1½lb floury potatoes
2 egg yolks
75g/3oz/¾ cup plain (all-purpose) flour
60ml/4 tbsp finely chopped fresh
  parsley, to garnish
For the sauce
25g/1oz/2 tbsp butter, melted
450g/1lb plum tomatoes, peeled,
  seeded and chopped
salt

1 Preheat the oven to 200°C/400°F/ Gas 6. Scrub the potatoes, then bake them in their skins in the oven for 1 hour or until the flesh feels soft when pricked with a fork.

2 While the potatoes are still warm, cut them in half and gently squeeze the flesh into a bowl, or use a spoon to scrape the flesh out of the shells. Mash the potato well, then season with a little salt. Add the egg yolks and mix lightly with a fork or spoon.

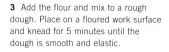

3 Add the flour and mix to a rough dough. Place on a floured work surface and knead for 5 minutes until the dough is smooth and elastic.

4 Shape the dough into small thumb-sized shapes by making long rolls and cutting them into segments. Press each of these with the back of a fork to give a ridged effect. Place the gnocchi on a floured work surface.

5 Preheat the oven to 140°C/275°F/ Gas 1. Cook the gnocchi in small batches in barely simmering, slightly salted water for about 10 minutes. Remove with a slotted spoon, drain well and tip into a dish. Cover and keep hot in the oven.

6 To make the sauce, heat the butter in a small pan for 1 minute, then add the tomatoes and cook over a low heat until the juice starts to run. Sprinkle the gnocchi with chopped parsley and serve with the sauce.

TOMATO <u>AND</u> RICH MEDITERRANEAN VEGETABLE HOT-POT

HERE'S A ONE-DISH MEAL THAT'S SUITABLE FOR FEEDING LARGE NUMBERS OF PEOPLE. IT'S LIGHTLY SPICED AND HAS PLENTY OF GARLIC — WHO COULD REFUSE?

SERVES FOUR

INGREDIENTS

60ml/4 tbsp extra virgin olive oil or
  sunflower oil
1 large onion, chopped
2 small–medium aubergines
  (eggplant), cut into small cubes
4 courgettes (zucchini), cut into
  small chunks
2 red, yellow or green (bell) peppers,
  seeded and chopped
115g/4oz/1 cup fresh or frozen peas
115g/4oz green beans
200g/7oz can flageolet (small
  cannellini) beans, rinsed and drained
450g/1lb new or salad potatoes,
  peeled and cubed
2.5ml/½ tsp cinnamon
2.5ml/½ tsp ground cumin
5ml/1 tsp paprika
4–5 tomatoes, peeled
400g/14oz can chopped tomatoes
30ml/2 tbsp chopped fresh parsley
3–4 garlic cloves, crushed
350ml/12fl oz/1½ cups vegetable stock
salt and ground black pepper
black olives, to garnish
fresh parsley, to garnish

1 Preheat the oven to 190°C/375°F/ Gas 5. Heat 45ml/3 tbsp of the oil in a heavy pan, and fry the onion until golden. Add the aubergines, sauté for 3 minutes, then add the courgettes, peppers, peas, beans and potatoes, and stir in the spices and seasoning. Cook for 3 minutes, stirring constantly.

2 Cut the tomatoes in half and scoop out the seeds. Chop the tomatoes finely and place them in a bowl. Stir in the canned tomatoes with the chopped fresh parsley, crushed garlic and the remaining olive oil. Spoon the aubergine mixture into a shallow ovenproof dish and level the surface.

3 Pour the stock over the aubergine mixture and then spoon over the prepared tomato mixture.

4 Cover the dish with foil and bake for 30–45 minutes until the vegetables are tender. Serve hot, garnished with black olives and parsley.

SPICY LEBANESE STEW

THIS IS A TRADITIONAL LEBANESE DISH THAT IS POPULAR ALL OVER THE MEDITERRANEAN.
HERE THE MOST IS MADE OF THE WONDERFUL COMBINATION OF TOMATOES AND SPICES.

SERVES FOUR

INGREDIENTS
   3 large aubergines (eggplant), cubed
   200g/7oz/1 cup chickpeas, soaked
   60ml/4 tbsp olive oil
   3 garlic cloves, chopped
   2 large onions, chopped
   2.5ml/½ tsp ground cumin
   2.5ml/½ tsp ground cinnamon
   2.5ml/½ tsp ground coriander
   3 x 400g/14oz cans chopped
     tomatoes
   200g/7oz fresh tomatoes, chopped
   salt and ground black pepper
   cooked rice, to serve
For the garnish
   30ml/2 tbsp olive oil
   1 onion, sliced
   1 garlic clove, sliced
   fresh coriander (cilantro) sprigs

1 Place the aubergines in a colander and sprinkle them with salt. Stand the colander in the sink and leave for 30 minutes, to allow any bitter juices to escape. Rinse with cold water and dry on kitchen paper. Drain the chickpeas and put in a pan with enough water to cover. Bring to the boil and simmer for about 1 hour, or until tender. Drain.

2 Heat the oil in a large pan. Add the garlic and onions; cook gently, until soft. Add the spices and cook, stirring, for a few seconds. Stir in the aubergine and stir to coat with the spices and onion. Cook for 5 minutes. Add the tomatoes and chickpeas, and season with salt and pepper. Cover and simmer for 20 minutes.

3 To make the garnish, heat the oil in a frying pan and, when very hot, add the sliced onion and garlic. Fry until golden and crisp. Serve the stew with rice, topped with the onion and garlic, and garnished with coriander.

COOK'S TIPS
• Tender, young aubergines will not need to be salted.
• When fat, flavoursome beefsteak tomatoes are in the shops, use them instead of canned tomatoes. You will need about 6 large tomatoes.
• If you are in a hurry, substitute 2 cans of chickpeas for dried. Rinse and drain before adding to the tomato mixture, and cook for about 15 minutes.

CHICKPEA TAGINE

A TAGINE IS A TYPE OF MOROCCAN STEW ORIGINALLY PREPARED BY LONG SIMMERING OVER AN OPEN FIRE. A TAGINE CAN BE SAVOURY OR SWEET AND SOUR.

SERVES SIX TO EIGHT

INGREDIENTS

150g/5oz/²/₃ cup chickpeas, soaked
  overnight, or 2 x 400g/14oz cans
  chickpeas, drained
30ml/2 tbsp sunflower oil or extra
  virgin olive oil
1 large onion, chopped
1 garlic clove, crushed or
  chopped (optional)
400g/14oz can chopped tomatoes
200g/7oz fresh tomatoes, peeled
  and puréed
5ml/1 tsp ground cumin
350ml/12fl oz/1½ cups vegetable
  stock
¼ preserved lemon
30ml/2 tbsp chopped fresh
  coriander (cilantro)
crusty bread, to serve

COOK'S TIP

To preserve lemons, quarter 6 unwaxed
lemons and layer them with 90ml/6 tbsp
sea salt in a sieve. Drain for 2 days, then
pack in preserving jars with 30ml/2 tbsp
black peppercorns, 4 bay leaves,
6 cardamom pods and a cinnamon stick.
Cover with sunflower oil, seal and leave
for 3–4 weeks before using.

1 If using dried chickpeas, drain and
cook in plenty of boiling water for
1–1½ hours until tender. Drain again.

2 Skin the chickpeas by placing them
in a bowl of cold water and rubbing
them between your fingers – the skins
will rise to the surface.

3 Heat the oil in a large pan or
flameproof casserole and fry the onion
and garlic, if using, for 8–10 minutes
until golden.

4 Stir in the tomatoes and cumin, then
pour over the stock and stir well. Cook
for 10 minutes.

5 Add the chickpeas and simmer,
uncovered, for 30–40 minutes more.

6 Rinse the preserved lemon and cut
away the flesh and pith. Cut the peel
into slivers and stir into the chickpeas
along with the coriander. Serve
immediately with crusty bread.

TOMATO AND LENTIL DHAL WITH ALMONDS

RICHLY FLAVOURED WITH SPICES, COCONUT MILK AND TOMATOES, THIS LENTIL DISH MAKES A FILLING SUPPER. SPLIT RED LENTILS GIVE THE DISH A VIBRANT COLOUR, BUT YOU COULD USE LARGER YELLOW SPLIT PEAS INSTEAD, IF YOU PREFER.

SERVES FOUR

INGREDIENTS
    30ml/2 tbsp vegetable oil
    1 large onion, finely chopped
    3 garlic cloves, chopped
    1 carrot, diced
    2.5cm/1in piece fresh ginger, grated
    10ml/2 tsp cumin seeds
    10ml/2 tsp yellow mustard seeds
    10ml/2 tsp ground turmeric
    5ml/1 tsp mild chilli powder
    5ml/1 tsp garam masala
    225g/8oz/1 cup split red lentils
    400ml/14fl oz/1⅔ cups water
    400ml/14fl oz/1⅔ cups coconut milk
    12 tomatoes, peeled, seeded
      and chopped
    juice of 2 limes
    60ml/4 tbsp chopped fresh
      coriander (cilantro)
    25g/1oz/¼ cup flaked (sliced)
      almonds, toasted
    salt and ground black pepper
    warmed naan bread and natural
      (plain) yogurt, to serve

1 Heat the oil in a large heavy pan. Sauté the chopped onion for 5 minutes until softened, stirring occasionally. Add the garlic, carrot, ginger, cumin and mustard seeds. Cook for 5 minutes, stirring, until the seeds begin to pop and the carrot softens slightly.

2 Stir in the ground turmeric, chilli powder and the garam masala, and cook for 1 minute or until the flavours mingle, stirring constantly to prevent the spices sticking and burning on the base of the pan.

3 Add the split red lentils, water, coconut milk and chopped tomatoes to the pan. Season well with salt and ground black pepper.

4 Bring to the boil, then reduce the heat and gently simmer, covered with a lid, for about 45 minutes, stirring occasionally to prevent the lentils from sticking to the base of the pan.

5 Stir in the lime juice and 45ml/3 tbsp of the fresh coriander, then check the seasoning adding more if necessary. Cook the mixture for a further 15 minutes until the lentils soften and become tender.

6 To garnish, sprinkle with the remaining coriander and the flaked almonds. Serve with warmed naan bread and natural yogurt.

COOK'S TIPS
• It is a good idea to cover the pan while the cumin seeds and mustard seeds are popping. It is surprising how far they can travel.
• Garam masala, which means "warming spices", is a mixture of cumin seeds, cinnamon, black peppercorns and cloves. It is available ready-mixed from ethnic food stores and larger supermarkets.

BEAN FEAST WITH TOMATO AND AVOCADO SALSA

THIS IS A VERY QUICK AND EASY RECIPE USING CANNED BEANS, ALTHOUGH IT COULD BE MADE WITH DRIED BEANS. THEY WOULD NEED TO BE SOAKED OVERNIGHT, BOILED HARD FOR 10 MINUTES, THEN SIMMERED FOR 1–1½ HOURS UNTIL TENDER.

SERVES FOUR

INGREDIENTS

15ml/1 tbsp olive oil
1 small onion, finely chopped
3 garlic cloves, finely chopped
1 fresh red Ancho chilli, seeded and finely chopped
1 red (bell) pepper, seeded and coarsely chopped
2 plum tomatoes, chopped
2 bay leaves
10ml/2 tsp chopped fresh oregano
10ml/2 tsp ground cumin
5ml/1 tsp ground coriander
2.5ml/½ tsp ground cloves
15ml/1 tbsp soft dark brown sugar
400g/14oz can red kidney beans, rinsed and drained
400g/14oz can flageolet (small cannellini) beans, rinsed and drained
400g/14oz can borlotti beans, rinsed and drained
300ml/½ pint/1¼ cups vegetable stock
salt and ground black pepper
fresh coriander (cilantro), to garnish

For the salsa

1 ripe, but firm, avocado
45ml/3 tbsp fresh lime juice
1 small red onion
1 small fresh hot green chilli
5 ripe plum tomatoes
45ml/3 tbsp chopped fresh coriander (cilantro)

2 Stir well and cook for a further 3 minutes, then add the sugar, beans and stock, and cook for 8 minutes. Season with salt and plenty of ground black pepper.

4 Chop the red onion and slice the chilli, discarding the seeds. Plunge the tomatoes into boiling water, leave for 30 seconds and then peel away the skin. Chop the tomatoes.

1 Heat the oil and fry the onion for 3 minutes, until transparent. Add the garlic, chilli, pepper, herbs and spices.

3 To make the salsa, peel the avocado, cut it in half around the stone (pit), then remove the stone by striking it with the blade of a large, sharp knife and lifting it out cleanly. Cut the flesh into 1cm/½in dice. Place in a mixing bowl with the lime juice and stir to mix.

5 Add the onion, chilli, tomatoes and coriander to the avocado. Season with black pepper and stir to mix. Spoon the beans into a warmed serving dish or into 4 serving bowls. Serve with the tomato and avocado salsa and garnish with sprigs of fresh coriander.

MEDITERRANEAN ROLLS <u>WITH</u> TOMATO SAUCE

THESE LITTLE ROLLS OF AUBERGINE WRAPPED AROUND A FILLING OF RICOTTA AND RICE MAKE AN INSPIRED ADDITION TO A SUMMER BUFFET TABLE OR A GREEK OR TURKISH-STYLE MEZE.

SERVES FOUR

INGREDIENTS

2 aubergines (eggplant)
olive oil, or sunflower oil for
shallow frying
75g/3oz/scant ½ cup ricotta cheese
75g/3oz/scant ½ cup soft goat's
cheese
225g/8oz/2 cups cooked long grain
white rice
15ml/1 tbsp chopped fresh basil
5ml/1 tsp chopped fresh mint, plus
mint sprigs, to garnish
salt and ground black pepper
For the tomato sauce
15ml/1 tbsp olive oil
1 red onion, finely chopped
1 garlic clove, crushed
400g/14oz can chopped tomatoes
120ml/4fl oz/½ cup vegetable stock
or white wine or a mixture
15ml/1 tbsp chopped fresh parsley

COOK'S TIP
Cut each aubergine into 4–5 slices,
discarding the two outer slices, which
consist largely of skin. If you prefer to
use less oil for the aubergines, brush
each slice with just a little oil, then grill
(broil) until evenly browned.

1 Make the tomato sauce. Heat the oil in a small pan and fry the onion and garlic for 3–4 minutes until softened. Add the tomatoes, vegetable stock and/or wine, and parsley. Season well. Bring to the boil, then lower the heat and simmer for 10–12 minutes until slightly thickened, stirring.

2 Preheat the oven to 190°C/375°F/ Gas 5. Slice the aubergines lengthways. Heat the oil in a large frying pan and fry the aubergine slices until they are golden brown on both sides. Drain on kitchen paper. Mix the ricotta, goat's cheese, rice, basil and mint in a bowl. Season well with salt and pepper.

3 Place a generous spoonful of the cheese and rice mixture at one end of each aubergine slice and roll up. Arrange the rolls side by side in a shallow ovenproof dish. Pour the tomato sauce over the top and bake for 10–15 minutes until heated through. Garnish with the mint sprigs and serve.

GRILLED TOMATO PARCELS

THESE ARE DELICIOUS LITTLE ITALIAN BUNDLES OF TOMATOES, MOZZARELLA CHEESE AND BASIL,
WRAPPED IN CREAMY SLICES OF PURPLE AUBERGINE.

SERVES FOUR

INGREDIENTS
2 large, long aubergines (eggplant)
225g/8oz mozzarella cheese
2 plum tomatoes
16 large fresh basil leaves
salt and ground black pepper
30ml/2 tbsp olive oil
For the dressing
60ml/4 tbsp olive oil
5ml/1 tsp balsamic vinegar
15ml/1 tbsp sun-dried tomato paste
15ml/1 tbsp lemon juice
To garnish
30ml/2 tbsp toasted pine nuts
torn fresh basil leaves

COOK'S TIP
The best cheese to use in these
delectable little parcels is undoubtedly
mozzarella. Look for the authentic moist
cheese, made from buffalo's milk, which
is sold packed in whey. If you can find it,
lightly smoked mozzarella would also
work well, and would add additional
flavour to the dish. It is labelled
mozzarella affumicata. Alternatively,
you could use a plain or smoked goat's
cheese. Look for one with a similar
texture to mozzarella.

1 Remove the stalks from the
aubergines and cut the aubergines
lengthways into thin slices – the aim is
to get 16 slices in total, disregarding the
outer 2 slices, which consist largely of
skin. (If you have a mandolin, it will cut
perfect, even slices for you – otherwise,
use a sharp, long-bladed cook's knife).

2 Bring a large pan of salted water to
the boil and cook the aubergine slices
for about 2 minutes. Drain the slices
thoroughly, then dry on kitchen paper.
Cut the mozzarella cheese into 8 slices.
Cut each tomato into 8 slices, not
counting the first and last slices.

3 Take 2 aubergine slices and place
on a flameproof dish or tray, in a cross.
Place a slice of tomato in the centre,
season with salt and pepper, then add
a basil leaf, followed by a slice of
mozzarella, another basil leaf, a slice of
tomato and more seasoning.

4 Fold the ends of the aubergine slices
around the mozzarella and tomato
filling. Repeat with the rest of the
ingredients to make 8 parcels. Chill the
parcels for about 20 minutes.

5 To make the tomato dressing, whisk
together the oil, vinegar, tomato paste
and lemon juice. Season to taste.

6 Preheat the grill (broiler). Brush the
parcels with olive oil and cook for about
5 minutes on each side until golden.
Serve hot, with the dressing. Garnish
with the pine nuts and basil.

POTATO RÖSTI <u>AND</u> TOFU <u>WITH</u> FRESH TOMATO <u>AND</u> GINGER SAUCE

ALTHOUGH THIS DISH FEATURES VARIOUS COMPONENTS, IT IS NOT DIFFICULT TO MAKE, AND THE FINISHED RESULT IS WELL WORTH THE EFFORT. MAKE SURE YOU MARINATE THE TOFU FOR AT LEAST AN HOUR TO ALLOW IT TO ABSORB THE FLAVOURS OF THE GINGER, GARLIC AND TAMARI.

SERVES FOUR

INGREDIENTS
   425g/15oz tofu, cut into 1cm/
      ½in cubes
   900g/2lb potatoes, peeled
   sunflower oil, for frying
   30ml/2 tbsp sesame seeds, toasted
   salt and ground black pepper
   mixed leaf salad, to serve
For the marinade
   30ml/2 tbsp tamari or dark soy sauce
   15ml/1 tbsp clear honey
   2 garlic cloves, crushed
   4cm/1½in piece fresh root
      ginger, grated
   5ml/1 tsp toasted sesame oil
For the sauce
   15ml/1 tbsp olive oil
   8 tomatoes, halved, seeded
      and chopped

1 Mix together all the marinade ingredients in a shallow dish and add the tofu. Spoon the marinade over the tofu and leave to marinate in the refrigerator for at least 1 hour. Turn the tofu occasionally in the marinade to allow the flavours to be absorbed.

2 To make the rösti, bring a pan of lightly salted water to the boil and par-boil the potatoes for 10–15 minutes until almost tender. Drain the potatoes well, leave to cool, then grate coarsely. Season well. Preheat the oven to 200°C/400°F/Gas 6.

3 Using a slotted spoon, remove the tofu from the marinade carefully to ensure that it does not break up. Reserve the marinade for later use. Spread out the tofu in an ovenproof dish and bake for 20 minutes, turning occasionally, until it is firm, golden and crisp on all sides.

4 Meanwhile, shape the rösti. Rinse your hands in cold water and shake them so that they are just damp. Take one-quarter of the potato mixture in your hands and form it into a rough, round cake. Repeat with the remaining mixture and shape into pieces the same size and shape as the first.

5 Heat a frying pan with just enough oil to cover the base. Place the rösti cakes in the frying pan and flatten the mixture slightly, using a wooden spatula to form rounds approximately 1cm/½in thick, though if you prefer, they can be up to 2cm/1in thick.

6 Cook the rösti over a medium heat for about 6 minutes until golden and crisp underneath. Using a fish slice or spatula, carefully turn the rösti over and cook for a further 6 minutes on the other side until they are golden brown all over.

7 Meanwhile, make the sauce. Heat the oil in a pan, add the reserved marinade and the tomatoes, and cook for 2 minutes, stirring.

8 Reduce the heat and simmer, covered, for 10 minutes, stirring occasionally, until the tomatoes break down. Press through a sieve to make a thick, smooth sauce.

9 Place a rösti on each of 4 warmed serving plates, arrange the tofu on top, spoon over the tomato sauce and sprinkle with sesame seeds. Serve with a mixed leaf salad.

COOK'S TIP
Tamari is a thick, mellow-flavoured Japanese soy sauce, which, unlike conventional Chinese soy sauce, is wheat-free and so is suitable for people who are on wheat- or gluten-free diets. It is sold in Japanese food stores and some larger health food stores.

ONIONS STUFFED <u>WITH</u> GOAT'S CHEESE <u>AND</u> SUN-DRIED TOMATOES

ROASTED ONIONS AND GOAT'S CHEESE ARE A WINNING COMBINATION. THESE STUFFED ONIONS MAKE AN EXCELLENT MAIN COURSE WHEN SERVED WITH A RICE OR CRACKED WHEAT PILAFF.

SERVES FOUR

INGREDIENTS
    4 large onions
    150g/5oz goat's cheese, crumbled
        or cubed
    50g/2oz/1 cup fresh breadcrumbs
    8 sun-dried tomatoes in olive oil,
        drained and chopped
    1–2 garlic cloves, finely chopped
    2.5ml/½ tsp chopped fresh
        thyme leaves
    30ml/2 tbsp chopped fresh parsley
    1 small egg, beaten
    45ml/3 tbsp pine nuts, toasted
    30ml/2 tbsp olive oil (from the jar of
        sun-dried tomatoes)
    salt and ground black pepper

1 Bring a large pan of lightly salted water to the boil. Add the whole onions in their skins and boil for 10 minutes. Drain and cool, then cut each onion in half horizontally and slip off the skins, keeping the onion halves intact.

2 Using a teaspoon to scoop out the flesh, remove the centre of each onion, leaving a thick shell. Reserve the flesh on a board and place the shells in an oiled ovenproof dish. Preheat the oven to 190°C/375°F/Gas 5.

3 Chop the scooped-out onion flesh and place it in a bowl. Add the goat's cheese, breadcrumbs, sun-dried tomatoes, garlic, thyme, half the parsley and egg. Mix well, then season to taste with salt and pepper, and add the toasted pine nuts.

4 Divide the stuffing among the onions and cover with foil. Bake for about 25 minutes. Uncover, drizzle with the oil and cook for another 30–40 minutes, until the filling is bubbling and the onions are well cooked. Baste occasionally during cooking. When cooked, sprinkle with the remaining parsley to garnish.

VARIATIONS
• Omit the goat's cheese and add 115g/4oz finely chopped mushrooms and 1 grated carrot.
• Substitute feta cheese for the goat's cheese and raisins for the pine nuts.
• Substitute smoked mozzarella for the goat's cheese and substitute pistachio nuts for the pine nuts.
• Use red and yellow (bell) peppers preserved in olive oil instead of sun-dried tomatoes.

STUFFED BEEFSTEAK TOMATOES <u>AND</u> RED <u>AND</u> YELLOW PEPPERS

COLOURFUL PEPPERS AND TOMATOES MAKE PERFECT CONTAINERS FOR VARIOUS STUFFINGS.
THIS RICE AND HERB VERSION USES TYPICALLY GREEK INGREDIENTS.

SERVES FOUR

INGREDIENTS

    2 large ripe tomatoes
    1 green (bell) pepper
    1 yellow or orange (bell) pepper
    60ml/4 tbsp olive oil
    2 onions, chopped
    2 garlic cloves, crushed
    115g/4oz/1 cup blanched
      almonds, chopped
    75g/3oz/generous ½ cup long grain
      white rice, boiled and drained
    15g/½oz fresh mint, roughly chopped
    15g/½oz fresh parsley, roughly chopped
    25g/1oz/3 tbsp sultanas (golden raisins)
    45ml/3 tbsp ground almonds
    salt and ground black pepper
    chopped fresh herbs,to garnish

VARIATION
Small aubergines (eggplant) or large
courgettes (zucchini) are also good for
stuffing. Halve and scoop out the
centres, then oil the vegetable cases and
bake for about 15 minutes. Chop the
centres, fry for 2–3 minutes to soften,
and add to the stuffing. Fill and bake as
in the main recipe.

1 Preheat the oven to 190°C/375°F/
Gas 5. Cut the tomatoes in half and
scoop out the pulp and seeds using a
teaspoon or round-ended knife. Leave
the tomato shells to drain on kitchen
paper, with cut sides down. Roughly
chop the tomato pulp and set it aside in
a small bowl.

2 Halve the peppers, leaving the cores
intact. Scoop out the seeds. Brush the
peppers with 15ml/1 tbsp of the oil and
bake on a baking sheet for 15 minutes.
Stand the peppers and tomatoes, hollows
uppermost, in a shallow ovenproof dish
and season with salt and pepper.

3 Fry the onions in the remaining oil
for 5 minutes. Add the garlic and
chopped almonds and fry for a
further 1 minute.

4 Remove the pan from the heat and
stir in the rice, chopped tomato pulp,
mint, parsley and sultanas. Spoon the
mixture into the tomatoes and peppers.

5 Pour 150ml/¼ pint/⅔ cup boiling
water around the tomatoes and peppers,
and bake, uncovered, for 20 minutes.
Sprinkle with the ground almonds and
drizzle over a little extra olive oil. Return
to the oven for a further 20 minutes.
Garnish with fresh herbs.

CHEESE SAUSAGES ^{WITH} TOMATO SAUCE

THESE ARE BASED ON THE WELSH SPECIALITY WHICH ARE TRADITIONALLY MADE USING BREADCRUMBS.
HOWEVER, ADDING MASHED POTATO LIGHTENS THE SAUSAGES AND MAKES THEM EASIER TO HANDLE.

SERVES FOUR

INGREDIENTS

    25g/1oz/2 tbsp butter or
    low-fat spread
    175g/6oz leeks or shallots,
    finely chopped
    90ml/6 tbsp cold mashed potato
    115g/4oz/2 cups fresh white or
    wholemeal (whole-wheat) breadcrumbs
    150g/5oz/1¼ cups grated (shredded)
    Caerphilly, Lancashire or Cantal cheese
    30ml/2 tbsp chopped fresh parsley
    5ml/1 tsp chopped fresh sage
    or marjoram
    2 large eggs, beaten
    pinch of cayenne pepper
    65g/2½oz/⅔ cup dry white
    breadcrumbs
    oil, for shallow frying
    salt and ground black pepper
For the sauce
    30ml/2 tbsp extra virgin olive oil or
    sunflower oil
    2 garlic cloves, thinly sliced
    1 fresh red chilli, seeded and finely
    chopped, or a good pinch of dried
    red chilli flakes
    1 small onion, finely chopped
    500g/1¼lb tomatoes, peeled, seeded
    and chopped
    a few fresh thyme sprigs
    10ml/2 tsp balsamic vinegar or red
    wine vinegar
    pinch of light muscovado (molasses) sugar
    15–30ml/1–2 tbsp chopped fresh
    marjoram or oregano

VARIATION
These sausages are also delicious served
with garlic mayonnaise or a confit of
slow-cooked red onions.

1 Melt the butter and fry the leeks for
4–5 minutes, until softened but not
browned. Tip into a bowl and add the
mashed potato, fresh breadcrumbs,
cheese, chopped fresh parsley and sage
or marjoram. Mix well. Add sufficient
beaten egg (about two-thirds of the
quantity) to bind the mixture. Season
well and add a good pinch of cayenne.

2 Shape the mixture into 12 sausage
shapes. Dip in the remaining egg, then
coat in the dry breadcrumbs. Chill the
coated sausages.

3 For the sauce, heat the oil over a low
heat and cook the garlic, chilli and
onion for 3–4 minutes. Add the
tomatoes, thyme and vinegar. Season
with salt, pepper and sugar.

4 Cook the sauce for 40–50 minutes,
until reduced. Remove the thyme and
purée the sauce in a blender. Reheat
with the marjoram or oregano, then
adjust the seasoning, adding more
sugar, if necessary.

5 Fry the sausages in shallow oil until
golden brown on all sides. Drain on
kitchen paper and serve with the sauce.

BAKED HERB CRÊPES ^{WITH} TOMATO SAUCE

TURN LIGHT HERB CRÊPES INTO SOMETHING SPECIAL. FILL WITH A SPINACH, CHEESE AND PINE NUT FILLING, THEN BAKE AND SERVE WITH A DELICIOUS TOMATO SAUCE.

SERVES FOUR

INGREDIENTS
    25g/1oz/½ cup chopped fresh herbs
    15ml/1 tbsp sunflower oil, plus extra
      for frying and greasing
    120ml/4fl oz/½ cup milk
    3 eggs
    25g/1oz/¼ cup plain
      (all-purpose) flour
    pinch of salt
For the sauce
    30ml/2 tbsp olive oil
    1 small onion, chopped
    2 garlic cloves, crushed
    400g/14oz can chopped tomatoes
    pinch of soft light brown sugar
For the filling
    450g/1lb fresh spinach, cooked
      and drained
    175g/6oz/¾ cup ricotta cheese
    25g/1oz/¼ cup pine nuts, toasted
    5 sun-dried tomato halves in olive
      oil, drained and chopped
    30ml/2 tbsp shredded fresh basil
    salt, grated nutmeg and ground
      black pepper
    4 egg whites

1 To make the crêpes, place the herbs and oil in a food processor and process until smooth. Add the milk, eggs, flour and salt, and process again until smooth. Leave to rest for 30 minutes.

2 Heat a small non-stick frying pan and add a very small amount of oil. Pour out any excess oil and pour in a ladleful of the batter. Swirl around until the batter covers the base evenly.

3 Cook the crêpe for 2 minutes, turn over and cook for a further 1–2 minutes. Make 7 more crêpes in the same way.

4 To make the sauce, heat the oil in a small pan, add the onion and garlic, and cook gently for 5 minutes. Stir in the tomatoes and sugar, and cook for about 10 minutes until thickened. Purée in a blender, then sieve and set aside.

5 To make the filling, put the spinach in a bowl and add the ricotta, pine nuts, tomatoes and basil. Season with salt, nutmeg and pepper, and mix well.

6 Preheat the oven to 190°C/375°F/ Gas 5. Whisk the 4 egg whites until they are stiff and stand in peaks. Stir one-third into the spinach mixture, then gently fold in the rest.

7 Place 1 crêpe at a time on a lightly oiled baking sheet, add a spoonful of filling and fold into quarters. Bake for 12 minutes until set.

8 Meanwhile, pour the tomato sauce into a small pan and reheat it gently, stirring occasionally. Serve with the crêpes.

MEXICAN TORTILLA PARCELS

SEEDED GREEN CHILLIES ADD JUST A FLICKER OF FIRE TO THE SPICY TOMATO FILLING IN THESE PARCELS, WHICH ARE PERFECT AS A MAIN COURSE, APPETIZER OR SNACK.

SERVES FOUR

INGREDIENTS

675g/1½lb tomatoes
60ml/4 tbsp sunflower oil
1 large onion, finely sliced
1 garlic clove, crushed
10ml/2 tsp cumin seeds
2 fresh green chillies, seeded
  and chopped
30ml/2 tbsp tomato purée (paste)
1 vegetable stock (bouillon) cube
200g/7oz can sweetcorn, drained
15ml/1 tbsp chopped fresh
  coriander (cilantro)
115g/4oz/1 cup grated Cheddar cheese
8 wheat tortillas
fresh coriander (cilantro), shredded
  lettuce and sour cream, to serve

1 Peel the tomatoes: place them in a heatproof bowl, add boiling water to cover and leave for 30 seconds. Lift out with a slotted spoon and plunge into a bowl of cold water. Leave for 1 minute, then drain. Slip the skins off the tomatoes and chop the flesh.

2 Heat half the oil in a frying pan and fry the onion with the garlic and cumin seeds for 5 minutes, until the onion softens. Add the chillies and tomatoes, then stir in the tomato purée. Crumble the stock cube over, stir well and cook gently for 5 minutes, until the chilli is soft but the tomato has not completely broken down. Stir in the sweetcorn and fresh coriander and heat gently to warm through. Keep warm.

3 Sprinkle grated cheese in the middle of each tortilla. Spoon some tomato mixture over the cheese. Fold over one edge of the tortilla, then the sides and finally the remaining edge, to enclose the filling completely.

4 Heat the remaining oil in a frying pan and fry the filled tortillas for 1–2 minutes on each side until golden and crisp. Lift them out carefully with tongs and drain on kitchen paper. Serve immediately, with coriander, shredded lettuce and sour cream.

COOK'S TIP
Mexican wheat tortillas (sometimes described as wheatflour tortillas) are available in most supermarkets. They are handy to keep in the pantry as a wrapping for a variety of vegetable mixtures.

MEDITERRANEAN ONE-CRUST PIE

THIS FREE-FORM PIE ENCASES A RICH TOMATO, AUBERGINE AND KIDNEY BEAN FILLING. IF YOUR PASTRY CRACKS, JUST PATCH IT UP — IT ADDS TO THE PIE'S RUSTIC CHARACTER.

SERVES FOUR

INGREDIENTS

500g/1¼lb aubergine (eggplant), cubed
1 red (bell) pepper
30ml/2 tbsp olive oil
1 large onion, finely chopped
1 courgette (zucchini), sliced
2 garlic cloves, crushed
15ml/1 tbsp chopped fresh oregano
  or 5ml/1 tsp dried, plus extra fresh
  oregano to garnish
200g/7oz can red kidney beans,
  rinsed and drained
115g/4oz/1 cup pitted black
  olives, rinsed
350ml/12fl oz/1½ cups passata
  (bottled strained tomatoes)
1 egg, beaten
30ml/2 tbsp semolina
salt and ground black pepper
For the pastry
75g/3oz/¾ cup plain (all-purpose) flour
75g/3oz/¾ cup wholemeal (whole-
  wheat) flour
75g/3oz/6 tbsp margarine
50g/2oz/⅔ cup freshly grated
  (shredded) Parmesan cheese

1 Preheat the oven to 220°C/425°F/ Gas 7. To make the pastry, sift the flours into a large bowl. Rub in the margarine until the mixture resembles breadcrumbs, then stir in the Parmesan. Mix in enough cold water to form a fine dough.

2 Turn out on to a lightly floured work surface and form into a smooth ball. Wrap the dough in clear film or place in a plastic bag. Chill for about 30 minutes.

3 To make the filling, place the cubed aubergine in a colander and sprinkle with salt, then leave for about 30 minutes. Rinse and pat dry with kitchen paper. Meanwhile, place the pepper on a baking sheet and roast in the oven for 20 minutes. Put the pepper in a plastic bag and leave until cool enough to handle. Peel and seed, then dice the flesh. Set aside.

4 Heat the oil in a large, heavy frying pan. Fry the onion for 5 minutes until softened, stirring occasionally. Add the aubergine and fry for 5 minutes, until tender. Add the courgette, garlic and oregano, and cook for a further 5 minutes, stirring frequently. Add the kidney beans and olives, stir, then add the passata and red pepper. Cook for 5 minutes, then set aside to cool.

5 Roll out the pastry to a rough round and place on a lightly oiled baking sheet. Brush with beaten egg, sprinkle over the semolina, leaving a 4cm/1½in border, then spoon over the filling. Gather up the edges of the pastry to partly cover the filling. Brush with the egg and bake for 30–35 minutes until golden. Garnish with oregano.

VEGETABLE TARTE TATIN

SAVOURY UPSIDE-DOWN TARTS ARE BECOMING INCREASINGLY POPULAR. THIS ONE COMBINES MEDITERRANEAN VEGETABLES WITH A MEDLEY OF RICE, GARLIC, ONIONS AND OLIVES.

SERVES TWO

INGREDIENTS

30ml/2 tbsp sunflower oil
25ml/1½ tbsp olive oil
1 aubergine (eggplant),
   sliced lengthways
1 large red (bell) pepper, seeded and
   cut into long strips
10 tomatoes
2 red shallots, finely chopped
1–2 garlic cloves, crushed
150ml/¼ pint/⅔ cup white wine
10ml/2 tsp chopped fresh basil
225g/8oz/2 cups cooked white or
   brown long grain rice
40g/1½oz/scant ½ cup pitted black
   olives, chopped
350g/12oz puff pastry, thawed
   if frozen
ground black pepper
salad leaves, to serve

COOK'S TIP
This tart would make a lovely lunch or
supper dish. Serve it hot with buttered
new potatoes and a green vegetable,
such as mangetouts (snow peas),
sugarsnap peas or green beans.

1 Preheat the oven to 190°C/375°F/
Gas 5. Heat the sunflower oil with
15ml/1 tbsp of the olive oil in a frying
pan and fry the aubergine slices, in
batches if necessary, for 4–5 minutes
on each side until golden brown. As
each aubergine slice softens and
browns, lift it out and drain on several
sheets of kitchen paper to remove as
much oil as possible.

2 Add the pepper strips to the oil
remaining in the pan, turning them to
coat. Cover the pan with a lid or foil
and sweat the peppers over a medium
high heat for 5–6 minutes, stirring
occasionally, until the pepper strips are
soft and flecked with brown.

3 Slice two of the tomatoes and set
them aside.

4 Plunge the remaining tomatoes into
boiling water for 30 seconds, then
drain. Peel them, cut them into quarters
and remove the core and seeds. Chop
them roughly.

5 Heat the remaining oil in the frying
pan and fry the shallots and garlic for
3–4 minutes until softened. Add the
chopped tomatoes and cook for a few
minutes until softened.

6 Stir in the wine and basil, with black
pepper to taste. Bring to the boil, then
remove from the heat and stir in the
cooked rice and pitted black olives,
making sure they are well distributed.

7 Arrange the tomato slices, aubergine
slices and peppers in a single layer over
the base of a heavy, 30cm/12in shallow
ovenproof dish. Spread the rice mixture
on top.

8 Roll out the pastry to a circle slightly
larger than the diameter of the dish and
place it on top of the rice, tucking the
overlap down inside the dish.

9 Bake for 25–30 minutes, until the
pastry is golden and risen. Cool slightly,
then invert the tart on to a large,
warmed serving plate. Serve in slices,
with a leafy green salad or simply
dressed lamb's lettuce or mâche.

VARIATIONS
• Use large courgettes (zucchini) instead
of aubergine slices.
• Instead of using only red pepper, use
a mixture of red, yellow and orange.
• Red shallots can be hard to come by;
substitute 1 red onion.
• Omit the black olives and add
currants instead.

TOMATO <u>AND</u> BASIL TART

THIS IS A VERY SIMPLE YET EXTREMELY TASTY TART MADE WITH RICH SHORTCRUST PASTRY, TOPPED WITH SLICES OF MOZZARELLA CHEESE AND TOMATOES, DRIZZLED WITH OLIVE OIL AND DOTTED WITH FRESH BASIL LEAVES. IT TASTES BEST HOT.

SERVES FOUR

INGREDIENTS
   150g/5oz mozzarella cheese,
     thinly sliced
   4 large tomatoes, thickly sliced
   about 10 fresh basil leaves
   30ml/2 tbsp olive oil
   2 garlic cloves, thinly sliced
   sea salt and ground black pepper
For the pastry
   115g/4oz/1 cup plain (all-purpose)
     flour, plus extra for dusting
   pinch of salt
   50g/2oz/¼ cup butter, at room
     temperature
   1 egg yolk, cold

1 To prepare the pastry, sift the flour and salt into a bowl. Rub in the butter until the mixture resembles fine breadcrumbs. Beat the egg yolk and add to the crumb-like mixture. Add a little water at a time, and mix together until the dough is smooth. Knead lightly on a floured work surface for a few minutes. Place in a plastic bag and chill for about 1 hour in a refrigerator.

2 Preheat the oven to 190°C/375°F/ Gas 5. Remove the pastry from the refrigerator, allow about 10 minutes for it to return to room temperature and then roll out into a 20cm/8in round. The pastry should be an even thickness all over.

3 Press the pastry into a 20cm/8in flan tin (tart pan). Bake in the oven for 10 minutes. Allow to cool. Reduce the oven temperature to 180°C/350°F/Gas 4.

4 Arrange the mozzarella slices over the pastry. On top, arrange the sliced tomatoes. Dip the basil leaves in olive oil and arrange them on the tomatoes.

5 Sprinkle the garlic on top, drizzle with the remaining oil and season. Bake the tart for 45 minutes, or until the pastry case is golden brown and tomatoes are well cooked. Serve hot.

SPICY TOMATO TART WITH TOMATO ROSES

SERVE THIS CHILLI-FLAVOURED TOMATO TART HOT OR COLD WITH A FRESH, CRISPY SALAD. FOR AN IMPRESSIVE FINISHING TOUCH, GARNISH WITH PRETTY TOMATO ROSES.

SERVES EIGHT TO TEN

INGREDIENTS
300g/11oz/2¾ cups self-raising
(self-rising) flour
200g/7oz/scant 1 cup butter, diced
45–60ml/3–4 tbsp cold water
salt and ground black pepper
tomato roses and a sprig of basil,
to garnish
For the filling
30ml/2 tbsp olive oil
2 onions, thinly sliced
1 garlic clove, crushed
1.3–1.6kg/3–3½lb tomatoes, peeled
and chopped
2 dried chillies, seeded and chopped
120ml/4fl oz/½ cup passata
(bottled strained)
30ml/2 tbsp sugar

1 Place the flour, a pinch of salt and the butter in a food processor or blender; process into breadcrumbs.

2 Add the water and process for another 5–10 seconds. Turn out on to a floured work surface and knead to a firm dough. Wrap in clear film and chill in the refrigerator for 30 minutes. Preheat the oven to 190°C/375°F/Gas 5.

3 Make the filling. Heat the olive oil in a large frying pan, add the onions and garlic and fry for 10 minutes. Stir in the chopped tomatoes and chillies. Bring to the boil, lower the heat and simmer for 20–25 minutes until thickened. Add the passata and sugar, and simmer for 5 minutes more. Season and cool.

4 On a lightly floured work surface, roll out the pastry and line a deep 25cm/ 10in flan tin (tart pan). Prick the base of the pastry, line with baking parchment and fill with baking beans. Bake blind for 15 minutes, then remove the beans and paper. Return the flan tin to the oven for a further 5 minutes.

5 Pour the tomato sauce into the pastry case, spreading it out evenly. Return the tomato tart to the oven and bake for 20–25 minutes.

6 Serve the tomato tart hot or at room temperature. Garnish with tomato roses and a sprig of basil.

TOMATO AND BLACK OLIVE TART

THIS DELICIOUS TART HAS A FRESH, RICH MEDITERRANEAN FLAVOUR. SINCE THE FLAVOUR OF THE TOMATOES IS QUITE OBVIOUS IN THIS DISH, IT IS PERFECT FOR TRYING DIFFERENT TOMATO VARIETIES.

SERVES FOUR

INGREDIENTS
   6 firm plum tomatoes, or other tasty
     tomatoes
   75g/3oz ripe Brie cheese
   about 16 black olives, pitted
   3 eggs, beaten
   300ml/½ pint/1¼ cups milk
   30ml/2 tbsp chopped fresh herbs,
     such as parsley, marjoram or basil
   salt and ground black pepper
   salad or cooked vegetables, to serve
For the pastry
   115g/4oz/½ cup butter
   225g/8oz/2 cups plain (all-purpose)
     flour, plus extra for dusting
   1 egg yolk

1 To make the pastry, rub together the butter and flour until it resembles fine breadcrumbs. Blend in the egg yolk and a little cold water, then mix thoroughly to form a smooth dough. Cover and leave for 10 minutes.

2 Preheat the oven to 190°C/375°F/ Gas 5. Roll out the pastry thinly on a lightly floured surface. Line a 28 x 18cm/ 11 x 7in loose-based rectangular flan tin (tart pan), trimming off any overhanging edges with a sharp knife.

3 Line the pastry case with greaseproof (waxed) paper and weigh it down with baking beans, and bake blind for 15 minutes. Remove the paper and beans, and bake for a further 5 minutes until the base is crisp.

4 Meanwhile, slice the tomatoes, cube the cheese, and slice the olives. Mix together the eggs, milk, seasoning and herbs.

5 Place the prepared flan case on a baking tray, arrange the tomatoes, cheese and olives on the base, then pour in the egg mixture.

6 Transfer carefully to the oven and bake for about 40 minutes until just firm and turning golden. Slice hot or cool in the tin and then serve with salad or cooked vegetables.

PEPPERY TOMATO PIZZA

PEPPERY ROCKET AND AROMATIC FRESH BASIL ADD COLOUR AND FLAVOUR TO THIS CRISP PIZZA, A PERFECT ADDITION TO ANY PICNIC, BUFFET OR OUTDOOR MEAL.

SERVES TWO

INGREDIENTS
10ml/2 tsp olive oil
1 garlic clove, crushed
150g/5oz can chopped tomatoes
2.5ml/½ tsp caster (superfine) sugar
30ml/2 tbsp torn fresh basil leaves
2 tomatoes, seeded and chopped
150g/5oz mozzarella cheese, sliced
20g/¾oz rocket (arugula) leaves
For the pizza base
225g/8oz/2 cups strong white
(bread) flour
5ml/1 tsp salt
2.5ml/½ tsp easy-blend (rapid-rise)
dried yeast
30ml/2 tbsp olive oil

1 Make the pizza base. Place the dry ingredients in a bowl. Add the oil and 150ml/¼ pint/⅔ cup warm water. Mix to form a soft dough.

2 Turn out the dough and knead until it is smooth and elastic. Place in an oiled bowl and cover. Leave in a warm place for 45 minutes or until doubled in bulk.

3 Preheat the oven to 220°C/425°F/ Gas 7. Make the topping. Heat the oil in a frying pan and fry the garlic for 1 minute. Add the canned tomatoes and sugar, and cook for 10 minutes.

4 Knead the risen dough lightly, then roll out to form a rough 30cm/12in round. Place on a lightly oiled baking sheet and push up the edges of the dough to form a shallow, even rim.

5 Season the tomato mixture and stir in the basil. Spoon it over the pizza base, then top with the chopped fresh tomatoes. Arrange the mozzarella slices on top of the tomato mixture. Season with sea salt and pepper and drizzle with a little olive oil.

6 Bake for 10–12 minutes until crisp and golden. Scatter the rocket leaves over the pizza just before serving.

MUSHROOM, SWEETCORN <u>AND</u> PLUM TOMATO WHOLEWHEAT PIZZA

THIS TASTY VEGETABLE PIZZA CAN BE SERVED HOT OR COLD WITH A MIXED BEAN SALAD AND FRESH CRUSTY BREAD OR BAKED POTATOES. IT IS ALSO IDEAL FOR PICNICS OR PACKED LUNCHES.

SERVES TWO

INGREDIENTS
30ml/2 tbsp tomato purée (paste)
10ml/2 tsp dried basil
10ml/2 tsp olive oil
1 onion, sliced
1 garlic clove, crushed or
   finely chopped
2 small courgettes (zucchini), sliced
115g/4oz mushrooms, sliced
115g/4oz/⅔ cup canned or
   frozen sweetcorn
4 plum tomatoes, sliced
50g/2oz/½ cup Red Leicester cheese,
   finely grated (shredded)
50g/2oz mozzarella cheese,
   finely grated
salt and ground black pepper
basil sprigs, to garnish
mixed bean salad and fresh
   crusty bread or baked potatoes,
   to serve
For the pizza base
225g/8oz/2 cups plain (all-purpose
   whole-wheat) wholemeal flour
pinch of salt
10ml/2 tsp baking powder
50g/2oz/4 tbsp margarine
about 150ml/¼ pint/⅔ cup milk

1 Preheat the oven to 220°C/425°F/ Gas 7. Grease a baking sheet with a little oil. Put the flour, salt and baking powder in a bowl and rub the margarine lightly into the flour until it resembles breadcrumbs.

2 Add enough milk to form a soft dough and knead. Roll the dough out to a circle about 25cm/10in in diameter.

3 Place the dough on the prepared baking sheet and make the edges slightly thicker than the centre. Spread the tomato purée over the base and sprinkle the basil on top.

4 Heat the oil in a frying pan, add the onion, garlic, courgettes and mushrooms, and cook gently for 10 minutes, stirring occasionally.

5 Spread the hot vegetable mixture over the pizza base, sprinkle over the sweetcorn and season with salt and ground black pepper. Arrange the tomato slices on top.

6 Mix together the Red Leicester and mozzarella cheeses and sprinkle over the pizza. Bake for 25–30 minutes, until the dough is cooked and the cheese is golden brown. Serve the pizza hot or cold in slices, garnished with basil sprigs, with bean salad and crusty bread or baked potatoes.

CLASSIC MARINARA PIZZA

THE COMBINATION OF SIMPLE INGREDIENTS, FRESH GARLIC, GOOD-QUALITY OLIVE OIL AND A FRESH TOMATO SAUCE GIVES THIS PIZZA AN UNMISTAKABLY ITALIAN FLAVOUR. ALTHOUGH PLAIN IN LOOKS, THE TASTE OF THE MARINARA IS UTTERLY DELICIOUS.

SERVES TWO

INGREDIENTS
    60ml/4 tbsp extra virgin olive oil or
      sunflower oil
    675g/1½lb plum tomatoes, peeled,
      seeded and chopped
    4 garlic cloves, cut into slivers
    15ml/1 tbsp chopped
      fresh oregano
    salt and ground black pepper
For the pizza base
    225g/8oz/2 cups plain (all-purpose)
      white flour
    pinch of salt
    10ml/2 tsp baking powder
    50g/2oz/4 tbsp margarine
    about 150ml/¼ pint/⅔ cup milk

1 Preheat the oven to 220°C/425°F/ Gas 7. Use non-stick baking parchment to line a baking sheet. Sieve the flour, salt and baking powder in a bowl and rub the margarine lightly into the flour until it resembles breadcrumbs.

2 Pour in enough milk to form a soft dough and knead. Roll the dough out to a circle about 25cm/10in in diameter.

3 Place the dough on the prepared baking sheet and make the edges slightly thicker than the centre.

4 Heat 30ml/2 tbsp of the oil in a pan. Add the seeded and chopped plum tomatoes and cook, stirring frequently for about 5 minutes until soft.

5 Place the tomatoes in a sieve over a bowl and leave to drain for about 5 minutes.

6 Empty the juice from the bowl and force the tomatoes through the sieve, into the bowl with the back of a spoon. You may also use a food processor or blender and beat until the tomatoes are smooth.

7 Brush the pizza base with half the remaining oil. Spoon over the tomatoes and sprinkle with garlic and oregano. Drizzle over the remaining oil and season with salt and pepper.

8 Bake for 15–20 minutes in the oven until the pizza is crisp and golden. Serve immediately.

CLASSIC MARGHERITA PIZZA

THIS TOMATO, BASIL AND MOZZARELLA PIZZA IS SIMPLE TO PREPARE. THE SWEET FLAVOUR OF SUN-RIPE TOMATOES WORKS WONDERFULLY WITH THE BASIL AND MOZZARELLA.

SERVES TWO

INGREDIENTS
   30ml/2 tbsp olive oil
   1 onion, finely chopped
   1 garlic clove, crushed
   400g/14oz can chopped tomatoes
   15ml/1 tbsp tomato purée (paste)
   pinch of granulated sugar
   15ml/1 tbsp chopped fresh basil
   150g/5oz mozzarella cheese
   4 ripe tomatoes, sliced
   6–8 fresh basil leaves
   30ml/2 tbsp grated Parmesan cheese
   salt and ground black pepper
For the pizza base
   225g/8oz/2 cups strong white
     (bread) flour
   5ml/1 tsp salt
   2.5ml/½ tsp easy-blend (rapid-rise)
     dried yeast
   15ml/1 tbsp olive oil
   150ml/¼ pint/⅔ cup warm water

1 Make the pizza base. Place the dry ingredients in a bowl. Add the oil and water. Mix to a soft dough and knead for 10 minutes. Cover and put in a warm place until doubled in bulk.

2 Preheat the oven to 220°C/425°F/ Gas 7. Make the topping. Fry the onion and garlic for 5 minutes in half the oil. Stir in the tomatoes, purée and sugar. Cook for 5 minutes. Stir in the basil and seasoning.

3 Knead the dough lightly for 5 minutes, then roll out to a round and place on a baking sheet.

4 Use a spoon to spread the tomato topping evenly over the base. Cut the mozzarella cheese and fresh tomatoes into thick slices. Arrange them in a circle, alternating the cheese with the tomato slices.

5 Roughly tear the basil leaves, add to the pizza and sprinkle with the Parmesan cheese. Drizzle over the remaining oil and season well with black pepper. Bake for 15–20 minutes until crisp and golden. Serve immediately.

SUN-DRIED TOMATO CALZONE

CALZONE IS A TRADITIONAL FOLDED PIZZA. IN THIS TASTY VEGETARIAN VERSION, YOU CAN ADD MORE OR FEWER RED CHILLI FLAKES, DEPENDING ON PERSONAL TASTE.

<u>SERVES TWO</u>

INGREDIENTS
    4 baby aubergines (eggplant)
    3 shallots, chopped
    45ml/3 tbsp olive oil
    1 garlic clove, chopped
    50g/2oz/⅓ cup sun-dried tomatoes
       in oil, drained
    1.5ml/¼ tsp dried red chilli flakes
    10ml/2 tsp chopped fresh thyme
    75g/3oz mozzarella cheese, cubed
    salt and ground black pepper
    15–30ml/1–2 tbsp freshly grated
       Parmesan cheese, plus extra to serve
For the dough
    225g/8oz/2 cups strong white
       (bread) flour
    5ml/1 tsp salt
    2.5ml/½ tsp easy-blend (rapid-rise)
       dried yeast
    15ml/1 tbsp olive oil
    150ml/¼ pint/⅔ cup warm water

1 Make the dough. Place the dry ingredients in a bowl and mix to form a soft dough with the oil and water. Knead for 10 minutes. Put in an oiled bowl, cover and leave in a warm place until doubled in size.

2 Preheat the oven to 220°C/425°F/ Gas 7. Dice the aubergines. Fry the shallots in a little oil until soft. Add the aubergines, garlic, sun-dried tomatoes, chilli, thyme and seasoning. Cook for 5 minutes. Divide the dough in half and roll out each piece on a lightly floured work surface to an 18cm/7in circle.

3 Spread the aubergine mixture over half of each circle, leaving a 2.5cm/1in border, then scatter over the mozzarella. Dampen the edges with water, then fold over the dough to enclose the filling. Press the edges firmly together to seal. Place on greased baking sheets.

4 Brush with half the remaining oil and make a small hole in the top of each calzone to allow steam to escape. Bake for 15–20 minutes until golden. Remove from the oven and brush with the remaining oil. Sprinkle over the Parmesan and serve immediately.

To give savoury dishes a kick, serve some salsa — from mild and fruity Guacamole to fiery Salsa, there are many variations on the basic theme. As for cold meats and cheeses, they become much more interesting when served with a dollop of Green Tomato Chutney or a spoonful of Apple and Tomato Chutney. Tomatoes can even be used to make striking cocktails and delicious home-made bread — for a real treat make Sun-dried Tomato Bread and eat it straight from the oven with butter.

Drinks, Salsas, and Breads

VIRGIN PRAIRIE OYSTER

THIS IS A DELICIOUS NON-ALCOHOLIC VERSION OF THE TOMATO COCKTAIL BASED ON THE BLOODY MARY AND THE VIRGIN MARY. IT CAN BE DRUNK WITHOUT THE RAW EGG YOLK, IF THAT DOES NOT APPEAL TO YOU. IF YOU CAN, USE ONLY FRESH, FREE-RANGE ORGANIC EGGS.

SERVES ONE

INGREDIENTS
  175ml/6fl oz/³⁄₄ cup tomato juice
  ice cubes
  10ml/2 tsp Worcestershire sauce
  5–10ml/1–2 tsp balsamic vinegar
  1 egg yolk
  cayenne pepper, to taste

VARIATION
Shake together equal quantities of fresh grapefruit juice and tomato juice with a dash of Worcestershire sauce. Strain into a tall and narrow highball glass.

1 Measure the tomato juice into a large glass and stir over plenty of ice, until well chilled.

2 Strain into a tall glass half-filled with ice cubes.

3 Add the Worcestershire sauce and balsamic vinegar, to taste, and use a stirrer to mix together.

4 Float the egg yolk on top and lightly dust with cayenne pepper.

COOK'S TIP
The very young, the elderly, pregnant women and those in ill-health or with a compromised immune system are advised against consuming raw eggs.

DICKSON'S BLOODY MARY

IT WAS IN NEW YORK THAT THE LIFE-ENHANCING DASH OF TABASCO SAUCE WAS FIRST ADDED TO THIS CLASSIC MORNING-AFTER REVIVER. IN CAJUN COUNTRY THEY MAKE THEIR BLOODY MARYS BY THE JUGFUL AND DRINK IT BY THE JUGFUL!

SERVES ONE

INGREDIENTS
  ice cubes
  45ml/3 tbsp vodka or chilli-flavoured
    vodka
  25ml/1½ tbsp *fino* sherry
  150ml/¼ pint/⅔ cup tomato juice
  25ml/1½ tbsp lemon juice
  10–15ml/2–3 tsp Worcestershire
    sauce
  2–3 dashes Tabasco sauce
  2.5ml/½ tsp creamed horseradish
    relish
  5ml/1 tsp celery salt
  celery stick, stuffed green olives and
    cherry tomato, to garnish

3 Take a chilled glass and half fill it with whole ice cubes or cracked ice, if preferred. Use either a sieve, colander or special straining lid and pour the tomato cocktail mixture into the chilled, long tumbler.

4 Add a decorative stick of celery that can be used to stir the drink. Finish off the cocktail by threading a cocktail stick or toothpick with stuffed green olives and a cherry tomato, and add to the rim of the glass.

1 Fill a tall glass with cracked ice and add the combined vodka, sherry and tomato juice. Stir well.

2 Add the lemon juice, Worcestershire sauce and Tabasco sauce. Mix the ingredients together well, then stir in creamed horseradish to taste, the celery salt, salt and black pepper. Stir.

CLASSIC TOMATO SALSA

THIS IS THE TRADITIONAL TOMATO-BASED SALSA THAT MOST PEOPLE ASSOCIATE WITH MEXICAN FOOD. THERE ARE INNUMERABLE RECIPES FOR IT, BUT THE BASIC INGREDIENTS OF ONION, TOMATO AND CHILLI ARE COMMON TO EVERY ONE OF THEM. SERVE THIS SALSA AS A CONDIMENT. IT GOES WELL WITH A WIDE VARIETY OF DISHES.

SERVES SIX AS AN ACCOMPANIMENT

INGREDIENTS
3–6 fresh Serrano chillies
1 large white onion
grated (shredded) rind and juice of
   2 limes, plus strips of lime rind,
   to garnish
8 ripe, firm tomatoes
large bunch of fresh coriander (cilantro)
1.5ml/¼ tsp sugar
salt

VARIATIONS
• Use spring onions (scallions) or mild red onions instead of white onion.
• For a smoky flavour, use chipotle chillies instead of Serrano chillies.

1 Use 3 chillies for a salsa of medium heat; up to 6 if you like it hot. To peel the chillies, spear them on a long-handled metal skewer and roast them over the flame of a gas burner until the skins blister and darken. Do not let the flesh burn. Alternatively, dry-fry them in a griddle pan until the skins are scorched.

2 Place the roasted chillies in a strong plastic bag and tie the top of the bag to keep the steam in. Set aside for about 20 minutes.

3 Meanwhile, chop the onion finely and put it in a bowl with the lime rind and juice. The lime juice will soften the onion considerably.

4 Remove the chillies from the bag and peel off the skins. Cut off the stalks, then slit the chillies and scrape out the seeds. Chop the flesh and set it aside in a small bowl.

5 Cut a small cross in the base of each tomato. Place in a heatproof bowl and pour over boiling water to cover.

6 Lift out the tomatoes and plunge them into a bowl of cold water. Drain well. Remove the skins.

7 Dice the peeled tomatoes and put them in a bowl. Add the chopped onion, which should by now have softened, together with any remaining lime juice and rind. Chop the coriander finely.

8 Add the chopped coriander to the salsa, with the chillies and the sugar. Mix gently until the sugar has dissolved and all the ingredients are coated in lime juice. Cover and chill for 2–3 hours to allow the flavours to blend. Garnish with the extra strips of lime rind just before serving.

COOK'S TIP
The salsa can be made ahead of time. The flavour will intensify on keeping. Scrape the salsa into a jar and cover tightly, or simply cover the bowl with a double thickness of clear film. Store in the refrigerator for 3–4 days.

ROASTED TOMATO SALSA

SLOW ROASTING THESE TOMATOES TO A SEMI-DRIED STATE RESULTS IN A VERY RICH, FULL-FLAVOURED SWEET SAUCE. THE COSTENO AMARILLO CHILLI IS MILD AND HAS A FRESH LIGHT FLAVOUR, MAKING IT THE PERFECT PARTNER FOR THE RICH TOMATO TASTE. THIS SALSA IS GREAT WITH TUNA OR SEA BASS AND MAKES A MARVELLOUS SANDWICH FILLING WHEN TEAMED WITH CREAMY CHEESE.

SERVES SIX AS AN ACCOMPANIMENT

INGREDIENTS
  500g/1¼lb tomatoes
  8 small shallots
  5 garlic cloves
  1 fresh rosemary sprig
  2 costeno amarillo chillies
  grated (shredded) rind and juice of
    ½ small lemon
  30ml/2 tbsp extra virgin olive oil
  1.5ml/¼ tsp soft dark brown sugar
  sea salt

1 Preheat the oven to 160°C/325°F/ Gas 3. Cut the tomatoes into quarters and place them on a baking sheet.

2 Peel the shallots and garlic, and add them to the baking sheet. Sprinkle with sea salt. Roast in the oven for 1¼ hours or until the tomatoes are beginning to dry. If necessary, reduce the oven temperature to 150°C/300°F/Gas 2. Do not let the tomatoes burn or blacken or they will have a bitter taste.

3 Leave the tomatoes to cool, then peel off the skins and chop the flesh finely. Place in a bowl. Remove the outer layer of skin from any shallots that have toughened during cooking.

4 Using a large, sharp knife, chop the shallots and garlic roughly; place them with the tomatoes in a bowl and mix.

5 Strip the rosemary leaves from the woody stem and chop them finely. Add half to the tomato and shallot mixture and mix lightly.

6 Soak the chillies in hot water for about 10 minutes until soft. Drain, remove the stalks, slit them and scrape out the seeds with a sharp knife. Chop the flesh finely and add it to the tomato mixture. Mix well.

7 Stir in the lemon rind and juice, the olive oil and the sugar. Mix well, taste, and add more salt if needed. Cover and chill for at least 1 hour before serving, sprinkled with the remaining rosemary. The salsa will keep for up to 1 week in the refrigerator.

COOK'S TIP
Use plum tomatoes or vine tomatoes for this salsa – they have more flavour than tomatoes that have been grown for their keeping properties rather than their taste. Cherry tomatoes make delicious roasted tomato salsa; you can roast them whole, and there is no need to peel them after roasting.

FRAGRANT ROASTED TOMATO SALSA

ROASTING THE TOMATOES GIVES A GREATER DEPTH TO THE FLAVOUR OF THIS SALSA, WHICH ALSO BENEFITS FROM THE WARM, ROUNDED FLAVOUR OF ROASTED CHILLIES.

SERVES SIX AS AN ACCOMPANIMENT

INGREDIENTS
    500g/1¼lb tomatoes, preferably
        beefsteak tomatoes
    2 fresh Serrano chillies or other fresh
        red chillies
    1 onion
    juice of 1 lime
    large bunch of fresh coriander (cilantro)
    salt

1 Preheat the oven to 200°C/400°F/ Gas 6. Cut the tomatoes into quarters and place them in a roasting pan. Add the chillies. Roast for 45 minutes to 1 hour, until the tomatoes and chillies are charred and softened.

2 Place the roasted chillies in a strong plastic bag. Tie the top to keep the steam in and set aside for 20 minutes. Leave the tomatoes to cool slightly, then use a small, sharp knife to remove the skins and dice the flesh.

3 Chop the onion finely, then place it in a bowl and add the lime juice and the diced tomatoes. Mix well with a wooden spoon.

4 Remove the chillies from the bag and peel off the skins. Cut off the stalks, then slit the chillies and scrape out the seeds with a sharp knife. Chop the chillies roughly and add them to the onion mixture. Mix well.

5 Chop the coriander and add most of it to the salsa. Add salt to season, cover and chill for at least 1 hour before serving, sprinkled with the remaining chopped coriander. This salsa will keep in the refrigerator for 1 week.

GUACAMOLE

ONE OF THE BEST-LOVED MEXICAN SALSAS, THIS BLEND OF CREAMY AVOCADO, TOMATOES, CHILLIES, CORIANDER AND LIME NOW APPEARS ON TABLES THE WORLD OVER. BOUGHT GUACAMOLE USUALLY CONTAINS MAYONNAISE, WHICH HELPS TO PRESERVE THE AVOCADO, BUT THIS IS NOT AN INGREDIENT THAT YOU ARE LIKELY TO FIND IN TRADITIONAL RECIPES.

SERVES SIX TO EIGHT

INGREDIENTS

  4 tomatoes
  4 ripe avocados, preferably *fuerte*
  juice of 1 lime
  ½ small onion
  2 garlic cloves
  small bunch of fresh coriander
    (cilantro), chopped
  3 fresh red fresno chillies
  salt
  tortilla chips or breadsticks, to serve

COOK'S TIP
Smooth-skinned *fuerte* avocados are native to Mexico, so would be ideal for this dip. If they are not available, use any avocados, but make sure they are ripe. To test, gently press the top of the avocado; it should give a little.

1 Cut a cross in the base of each tomato. Place the tomatoes in a heatproof bowl and pour over boiling water to cover. The easiest way to do this is to use a kettle, but some people prefer just a pan of boiling water.

2 Leave the tomatoes in the water for 30 seconds, then lift them out using a slotted spoon and plunge them into a bowl of cold water. Drain. The skins will have begun to peel back from the crosses. Remove the skins completely. Cut the tomatoes in half, remove the seeds with a teaspoon, then chop the flesh roughly and set it aside.

3 Cut the avocados in half then remove the stones (pits). Scoop the flesh out of the shells and place it in a food processor or blender. Process until almost smooth, then scrape into a bowl and stir in the freshly squeezed lime juice.

4 Chop the onion finely, then crush the garlic. Add both to the avocado and mix well. Stir in the coriander.

5 Remove the stalks from the chillies, slit them and scrape out the seeds with a small, sharp knife. Chop the chillies finely and add them to the avocado mixture, with the roughly chopped tomatoes. Mix well.

6 Taste the guacamole and add salt if needed. Cover closely with clear film or a tight-fitting lid and chill for 1 hour before serving as a dip with tortilla chips or breadsticks. If it is well covered, guacamole will keep in the refrigerator for 2–3 days.

AROMATIC GUACAMOLE

GUACAMOLE IS OFTEN SERVED AS A FIRST COURSE WITH CORN CHIPS FOR DIPPING. THIS CHUNKY VERSION IS A GREAT ACCOMPANIMENT FOR GRILLED FISH, POULTRY OR MEAT, ESPECIALLY STEAK.

SERVES FOUR

INGREDIENTS

  2 large ripe avocados
  1 small red onion, very finely chopped
  1 red or green chilli, seeded and very
    finely chopped
  ½–1 garlic clove, crushed with a
    little salt
  finely shredded rind of ½ lime and
    juice of 1–1½ limes
  pinch of sugar
  225g/8oz tomatoes, seeded
    and chopped
  30ml/2 tbsp roughly chopped fresh
    coriander (cilantro)
  2.5–5ml/½–1 tsp ground toasted
    cumin seeds
  15ml/1 tbsp olive oil
  15–30ml/1–2 tbsp sour cream
    (optional)
  salt and ground black pepper
  lime wedges dipped in sea salt, and
    fresh coriander (cilantro) sprigs,
    to garnish

1 Cut 1 avocado in half and lift out and discard the stone (pit). Scrape the flesh from both halves into a bowl and mash it roughly with a fork.

2 Stir in the onion, chilli, garlic, lime rind, sugar, tomatoes and coriander. Add the ground cumin and seasoning to taste, then stir in the olive oil.

3 Halve and stone (pit) the remaining avocado. Dice the flesh and stir it into the guacamole.

4 Squeeze in fresh lime juice to taste, mix well, then cover and leave to stand for 15 minutes so that the flavour develops. Stir in the sour cream, if using. Serve with lime wedges dipped in sea salt, and fresh coriander sprigs.

COOK'S TIP
To crush garlic, place a peeled clove on a chopping board and chop it roughly. Sprinkle over a little sea salt and, using the flat side of a large knife blade, gradually work the salt into the garlic.

SMOKY TOMATO SALSA

THE SMOKY FLAVOUR IN THIS RECIPE COMES FROM THE SMOKED BACON AND THE COMMERCIAL LIQUID SMOKE MARINADE. SERVED WITH SOUR CREAM, THIS SALSA MAKES A GREAT BAKED POTATO FILLER.

SERVES FOUR

INGREDIENTS
  450g/1lb tomatoes
  4 rindless smoked streaky (fatty)
    bacon strips
  15ml/1 tbsp vegetable oil
  45ml/3 tbsp chopped fresh coriander
    (cilantro) leaves or parsley
  1 garlic clove, finely chopped
  15ml/1 tbsp liquid smoke marinade
  freshly squeezed juice of 1 lime
  salt and ground black pepper

1 Plunge the tomatoes into boiling water for 30 seconds. Remove with a slotted spoon, dunk in cold water and then remove the skins. Halve the tomatoes, scoop out and discard the seeds, then finely dice the flesh.

2 Cut the bacon into small pieces. Heat the oil in a frying pan and cook the bacon for 5 minutes, stirring occasionally, until crisp and browned. Remove from the heat and drain on kitchen paper. Leave to cool for a few minutes, then place in a mixing bowl.

3 Add the finely diced tomatoes and the chopped fresh coriander or parsley to the bowl. Stir in the finely chopped garlic, then add the liquid smoke and freshly squeezed lime juice. Season the salsa with salt and pepper to taste and mix well, using a wooden spoon or plastic spatula.

4 Spoon the smoky salsa into a serving bowl, cover with clear film and chill until ready to serve.

VARIATION
Give this smoky salsa an extra kick by adding a dash of Tabasco sauce or a pinch of dried chilli flakes.

FRESH TOMATO <u>AND</u> TARRAGON SALSA

PLUM TOMATOES, GARLIC, OLIVE OIL AND BALSAMIC VINEGAR MAKE FOR A VERY MEDITERRANEAN SALSA — TRY SERVING THIS WITH GRILLED LAMB CUTLETS OR TOSS IT WITH FRESHLY COOKED PASTA.

<u>SERVES FOUR</u>

INGREDIENTS

8 plum tomatoes, or 500g/1¼lb
  sweet cherry tomatoes
1 small garlic clove
60ml/4 tbsp olive oil or
  sunflower oil
15ml/1 tbsp balsamic vinegar
30ml/2 tbsp chopped fresh tarragon,
  plus extra shredded leaves,
  to garnish
salt and ground black pepper

1 Plunge the tomatoes into boiling water for 30 seconds. Remove with a slotted spoon; cool in cold water.

2 Slip off the tomato skins and finely chop the flesh.

3 Using a sharp knife, crush or finely chop the garlic.

4 Whisk together the oil, balsamic vinegar and plenty of salt and pepper.

5 Add the chopped fresh tarragon to the oil mixture.

6 Mix the tomatoes and garlic in a bowl and pour the tarragon dressing over. Leave to infuse (steep) for at least 1 hour before serving at room temperature. Garnish with shredded tarragon leaves.

COOK'S TIP
Be sure to serve this salsa at room temperature as the tomatoes taste less sweet, and rather acidic, when chilled.

GRILLED CORN-ON-THE-COB SALSA

THIS IS AN UNUSUAL SALSA AND CONTAINS DELICIOUSLY SWEET VEGETABLES. USE CHERRY TOMATOES FOR AN EXTRA SPECIAL FLAVOUR, AND COMBINE WITH THE RIPEST AND FRESHEST CORN ON THE COB.

SERVES FOUR

INGREDIENTS
2 corn on the cob
30ml/2 tbsp melted butter
4 tomatoes
8 spring onions (scallions)
1 garlic clove
30ml/2 tbsp fresh lemon juice
30ml/2 tbsp olive oil
Tabasco sauce, to taste

1 Remove the husks and silky threads covering the corn on the cob. Brush the cobs with the melted butter and gently cook on the barbecue or grill (broil) them for 20–30 minutes, turning occasionally, until tender and tinged brown.

2 To remove the kernels, stand each cob upright on a chopping board and use a large, heavy knife to slice down the length of the cob.

3 Plunge the tomatoes into boiling water for 30 seconds. Remove with a slotted spoon; cool in cold water. Slip off the skins and dice the tomato flesh.

4 Place 6 spring onions on a chopping board and chop finely. Crush and chop the garlic and then mix together with the corn and tomato in a small bowl.

5 Stir the lemon juice and olive oil together, adding Tabasco sauce, salt and pepper to taste.

6 Pour this mixture over the salsa and stir well. Cover the salsa and leave to steep at room temperature for 1–2 hours before serving. Garnish with the remaining spring onions.

COOK'S TIP
Make this salsa in summer when fresh cobs of corn are readily available.

FIERY SALSA

THIS IS A SCORCHINGLY HOT SALSA FOR ONLY THE VERY BRAVE! SPREAD IT SPARINGLY ON TO COOKED MEATS AND BURGERS OR ADD A TINY AMOUNT TO A CURRY OR POT OF CHILLI.

SERVES FOUR TO SIX

INGREDIENTS

6 Scotch bonnet chillies
2 ripe tomatoes
4 standard green jalapeño chillies
30ml/2 tbsp chopped fresh parsley
30ml/2 tbsp olive oil
15ml/1 tbsp balsamic vinegar or
   sherry vinegar
salt

1 Skin the Scotch bonnet chillies, either by holding them in a gas flame for 3 minutes until the skin blackens and blisters, or by plunging them into boiling water. Then, using rubber gloves, rub off the skin from the chilli.

2 Hold each tomato in a gas flame for 3 minutes until it starts to come away, (or plunge them into a container of boiling water, if you prefer). Remove the skins, halve the tomatoes, and remove the seeds. Chop the flesh very finely.

3 Try not to touch the Scotch bonnet chillies with your bare hands: use a fork to hold them and slice them open with a sharp knife. Scrape out and discard the seeds, then finely chop the flesh.

4 Halve the jalapeño chillies, remove their seeds and finely slice them widthways into tiny strips. Mix both types of chillies, the tomatoes and the chopped parsley in a bowl.

5 In a small bowl, whisk the olive oil with the vinegar and a little salt. Pour this over the salsa and cover the dish. Chill for up to 3 days.

BLOODY MARY SALSA

*SERVE THIS PERFECT PARTY SALSA WITH STICKS OF CRUNCHY CELERY OR FINGERS OF CUCUMBER OR,
ON A REALLY SPECIAL OCCASION, WITH FRESHLY SHUCKED OYSTERS.*

SERVES TWO

INGREDIENTS
4 ripe tomatoes
1 celery stick
1 garlic clove
2 spring onions (scallions)
45ml/3 tbsp tomato juice
Worcestershire sauce, to taste
Tabasco sauce, to taste
10ml/2 tsp horseradish sauce
15ml/1 tbsp vodka
1 lemon
salt and ground black pepper

VARIATION
Blend 1–2 seeded, fresh red chillies with
the tomatoes, instead of stirring in the
Tabasco sauce.

1 Halve the tomatoes, celery and
garlic. Trim the spring onions.

2 Put the tomatoes, celery, garlic and
spring onions in a blender or food
processor. Process until finely chopped,
then transfer the vegetable mixture to a
serving bowl.

3 Stir in the tomato juice, a little at a
time, then add a few drops of
Worcestershire sauce and Tabasco
sauce to taste. Mix well and set aside
for 10–15 minutes.

4 Stir in the horseradish sauce and
vodka. Squeeze the lemon and stir the
juice into the salsa. Add salt and ground
black pepper, to taste. Serve immediately,
or cover and chill for 1–2 hours.

ORANGE, TOMATO <u>AND</u> CHIVE SALSA

FRESH CHIVES AND SWEET ORANGES PROVIDE A VERY CHEERFUL COMBINATION OF FLAVOURS. AN UNUSUAL SALSA THAT IS A VERY GOOD ACCOMPANIMENT TO SALADS.

SERVES FOUR

INGREDIENTS

 2 large, sweet oranges
 1 beefsteak tomato, or 2 plum
 tomatoes if not available
 bunch of fresh chives
 1 garlic clove
 30ml/2 tbsp extra virgin olive oil or
 grapeseed oil
 sea salt

1 Slice the base off 1 orange so that it will stand firmly on a chopping board. Using a large sharp knife, remove the peel by slicing from the top to the bottom of the orange. Repeat with the second orange.

2 Working over a bowl, segment each orange in turn. Slice towards the middle of the fruit, and slightly to one side of a segment, and then gently twist the knife to release the orange segment. Repeat. Squeeze any juice from the remaining membrane.

3 Roughly chop the orange segments and add them to the bowl with the collected orange juice. Halve the tomato and use a teaspoon to scoop the seeds into the bowl. With a sharp knife, finely dice the flesh and add to the oranges and juice in the bowl.

4 Hold the bunch of chives neatly together and use a pair of kitchen scissors to snip them into the bowl.

5 Thinly slice the garlic and stir it into the orange mixture. Pour over the olive oil, season with sea salt and stir well to mix. Serve the salsa within 2 hours.

TART TOMATO RELISH

THE WHOLE LIME USED IN THIS RECIPE ADDS A PLEASANTLY SOUR AFTERTASTE. SERVE THIS TASTY RELISH WITH GRILLED OR ROAST PORK OR LAMB. IT ALSO GOES WELL WITH OILY FISH, LIKE MACKEREL.

SERVES FOUR

INGREDIENTS

2 pieces stem (crystallized) ginger
1 lime
450g/1lb cherry tomatoes
115g/4oz/½ cup light brown sugar
105ml/7 tbsp white wine vinegar
5ml/1 tsp salt

COOK'S TIP
Jars of this relish make marvellous presents at any time of the year. Next time you are invited to dinner, take along some tart tomato relish instead of the customary bottle of wine and see how welcome it will be. Label the jar with the contents, and don't forget the storage instructions.

1 Coarsely chop the ginger. Slice the whole lime thinly, then chop it into small pieces; do not remove the rind.

2 Place the whole cherry tomatoes, sugar, vinegar, salt, ginger and lime in a pan.

3 Bring to the boil, stirring until the sugar dissolves, then simmer rapidly for 45 minutes. Stir regularly until the liquid has evaporated and the relish is thickened and pulpy.

4 Allow the relish to cool for about 5 minutes, then spoon it into clean jars. Cool completely, cover and store in the refrigerator for up to 1 month. Spoon into a bowl to serve.

TOMATO AND RED PEPPER RELISH

THIS SPICY RELISH WILL KEEP FOR AT LEAST A WEEK IN THE REFRIGERATOR. IT IS PARTICULARLY GOOD WITH SAUSAGES AND BURGERS, BUT ALSO MAKES A GREAT ACCOMPANIMENT FOR A MATURE CHEDDAR.

SERVES EIGHT

INGREDIENTS

1 onion
1 red (bell) pepper, seeded
2 garlic cloves
6 tomatoes
30ml/2 tbsp extra virgin olive oil or
  sunflower oil
5ml/1 tsp ground cinnamon
about 5ml/1 tsp chilli flakes
5ml/1 tsp ground ginger
5ml/1 tsp salt
2.5ml/½ tsp ground black pepper
75g/3oz/⅓ cup light brown sugar,
  or other dark sugar
75ml/5 tbsp cider vinegar
handful of fresh basil leaves

COOK'S TIPS
• This relish thickens slightly on cooling
so do not worry if the mixture seems a
little thin after being simmered for
20 minutes.
• The precise amount of chilli flakes
added depends upon personal taste.
Chillies can be omitted entirely, if a
milder taste is preferred. On the other
hand, the chilli flavour can be
intensified, either by adding more flakes,
or by substituting 1–2 chopped fresh
chillies for the red pepper.

2 Using a small, sharp knife, scrape
and peel off the skins from each tomato
in turn. They should slip off fairly easily,
but you may need to slice off the skin if
it sticks. Chop the tomatoes.

3 Chop the onion, pepper and garlic.
Gently heat the oil in a pan. Add the
onion, pepper and garlic to the pan.

5 Stir in the cinnamon, chilli flakes,
ginger, salt, pepper, sugar and vinegar.
Bring to the boil over a low heat,
stirring constantly until all the sugar
has dissolved.

6 Simmer the relish mixture,
uncovered, for 20 minutes, until it
becomes pulpy. Stir in the basil leaves
and check the seasoning.

1 Put the tomatoes in a heatproof bowl.
Boil some water in a kettle or pan and
then pour it over the tomatoes. Leave
for 30 seconds. Remove the tomatoes
with a slotted spoon and cool in cold
water. Drain well.

4 Cook gently for 5–8 minutes, until
the pepper has softened, but still
retains its shape. Add the chopped
tomatoes. Cover and cook for
5 minutes, stirring often, until the
tomatoes release their juices.

7 Allow the relish to cool completely,
then transfer it to a glass jar or a plastic
container with a tightly fitting lid. Cover
tightly, label if necessary and store in
the refrigerator.

TOMATO CHUTNEY

THIS SPICY CHUTNEY IS DELICIOUS SERVED WITH A SELECTION OF CHEESES AND CRACKERS, OR WITH COLD MEATS. IT IS VERY GOOD WITH BAKED HAM.

MAKES ABOUT 1.8KG/4LB

INGREDIENTS
    900g/2lb tomatoes
    225g/8oz/1⅓ cups raisins
    225g/8oz onions, chopped
    225g/8oz/1 cup caster
     (superfine) sugar
    600ml/1 pint/2½ cups malt vinegar

COOK'S TIPS
• Tomatoes make good chutney and it is interesting to compare the difference in flavour between that made with ripe red tomatoes and green tomatoes.
• The chutney will keep, unopened, for up to a year. Once opened, store in the refrigerator and consume within a week.

1 Put the tomatoes in a heatproof bowl and pour over boiling water to cover. Leave for 30 seconds, then lift out each tomato in turn with a slotted spoon and place in a bowl of cold water. Drain, then slip off the skins.

2 Chop the tomatoes roughly. Put them in a preserving pan or a large, heavy pan.

3 Add the raisins, onions and caster sugar to the pan.

4 Pour over the vinegar. Bring to the boil, then reduce the heat and let the mixture simmer for 2 hours, uncovered. Spoon the hot chutney into warm sterilized jars. Seal each jar with a waxed circle and cover with a tightly fitting cellophane top. Store in a cool, dark place for at least 1 month before using.

GREEN TOMATO CHUTNEY

THIS IS A CLASSIC CHUTNEY TO MAKE AT THE END OF SUMMER WHEN THE LAST TOMATOES ON THE PLANTS IN THE GARDEN REFUSE TO RIPEN. LOOK OUT FOR GREEN TOMATOES ON MARKET STALLS, TOO.

MAKES ABOUT 2.5KG/5½LB

INGREDIENTS
450g/1lb cooking apples
1.8–2kg/4–4½lb green and red
  tomatoes, roughly chopped
450g/1lb onions, chopped
2 large garlic cloves, crushed
15ml/1 tbsp salt
45ml/3 tbsp pickling spice
600ml/1 pint/2½ cups cider vinegar
450g/1lb/2 cups sugar

1 Quarter the apples and use a sharp knife to remove the core from each piece. Remove the skin from the apples, then chop each wedge into small pieces.

2 Place the tomatoes, apples, onions and garlic in a preserving pan or a large, heavy pan. Add the salt. Tie the pickling spice in a piece of muslin (cheesecloth) and add it to the pan.

3 Pour in half the vinegar and bring to the boil. Lower the heat and simmer for 1 hour, or until the chutney is thick, stirring frequently.

4 Dissolve the sugar in the remaining vinegar and add to the chutney. Simmer for 1½ hours until the chutney is thick, stirring occasionally. Remove the muslin bag from the chutney.

5 Spoon the hot chutney into warm, sterilized jars. Seal each jar with a waxed circle and cover with a tightly fitting cellophane top. Store in a cool, dark place for at least 1 month before using.

COOK'S TIPS
• To make it easier to retrieve the muslin bag filled with pickling spice, tie it with a piece of string to the handle of the pan.
• Use a jam funnel to transfer the chutney into the jars. Wipe the jars and label them when cold.

APPLE ^AND^ TOMATO CHUTNEY

THIS MELLOW, GOLDEN, SPICY CHUTNEY TRANSFORMS AN ORDINARY LUNCH INTO A REAL TREAT. ANY TYPE OF TOMATOES CAN BE USED SUCCESSFULLY IN THIS RECIPE.

MAKES ABOUT 1.8KG/4LB

INGREDIENTS
    1.3kg/3lb cooking apples
    1.3kg/3lb tomatoes
    2 large onions, 2 garlic cloves
    250g/9oz pitted dates
    2 red (bell) peppers
    3 dried red chillies
    15ml/1 tbsp black peppercorns
    4 cardamom pods
    15ml/1 tbsp coriander seeds
    10ml/2 tsp cumin seeds
    10ml/2 tsp ground turmeric
    15ml/1 tbsp salt
    600ml/1 pint/2½ cups distilled
      malt vinegar
    1kg/2¼lb/4½ cups granulated sugar

1   Peel and chop the apples. Peel and chop the tomatoes, onions and garlic. Quarter the dates. Core and seed the peppers, then cut into chunky pieces. Put all the prepared ingredients, except the red peppers, into a preserving pan.

2   Slit the chillies. Put the peppercorns and remaining spices into a mortar and roughly crush with a pestle. Add the chillies, spices and salt to the pan.

3   Pour in the vinegar and sugar. Leave to simmer for 30 minutes, stirring occasionally. Add the red pepper and cook for a further 30 minutes, stirring more frequently as the chutney becomes thick and pulpy.

4   Spoon into warm, dry, sterilized jars. Seal each jar with a waxed circle and cover with a tightly fitting cellophane top. Leave to cool.

SOUR CREAM DIP

THIS COOLING TOMATO AND PEPPER DIP IS A PERFECT ACCOMPANIMENT TO HOT AND SPICY DISHES.
ALTERNATIVELY, SERVE IT AS A SNACK WITH THE FIERIEST TORTILLA CHIPS YOU CAN FIND.

SERVES TWO

INGREDIENTS
  1 small yellow (bell) pepper
  2 tomatoes
  30ml/2 tbsp chopped fresh parsley
  150ml/¼ pint/⅔ cup sour cream
  grate (shredded) lemon rind,
    to garnish

VARIATIONS
• Vary the colour combinations by using
yellow, orange or red peppers with red
or yellow tomatoes. Green pepper with
yellow tomatoes looks good with the
chopped parsley.
• Use Greek (US strained plain) yogurt or
crème fraîche instead of sour cream.
• Use finely diced avocado or cucumber
in place of the pepper.

1 Halve the pepper lengthways.
Remove the core and seeds, then cut
the flesh into tiny dice.

2 Halve the tomatoes, then scoop out
and discard the seeds and cut the flesh
into tiny dice.

3 Stir the pepper and tomato dice and
the chopped parsley into the sour
cream and mix well.

4 Spoon the dip into a small bowl and
chill. Garnish by sprinkling with grated
lemon rind before serving.

THOUSAND ISLAND DIP

THIS VARIATION ON THE CLASSIC THOUSAND ISLAND DRESSING IS FAR REMOVED FROM THE ORIGINAL VERSION, BUT CAN BE SERVED IN THE SAME WAY — WITH SHELLFISH LACED ON TO BAMBOO SKEWERS FOR DIPPING OR WITH A SIMPLE MIXED SALAD.

SERVES FOUR

INGREDIENTS

    4 sun-dried tomatoes in oil
    4 plum tomatoes, or
      2 beefsteak tomatoes
    150g/5oz/²⁄₃ cup mild soft cheese, or
      mascarpone or fromage frais
    60ml/4 tbsp mayonnaise
    30ml/2 tbsp tomato purée (paste)
    30ml/2 tbsp chopped fresh parsley
    1 lemon
    Tabasco sauce, to taste
    5ml/1 tsp Worcestershire sauce or
      soy sauce
    salt and ground black pepper

COOK'S TIP

Tabasco sauce packs quite a punch, so use it with care. Add just a couple of drops at first, beat it in and leave for a minute or so to allow the flavour to develop. Taste the dip and add more Tabasco if needed. Continue this process until you feel it has the correct amount of flavouring.

1 Use a slotted spoon to scoop the sun-dried tomatoes out of the jar and place them on a double sheet of kitchen paper to absorb the excess oil. Blot them all over with the paper.

2 Transfer them to a chopping board and check that the stalk and blossom ends of each tomato have been removed; if not, trim them and then cut the sun-dried tomatoes into small pieces.

3 Cut a cross in the base of each fresh tomato. Bring a small pan of water to the boil. Remove it from the heat and add the tomatoes. Leave for 30 seconds, then lift the tomatoes out with a slotted spoon and put them into a bowl of cold water. Drain. The skin will have begun to peel back from the crosses. Remove it, then cut the tomatoes in half and squeeze out the seeds. Chop the flesh finely.

4 Put the soft cheese in a bowl. Beat it until it is creamy, then gradually beat in the mayonnaise. Add the tomato purée in the same way.

VARIATIONS
• Stir in 2.5ml/¹⁄₂ tsp cayenne pepper or a chopped fresh chilli for a fiery dip.
• To add a more exotic flavour to this dip, you can vary the ingredients slightly – try using freshly squeezed lime juice instead of lemon juice, and swap the parsley for a few sprigs of aromatic coriander (cilantro) or try orange juice and very finely chopped lemon grass.

5 Stir in the parsley and sun-dried tomatoes, then the fresh tomatoes. Mix well so that the dip is evenly coloured.

6 Grate (shred) the lemon finely and add the rind to the dip. Mix well. Squeeze the lemon and add the juice to the bowl, with Tabasco sauce to taste. Stir in the Worcestershire sauce or soy sauce, and salt and pepper to taste.

7 Spoon the dip into a serving bowl, swirling the surface attractively. Cover with clear film and chill in the refrigerator until ready to serve.

SUN-DRIED TOMATO BREAD

IN THE SOUTH OF ITALY, TOMATOES ARE OFTEN DRIED IN THE HOT SUN. THEY ARE THEN PRESERVED IN
OIL, OR HUNG UP IN STRINGS IN THE KITCHEN, FOR USE IN THE WINTER. THIS RECIPE USES THE TYPE
IN OIL TO MAKE FOUR DELICIOUS LOAVES.

MAKES FOUR SMALL LOAVES

INGREDIENTS
   675g/1½lb/6 cups strong white
     (bread) flour, plus extra for dusting
   10ml/2 tsp salt
   30ml/2 tbsp sugar
   25g/1oz fresh yeast
   400–475ml/14–16fl oz/1⅔–2 cups
     warm milk
   15ml/1 tbsp tomato purée (paste)
   75g/3oz/1½ cups sun-dried
     tomatoes, drained and chopped,
     plus 75ml/5 tbsp oil from the jar
   75ml/5 tbsp extra virgin olive oil, or
     sunflower oil
   1 large onion, finely chopped

COOK'S TIP
Use a pair of sharp kitchen scissors to
cut up the sun-dried tomatoes – serrated
ones work best.

1 Sift the flour, salt and sugar into a
bowl, and make a well in the centre.
Crumble the yeast, mix with 150ml/
¼ pint/⅔ cup of the warm milk and add
to the flour.

2 Mix the tomato purée into the
remaining milk, until evenly blended,
then add to the flour with the tomato oil
and olive oil.

3 Gradually mix the flour into the
liquid ingredients, until you have a
dough. Turn out on to a floured work
surface, and knead for about 10 minutes,
until the dough is smooth and elastic.

4 Return the dough to the clean bowl,
cover with a clean dishtowel or clear
film and leave to rise in a warm place
for about 2 hours.

5 Punch the dough back down, and
add the tomatoes and onion. Knead
until evenly distributed through the
dough. Shape into four rounds and
place on a greased baking sheet. Cover
with a dishtowel and leave in a warm
place to rise again for about 45 minutes.

6 Preheat the oven to 190°C/375°F/
Gas 5. Bake the bread for 45 minutes,
or until the loaves sound hollow when
you tap them underneath with your
fingers. Leave to cool on a wire rack.
Eat warm or cut into thick slices and
toast. Serve with mozzarella cheese
grated on top, if liked.

HERBY TOMATO BREAD

THIS MOUTHWATERING ITALIAN-STYLE BREAD, FLAVOURED WITH BASIL, ROSEMARY, OLIVE OIL AND SUN-DRIED TOMATOES, IS ABSOLUTELY DELICIOUS SERVED WARM WITH A FRESH SALAD AND SLICED SALAMI OR PROSCIUTTO. THE OLIVE OIL, AS WELL AS ADDING FLAVOUR, HELPS IT TO KEEP LONGER.

MAKES THREE LOAVES

INGREDIENTS
50g/2oz/½ cup sun-dried
   tomatoes, drained
fresh rosemary and basil, or other
   fresh herbs
5ml/1 tsp sugar
900ml/1½ pints/3¾ cups warm water
15ml/1 tbsp dried yeast
1.3kg/3lb/12 cups strong white
   (bread) flour
15ml/1 tbsp salt
150ml/¼ pint/⅔ cup extra virgin olive
   oil or grapeseed oil
extra virgin olive oil, rosemary leaves
   and sea salt flakes, to garnish

COOK'S TIP
Use a sharp cook's knife to slash the
tops of the loaves just before the final
rising. Make a criss-cross pattern, cutting
about 1cm/½in deep.

1 Put the sun-dried tomatoes on a board and chop them roughly. Strip the leaves from the rosemary and chop them with enough fresh basil to yield about 75ml/5 tbsp altogether.

2 Put the sugar into a small bowl, pour on 150ml/¼ pint/⅔ cup of the warm water, then crumble the yeast over the top. Leave in a warm place for 10–15 minutes, until frothy. Put the flour, salt, herbs and sun-dried tomatoes into a large bowl. Add the oil and frothy yeast mixture, then gradually mix in the remaining warm water.

3 As the mixture becomes stiffer, bring it together with your hands. Mix to a soft but not sticky dough, adding a little extra water if needed. Turn the dough out on to a lightly floured work surface and knead for 5 minutes until smooth and elastic. Put the dough back into the bowl, cover it loosely with oiled clear film and put in a warm place for 30–40 minutes or until doubled in bulk.

4 Knead again, then cut into 3 pieces. Shape each into an oval loaf and place on oiled baking sheets. Slash the top of each loaf. Loosely cover and leave in a warm place for 15–20 minutes until well risen. Preheat the oven to 220°C/425°F/ Gas 7. Brush the loaves with a little olive oil and sprinkle with rosemary leaves and salt flakes. Bake for 25–30 minutes.

FOCACCIA <u>WITH</u> SUN-DRIED TOMATOES

A DIMPLED SURFACE IS FOCACCIA'S FAMOUS TRADEMARK. THIS VERSION MAKES A WONDERFUL TOMATO SANDWICH, OR TRY IT TOASTED, WITH COOKED TOMATOES ON TOP.

<u>SERVES EIGHT</u>

INGREDIENTS

300ml/½ pint/1¼ cups warm water
5ml/1 tsp dried yeast
pinch of caster (superfine) sugar
450g/1lb /4 cups strong white
  (bread) flour, plus extra for dusting
5ml/1 tsp salt
1.5ml/¼ tsp ground black pepper
15ml/1 tbsp pesto
115g/4oz/1 cup black olives, chopped
25g/1oz/3 tbsp drained sun-dried
  tomatoes in oil, chopped, plus
  15ml/1 tbsp oil from the jar
5ml/1 tsp coarse sea salt
5ml/1 tsp roughly chopped
  fresh rosemary

1 Lightly grease a 33 x 23cm/13 x 9in baking tray. Put the water in a bowl. Sprinkle the yeast on top. Add the sugar, mix well and leave for 10 minutes.

2 Sift the flour, salt and pepper into a bowl and make a well in the centre. Add the yeast mixture with the pesto, olives and sun-dried tomatoes.

3 Mix to a soft dough, adding a little extra water if necessary. Turn the dough on to a floured surface and knead for 5 minutes until smooth and elastic.

4 Return the bread dough to a clean bowl, cover with a clean damp dishtowel or oiled plastic and leave in a warm place to rise for about 2 hours, or until doubled in bulk. Preheat the oven to 220°C/425°F/Gas 7.

5 Turn the dough on to a floured surface, knead briefly, then roll out to a 33 x 23cm/13 x 9in rectangle. Place in the prepared tray.

6 Using your fingertips, dimple the dough. Brush with the oil from the sun-dried tomatoes, then sprinkle with the salt and rosemary. Leave to rise for 20 minutes, then bake for 20–25 minutes, or until golden. Serve warm.

SUN-DRIED TOMATO LOAF

THERE'S SOMETHING VERY APPEALING ABOUT A BRAIDED LOAF. RED PESTO, PARMESAN AND SUN-DRIED TOMATOES MAKE THIS ONE EXTRA SPECIAL.

SERVES EIGHT TO TEN

INGREDIENTS

300ml/½ pint/1¼ cups warm water
5ml/1 tsp dried yeast
pinch of sugar
225g/8 oz/2 cups wholemeal
    (whole-wheat) flour
225g/8oz/2 cups strong white
    (bread) flour, plus extra for dusting
5ml/1 tsp salt
1.5ml/¼ tsp ground black pepper
115g/4oz/1 cup drained sun-dried
    tomatoes in oil, plus 15ml/1 tbsp
    oil from the jar
25g/1oz/⅓ cup freshly grated
    (shredded) Parmesan cheese
30ml/2 tbsp red pesto
5ml/1 tsp coarse sea salt

COOK'S TIP
These two breads can be made using easy-blend (rapid-rise) dried yeast. Mix all the dry ingredients, including the yeast, then add the lukewarm water. Mix to a dough, working in any other ingredients.

1 Put half the warm water in a bowl. Sprinkle the yeast on top. Add the sugar, mix well and leave to stand for about 10 minutes.

2 Put the wholemeal flour in a mixing bowl. Sift in the white flour, salt and pepper. Make a well in the centre and add the yeast mixture, sun-dried tomatoes, oil, Parmesan, pesto and the remaining water. Gradually incorporate the flour and mix to a soft dough, adding a little extra water if necessary.

3 Turn the dough on to a floured surface and knead for 5 minutes until smooth and elastic. Return to the clean bowl, cover with a clean, damp dishtowel and leave in a warm place to rise for about 2 hours until doubled in bulk. Lightly grease a baking sheet.

4 Turn the dough on to a lightly floured surface and knead for a few minutes. Divide the dough into 3 equal pieces and shape each into a sausage, about 33cm/13in long.

5 Join the three sausages on one end. Braid them together loosely, then press them together at the other end. Place on the baking sheet, cover and leave in a warm place for about 30 minutes until well risen. Preheat the oven to 220°C/425°F/Gas 7.

6 Sprinkle the braid with sea salt. Bake for 10 minutes, then lower the oven temperature to 200°C/400°F/Gas 6 and bake for a further 15–20 minutes or until the loaf sounds hollow when tapped.

INDEX

ACKNOWLEDGEMENTS AND SUPPLIERS

The author and publisher would like to thank Jim Buckland and Sarah Wain of West Dean Gardens for their generous assistance. Many of the varieties of tomato photographed came from their gardens, which are open to the public. They host a tomato show in September every year. For recorded information on opening times and charges for the gardens, telephone: 00 44 (0) 1243 818210 or write to West Dean Gardens, West Dean, Chichester, West Sussex, PO18 0QZ, UK.

Totally Tomatoes, PO Box 202, Newton Abbot, TQ12 6ZH, UK, telephone: 00 44 (0) 1803 389516, is an excellent source of tomato seeds in the UK, carrying more than 200 varieties from all over the world. Their website is www.totallytomatouk.com. Simpson's Seeds, run by Colin, Jane and Matt Simpson, is a supplier, specializing in the most flavoursome varieties. Selling plants and seeds by mail order, the address is 27 Meadowbrook, Old Oxted, Surrey, RH8 9LT, UK, telephone: 00 44 (0) 13 715242. Another good source of seeds in the UK, is E W King & Co Ltd, Monk's Farm, Kelvedon, Colchester, Essex, CO5 9PG, UK, telephone 00 44 (0) 1376 570000. For rare varieties, contact Ferme de Sainte Marthe at PO Box 358, Walton, Surrey KT12 4YX, (telephone: 00 44 (0) 1932 266630). For US readers, heirloom tomato seeds can be supplied by The Cook's Garden, PO Box 5010, Hodges, SC 29653, USA, telephone: 001 (0) 800 457 9703, or www.cooksgarden.com. Also Seed Savers Exchange, 3076 North Winn Road, Decorah, IA 52101, USA, telephone: 00 1 (0) 319 382 5990. Their website is www.seedsavers.com. Another company supplying seeds is Heirloom Seeds, PO Box 245, West Elizabeth, PA 15088, USA, telephone: 00 1 (0) 412 384 0852 or www.heirloomseeds.com.

Lakeland Limited, Alexandra Buildings, Windermere, Cumbria, LA23 1BQ, UK. www.lakelandlimited.com, is a good source of equipment

Picture Acknowledgements
The Art Archive: pp6 both & 7 both; Cephas p8 top.

NOTES

NOTES

NOTES

NOTES

NOTES

NOTES

NOTES

NOTES